T0132867

Singular Creatures

MARK KINGWELL

SINGULAR CREATURES

Robots, Rights, and the Politics of Posthumanism

McGill-Queen's University Press

Montreal & Kingston • London • Chicago

ISBN 978-0-2280-1434-8 (cloth)
ISBN 978-0-2280-1537-6 (ePDF)
ISBN 978-0-2280-1538-3 (ePUB)

Legal deposit fourth quarter 2022
Bibliothèque nationale du Québec

Printed in Canada on acid-free paper that is 100% ancient forest
free (100% post-consumer recycled), processed chlorine free

This book has been published with the help of a grant from the
Canadian Federation for the Humanities and Social Sciences,
through the Awards to Scholarly Publications Program, using
funds provided by the Social Sciences and Humanities Research
Council of Canada.

Funded by the   Financé par le
Government   gouvernement
of Canada   du Canada

Canada

Canada Council   Conseil des arts
for the Arts   du Canada

We acknowledge the support of the Canada Council for the Arts.
Nous remercions le Conseil des arts du Canada de son soutien.

Library and Archives Canada Cataloguing in Publication

Title: Singular creatures : robots, rights, and the politics of post-
    humanism / Mark Kingwell.
Names: Kingwell, Mark, 1963- author.
Description: Includes bibliographical references and index.
Identifiers: Canadiana (print) 20220234663 | Canadiana (ebook)
    20220234779 | ISBN 9780228014348 (cloth) | ISBN 9780228015376
    (ePDF) | ISBN 9780228015383 (ePUB)
Subjects: LCSH: Technology—Philosophy. | LCSH: Human
    beings—Philosophy. | LCSH: Posthumanism.
Classification: LCC T14 .K56 2022 | DDC 601—dc23

Contents

Preface

There are many excellent books about emerging artificial intelligence.[1] These include serious social-philosophical considerations of artificial intelligence, technical and popular studies, treatises devoted to programming problems, and wild speculations about the shape of things to come. This book offers a different emphasis. Short and I hope accessible in language and context, it aims to be a series of meditations for those concerned that technology too often advances beyond the horizon of human reflection, especially when it comes to work, foreignness, foreign workers, and associated justice issues. Here, the robot becomes a flashpoint for larger worries about exploitation, fulfillment, and autonomy. The central problem is as old as Prometheus, the ancient Greek titan who was the bringer of Olympian fire to humankind but also a notorious trickster. There has proven no better figure to embody the twinned temptations and rewards of instrumental reason, the wielding of tools, and the advances of human cleverness. We tend to believe, without much reflection, that technology is under our control, since after all it is a product of our emergent desires; but devices fashioned from such desires may acquire a life of their own, even when enjoying a status well short of "intelligence." The things we make are not neutral properties. They are forever outstripping our ability to consider the deep consequences of what is blithely celebrated as unstoppable "progress." The issues the present book addresses are, therefore, distinct and existential ones concerning the nature of consciousness, life, and value. Its politics, construed here in a wide sense, are my own, naturally. But I believe that any amount of sustained reflection on our current techno-capitalist immersion will prompt at least some of the doubts and questions entertained here.

Despite its generally critical stance, then, the discussion that follows nevertheless aims at a rapprochement between, or anyway partial sublation of, the ubiquitous binary that separates *technophiles* and *technophobes*. Like many if not most people, I consider myself neither of these exclusively nor would I want to be or know someone who did. Indeed, this presumed chasm is almost always invoked as an aspect of special pleading with respect to privilege and profit or wielded as a weapon of demonization against subordinate groups (the unsavvy, late- or non-adopters, principled refuse-niks, and so on). This last move is especially popular when attitudes to techno-immersion are allowed to dominate distinct markers of identity such as birth year ("You're too old to understand."), social status ("I have *n*-thousand InstaTwitTok followers!"), and fashion sense or knowingness ("The 1990s called, they want their slang back."). These habituated conjoinings, so much fun for their users and so typical of lazy public discourse about technology, must be recognized for what they are: namely, toxic and sometimes gleeful age-based category slippage in lockstep with the current arrangement. It is of course true, per Bourdieu and Veblen among others, that these judgmental vectors can be reversed by subsequent moves in the larger status game. Witness resurgent interest in "obsolete" platforms such as turntables and vinyl records, hand-knit accessories, and flip phones or the rising tide of youth preference for off-grid activities, printed books, and mending. Today's cutting-edge hip kid may well be tomorrow's sad striver. So it goes in the game of distinction: coolness is a receding horizon, forever outpacing anyone's ability to stay out front.

More specifically for present purposes, and more seriously too, there is much biased and often superficial rhetoric that attends any mention of artificial intelligence, not just in the media but also in policy discussions and academic circles. The general run of discussion concerning culture and technology is not reassuring, lacking not only political and economic context but also frequently unmoored from longstanding and useful philosophical mediations from Heidegger, Mumford, and Marcuse to Ellul, McLuhan, and Haraway. It can often seem, as one scans the daily websites and discussion groups devoted to tech subjects, that their searching investigation of what Heidegger called "die Frage nach der Technik" had never been put on record, so absent are the insights from reductive focus on feature details, profit margin, processing speed, or breezy dismissal of any and all skepticism. That erasure of philosophical depth needs daily correction and realignment, especially with respect to the far-reaching idea of a truly sentient non-human entity. But at the same time this limitation offers new urgency for the pursuit of basic philosophical questions.[2] A machine-learning program can solve the Turing test, for example, reliably imitating human consciousness, without being able to explain that consciousness in any illuminating manner. That should come as no surprise: we human agents cannot entirely explain our own experience of first-person existence either. These evolving natural-language programs can imitate consciousness through written texts and do so ever more ably by the year if not the month.[3] (A documentary about the late celebrity chef Anthony Bourdain contained dialogue attributed to him voiced by a deep-fake AI.[4]) But do we really need to worry about natural-language algorithms, except in contexts like university evaluation or single-author text production, that mimic human writing? Why not simply welcome them to the discursive field, just as writing itself supplements oral traditions? This openness might then be considered an early stage in the transition to posthumanism, the future towards which we are inevitably headed, indeed already substantially inhabit.[5]

The intellectual difficulty of consciousness attempting its own self-understanding, once compared to a flashlight attempting to illuminate its own batteries at work, together with the ethico-political challenges of encountering potential new forms of conscious life are the orienting concerns of this text. Current uncertainties, issues encountered almost daily if one is paying attention, create apparently new conundrums of thought and action that are in fact, upon examination, revealed as philosophically venerable. My aim here is to trace at least some of those backward and forward connections throughout the following assessment. This is therefore a kind of reflective report on where we stand in the second decade of the twenty-first century. My own proclivities and philosophical commitments will become obvious in what follows, but my hope is that the discussion is thoughtful enough to engage even hard-core skeptics about artificial intelligence or, from the other side, those who live in daily fear of robot revolution.

Most general posthumanist reflection has focussed on two issues: (a) cyborg-style enhancements of the human physical form (already very much in evidence) that alter our default understanding of humanness; this is more properly transhumanist aspiration, contemplated for good and ill by many as their bodies fail or fall short of desire, and usually figured as a luxury commodity; and (b) anxiety about the emergence of a parallel non-biological sentient species that threatens our assumed primacy as humans. Both issues have some basis in fact, but neither is so far reliably assessed by philosophical reflection. A third issue, concerning the ethical rights of mind clones and non-human animals, or the digital uploading of human consciousness in pursuit of immortality, is closer to present concerns but still distinct, since such clones are copies of already extant persons rather than *de novo* artificial entities.[6] One final note worth entering here is that, given widespread acceptance of ethical and political claims made on behalf of non-human forms of life, both animals and natural features of the world around us (reefs, lakes, forests) – not to mention abstract legal entities such as corporations and trusts – it is fair to say that we already inhabit a post-human universe of a kind. But the real test case has always been, and still remains, the status of the robot. The status and the threat level.

And so what I have called "robots, rights, and the politics of posthuman-ism" delineate the questions that require urgent philosophical attention, if not solution, in our somewhat confused present moment. Karel Čapek's play *R.U.R.: Rossum's Universal Robots* (orig. *Rossumovi Univerzální Robot*) introduced the Czech-derived word *robota*, meaning worker or indentured servant, perhaps even carceral labour or slavery, in 1920 (first public per-formance 1921). The play, intended as a critique of Soviet Communist forced-labour regimes, also acts, in its long and sometimes uneven influence, as a subtle critique of scientism, a satire of neo-liberal overproduction, and a thoughtful meditation on the line where dignified work might sink into misery. The term *robot*, meanwhile, enters into more and more common usage over the century since, for decades freely substituted with other mean-ings of android or artificial being. Even before Čapek's play, automated life-forms have been associated with questions of work and its relation to human existence. There have likewise been, from the earliest beginnings, anxieties as well as pleasures to be contemplated with the possible arrival of these new planetary denizens. Would the robots set us free from toil, boredom, and drudgery? Would they make human life more comfortable, easier, better in all aspects? How advanced would they have to become to answer to our needs, and what dangers lay therein? Would the machines organize and revolt with a new-found workers' class consciousness, perhaps ending up by destroying their makers, which is to say the feeble, feckless, and lazy humans who heedlessly cobbled them into existence, on the way to new evolutionary peaks of performance and self-realization? Everyone knows the questions now, even if they are routinely consigned to the remainder bins of B-movie streaming sites and tired science-fiction novel outlines.

My view here is that the issues are too important to be allowed to remain of merely cultural interest, still less to stultify as so much forgotten intellectual compost. Despite skepticism in many quarters, I maintain that the questions of robots, rights, and posthumanism are live and tractable, urgent and coherent. That said, we are forced to exercise philosophical caution on approach. The results of such questions must always be considered conditional and speculative, awaiting further evidence and possible rebuttal, even as they shed light on existing political issues of rights more generally, especially as those rights concern neglected humans as well as non-human animals. This is the double payoff of this speculative philosophical exercise: illumination of both present and future, guided by an in-principle welcoming of new forms of life, new styles of personhood. Some thinkers believe the term "posthuman" is more aesthetic than technical. It should be considered, usefully, a combination of both. This is an existential issue that has been given new sharpness with the advent of recent technological changes that reach both backwards and forwards. How do we *even make sense* of first-person carbon-based existence, also known to us as human personhood, as technological change swiftly alters the terrain of everyday life? And is the first-person perspective so presumptively privileged anyway? Ethics and politics in the European tradition have long assumed that the relevant subject for any discussion of agency, responsibility, justice, and reparation is some version of a Cartesian self-reflective ego, otherwise known as the sovereign individual.

There can be little confidence at the moment in solving what is known as the alignment problem, that troubling region where machine learning has become very advanced but perhaps not necessarily lining up with human-style values and expectations.[7] A conscious, human-figured artificial intelligence remains well beyond the reach of current technology, and yet we continue almost heedlessly to integrate human persons with technological systems that greatly outpace our own "natural" abilities. (Nothing is natural until we make it so.) Nor is it obvious that even the most sophisticated artificial consciousness would possess the *intentionality*, or inherent "aboutness," of human mental states.[8] At the same time, emergent challenges from other philosophical traditions – Indigenous, collectivist, anarchist, animal welfarist, and perhaps eventually non-human sentient – suggest that the primacy of the private individual is an architecture of ethico-political thought whose time has gone the way of all things. The fallback position of white, male, European-descended individuality has long been criticized within the discourse of ethics and politics. These theoretical disputes now have data-driven arguments to demonstrate these biases, not just assert them. Artificial intelligence, in all its aspects including machine learning and data-gathering, is for these purposes the gateway rather than the destination of existential reflection. The relevant terms of reference now are mainly philosophical, not technological.

Posthumanism can be approached in many ways, including radical activism, gender fluidity, and debates about recognition or identity politics. There is also, alas, the Big Tech version of trans- or posthumanism, which relies on fleeting desire, disposable income, and transglobal mega-corporate greed. Our particular path to techno-human interaction links many aspects of the various critical debates in a manner that may be useful and perhaps less divisive. Not everyone, for example, is open to the ideas of gender-fluid identities, late-life transitioning, performativity, and multiple subject positions.[9] Nor is cyborg transformation, or technological upload, comfortable goals for those of us currently alive. Uploading consciousness to extend life strikes many humans as bizarre, if not sacrilegious, just as more complete integration with technology can seem grotesque, centred on the wrong global concerns.[10]

Almost everyone is aware that the current and evolving capito-technological regime is changing the way that we all live and think about ourselves. We are already integrated with technology in multiple forms. Already the inequities of access and distribution are brutally obvious, as are challenges to complacent human-centric personhood. The real question is how we continue to do so, and at what associated costs. The underlying and fundamental existential concern must be this: *how do we do philosophy* when the rules of the game seem to be changed so decisively by growing human/non-human interaction? I offer large and small speculative arguments throughout this book, but the general conversation must naturally continue in every possible venue.

A note on citations. Some of these, labelled with the heading [LF], are the result of conversations between me [MK] and my recent research assistant and co-instructor Logan Fletcher; see the acknowledgments for further detail. I include these in part because Logan, who is younger by what most people would call a generation, offered so many interesting ideas to the overall discussion that could not be included in the main text, and in part to illustrate the invigorating dialogue that can ensue when two people with divergent intellectual backgrounds but shared political and ethical concerns pause to think about who and what we are and want to become.

Singular Creatures

The Burning Boards, performance
art piece by Glenn Kaino at
Whitney Museum of American
Art, New York City, 2007.
Image by Austin Miller.

1

Past Perfect
Status Report: Speculative, Intrepid, Ludic

1.1 PERSONAL

When I was young, perhaps twelve or thirteen, I developed a passion for chess. I never considered this a serious talent. But even if I had, my initiation to the game was already late in the day for any potential professional career, considering the tales we know of the great players. They show their genius at ten or even nine years old, and get better and better over several decades. Recent research also suggests, however, that like pure mathematicians and football quarterbacks, chess players peak early by human lifetime standards. Which is to say that between twenty-five and thirty-five years of age is now the accepted range of greatness for certain undertakings, including chess, mathematics, formal logic, and football.[1] Early chess prodigies may develop into successful grandmasters, but then they decline even more quickly into wily, maybe wise, but increasingly unsuccessful, veterans. To be sure, this can be hard for them and their fans to accept.

So it goes in many fields of human achievement or social status. Physical beauty, confident brashness, vertical leap, personal risk tolerance, and mastery of slang are among the many things governed by an apparent tyranny of callow youth and its cultural twin, relentless novelty. To a large and growing extent, and despite pushback in certain sectors such as climate and public health, contemporary culture is an elaborate temple erected in the service of this joint tyranny, by which all must fall sooner or later – and usually sooner. That is why its supplicants at any given moment are acting in basic error, though they cannot know it in the moment of their temporary ascendancy. The rosy celebrants of today are the forgotten body count of tomorrow. One can deny this, but one cannot escape it. And yes, I know that saying any of this makes me sound old. But that's the point.

Like many members of my professional tribe, or this discursive node in intellectual production and consumption, I would like to believe that philosophy is an exception to this general generational rule of disdain, perhaps in common with artworks, red wine, Scotch whisky, some cheeses, good leather, kilims, cast-iron skillets, aesthetic judgment, first editions, and success at trivia quizzes. This maybe quixotic conviction about philosophical longevity is sustained only by the persistent influence of canonical thinkers in given traditions of thought, revived every year in university classes and journal articles throughout the world: Plato, Aquinas, Descartes, Hume, Kant. If they are not quite household names, these long-living philosophers are certainly familiar classroom names. They seem to withstand the test of time, at least across decades, centuries, and even sometimes millennia.[2] And yet, we must acknowledge that celebrating this longevity might just be indulging an ageist egotistical fetish for thinking that philosophical reflection outlives the cruel norms of cultural novelty. That indulgence is itself a cruel double-down, in its own fashion.

After all, we cannot ever be sure how this dynamic of intellectual production and consumption, at ground level, evaluates the work of any of the current or recent figures in the academic profession. How could anyone, know that? Students sometimes complain that contemporary philosophy seems to lack major figures on the order of the aforementioned luminaries. They are likely correct: we do not operate in that comprehensive world-building register, even considering leading thinkers such as Bertrand Russell, W.V.O. Quine, Charles Taylor, Donna Haraway, or J.L. Austin – not to mention Marx or Nietzsche. Depending on your sympathies, Jacques Derrida, Ludwig Wittgenstein, or Martin Heidegger might be the last philosophers who altered the currents of thought in a lasting way. Even there the influence is at best temporary. Everyone could add other names, or subtract from those mentioned. (Say Jean-Paul Sartre and, after him, Gilles Deleuze?) This sort of comparative exercise is a matter of extended and impossible debate, but all of these thinkers will emerge as important data points in the general argument about human consciousness even if their names are not common currency everywhere.

By same the same token, someone who is considered quite important and influential at the present moment just doesn't offer the same expansive heft of thought and therefore might well prove to be a damp squib over time – even as someone once neglected could emerge as the signature figure of a moment when viewed from some distant temporal perspective.[3] This is more obvious in literature than in philosophy. Who today reads Elizabeth Daly, J.G. Farrell, or Charles Hamilton, all renowned and even household names in their time?[4] As the sociologist Randall Collins has said about intellectual work, echoing received wisdom, almost all thinkers and writers are destined to be forgotten sooner rather than later.[5] Our students are sometimes more prescient than we know, not because they are in control of legacy but precisely because they recognize that they are not. As one recent popular culture source has it, "Age is no guarantee of efficiency ... and youth is no guarantee of innovation."[6] As ever, posterity will judge us all, with suitable ruthlessness.

What is *certainly* true, from my own limited ground level, is that I absolutely knew from the start that I was not remotely a genius, a modest talent, or an enthusiastic amateur, at the game of chess. I was a piker. I lost a lot more matches than I won. I mean, *a lot*. But these mundane travails taught me how much I admired the game and its fabled players, and, as with watching high-percentile athletes perform, I could tell what separated genius from talent, even if I could aspire to neither. So it goes. I would wager that many if not most of my academic colleagues, and likewise many if not most of the presumed readers of this book, have similar stories to tell. Nerds find each other, after all, under cover of coded word systems, puzzle blankets, linked references, and arcane trivia.[7] Chess, through all this, is a classic non-physical battle of the life of the mind. Fellow nerds will recall that, during July and August of 1972, eccentric master Bobby Fischer had squared off against Soviet champion Borıs Spassky in Reykjavik, a match that was widely viewed as an exercise in Cold War politics as much as chess. This World Championship pairing featured twenty-one matches between the two grandmasters and had also entertained various weird distractions: tactical adjournments, demands by Fischer for more prize money, delays on arrival to the matches, and requests for a particular moulded chess set from a specific London maker.[8]

Iceland's capital city was technically neutral even though there was a NATO airbase nearby in Keflavik. *Time* magazine laid out the moves of the decisive Fischer–Spassky match in a visual insert. I replayed them over and over again on my small discount-store chessboard, with its cheap plastic pieces. Fischer's victory made him, at age twenty-nine and after twenty-four unbroken years of Soviet dominance, just the second American world champion, and the first born in the United States. Chess was world news in that early-1970s moment, something perhaps hard to believe now. *Sports Illustrated* and *Der Spiegel*, among others, covered both the matches and the political resonances around them. I devoured all the coverage with typical youthful avidness.

1.2 PHILOSOPHICAL

Many years later, I had the good fortune to sit next to Russian grandmaster Garry Kasparov at a lunch event in Toronto. Kasparov had been, at age twenty-two, the youngest ever undisputed world champion in the history of chess when he defeated Anatoly Karpov in 1985. He was quoted as noting that the Fischer–Spassky contest, the Match of the Century, was "a crushing moment in the midst of the Cold War": a late-model endorsement of the dominant position. He is also well known as the human who took on the AI chess programs designed by IBM known as Deep Thought and, later, Deep Blue and Deep Junior. In May 1997, Deep Blue defeated Kasparov, despite some protests about human intervention and rule changes that denied Kasparov access to Deep Blue's playing style.

This was documented everywhere as a significant moment in the history of artificial intelligence, especially because earlier versions of chess programs had relied on full-crunch bulldozing and brute-force algorithms, using programming speed to defeat all possible moves. These early brute-force programs could track three million possible positions per second, something no human can do. Expert human chess players are said to "chunk" possible moves, organizing clusters of responses into fields of contingent action, disregarding unsuccessful chances as irrelevant. But they can't think as fast as massive operating systems. The later IBM programs added the significant ability to go off-book, in effect mimicking or creatively reproducing some aspects of the intuitive or creative style that distinguishes some masters of the game: which is to say, the ability to see an opening without calculating the precise moves ahead. This kind of off-kilter-creativity, added to huge processing power, makes these programs extremely difficult for any human to beat.

Over this lunch Kasparov spoke about chess, naturally, as well as artificial intelligence and the future of democratic politics, the latter his ruling passion still. I told him how I had often tried to beat my best friend, Bruce Millar, during long winter afternoons on a remote air force base in Prince Edward Island, when we were both teenagers. Bruce was what is sometimes known as a muscular player, and I could now and then win against his aggressive game if I was guileful and deceptive enough – but that was not often. I mentioned to Kasparov how, after many years of not playing at all, I took on my niece Natalie, who was thirteen at the time. She mopped the floor with me, I told him, using a pretty basic Sicilian opening that I had either forgotten or failed to recognize. This sad defeat reminded me of how I used to watch speed-chess matches parlayed on the stone chess boards to be found in the southwestern corner of Washington Square Park in Manhattan. I never tried to play against those raffish ruffian "I-got-next" chess pirates, who sometimes maintained control over three or four matches at once. Instead, I would watch as some overbright chancer from out of town would arrive in the park with what he thought was a perfect opening gambit and within minutes was pinned and pincered, pretty much embarrassed in every one of the sixty-four squares of the board. The pirates always won and took the folded Andrew Jacksons as bounty. It's not gambling for money; it's just a fee for rather harsh lessons in life.

When I told Kasparov the story about being thrashed by my young niece and those hapless hopefuls in Washington Square, he laughed so hard I thought he was going to choke on his hotel-kitchen salmon fillet. But chess defeat is so common that it cannot sustain good narrative for long: there are so many ways to lose and so many celebrated losses. We switched to a discussion of chess in films, especially his favourite, the one between Dr Frank Poole (Gary Lockwood) and HAL-9000 in *2001: A Space Odyssey* (1968, dir. Stanley Kubrick), which inspired Kasparov's own celebrated encounters with the IBM algorithms. He was not bitter or disillusioned about the Deep Blue defeats, just very thoughtful about technology and politics.[9]

Kasparov also talked about the riskiest mortal chess match in cinema, Max von Sydow's ex-Crusader Antonius Block setting up against Death (Bengt Ekerot) in *The Seventh Seal* (Bergman). This existential game is, alas for cinema-loving game purists, full of chess anachronisms, not least the range of the queen's moves, which were not then allowed. And chess people ask you never to mention *Knight Moves* (Schenkel), the Christopher Lambert murder-thriller that even a chess piker like me can tell is stupid. A further popular depiction of the game from 2020, the television series *The Queen's Gambit*, starred Anya Taylor-Joy as Beth Harmon, an orphaned, addictive, and self-torturing prodigy. Kasparov was a consultant for the show. Beth Harmon becomes a fashion-plate celebrity chess genius during the Cold War, and this was dramatic, sometimes thrilling, and for the most part technically correct. The series recognized, among other things, the Sicilian Defence, the Scholar's Mate, Alekhine's Defence, forking tactics, and pawn deployment during endgame. This attention to detail earned it the admiration of many real chess players, though also the objections of some purists.[10] Meanwhile, its 1950s production design seemed pretty flawless, right down to the teak furniture, flocked wallpaper, pseudo-Modernist hotel suites, and vintage airplanes.

But I could not help noticing, even as an amateur, that it nevertheless showed some boards that did not quite match the Hollywood-style dialogue of the television drama. An abstract game of intellect based on military tactics and strategy, chess is by dint of that combination very hard to dramatize on the screen. It is a game of the mind and imagination, executed within tight boundaries driven by almost limitless possibility.[11] *The Queen's Gambit* got this right in one sense, namely the ceiling-visualized games of the troubled young player, viewed at night as she lay in bed unable to sleep. But a screenwriter needed to add childhood trauma, mental illness, alcohol dependency, espionage, and devotion to fashion to make it screen worthy. We accept that chess is a vehicle of human understanding and competition, rather than a set of historical facts. And we further know that AI chess programs such as Deep Blue do not have any equivalent versions of the human distractions or desires that make for chess drama. They just play. That is why we might find them fearful and strange.

But per Ingmar Bergman, one cannot dare to speak yet of any match with Death. That final game belongs to a different register altogether, and the board is a metaphor, not a physical thing. We cannot defeat an opponent in a game designed to reap our fragile bodies, vehicles of self.

1.3 POLITICAL

Garry Kasparov has become an inspiration both for his formidable chess genius and for his recent political insight and activism.[12] In 2011, he succeeded former Czech president Václav Havel as chairman of the New York–based Human Rights Foundation. This conjunction of open intellectual contest with algorithms and concern for human rights is apposite to current events, including those registered in this text. In a similar spirit, these pages attempt, as their title suggests, to be a substantial but also accessible meditation on the *ethics and politics* of emergent artificial intelligence technology (AI throughout what follows), in its effects on human beings, using among other frameworks the regime of international human rights.

The aim is therefore not technological as such. It is, rather, to reflect critically, during this crucial stage of development and dissemination, on the far-reaching implications of creating programs and algorithms. These programs and algorithms may, at some future point, acquire individual consciousness and therefore be relevant subjects of traditional discourses concerning rights and responsibilities. Upstream of this possibility lie urgent ethical and political questions about technology more generally and how its influence is spread and, sometimes, regulated. What I hope is distinctive in what follows is a philosophical perspective that draws from longstanding scholarship about ethics, politics, and technology, and an appreciation for the cultural and social aspects of the linked questions. The former branch includes work by traditional theorists of the idea of technology (the usual suspects, some named already: Heidegger, Ellul, Mumford, Haraway) and of AI in particular (the Churchlands, Daniel Dennett, John Searle, David Chalmers). The latter branch likewise includes reflection on cultural sources such as films and television, science fiction literature, and video games (Isaac Asimov, Octavia Butler, Ann Leckie, Jonathan Lethem, Philip K. Dick, Wesley Wark, Bernard Suits).[13]

The central argument here is that *now is the moment for keen reflection on the status of potential non-human individual persons*, when they remain in the speculative frame but when, likewise, accelerating technology seems to make AI more and more proximate to issues of everyday life. If we are creating, somewhat willy-nilly, a posthuman future, this is the time to think hard about what that means and what, exactly, we should or could want from such a future.[14] This is likewise the moment *for keen reflection on the nature and viability of artificial consciousness of any kind* – and that is a much larger metaphysical and epistemological challenge that nevertheless shadows near-term ethical and political concerns.

In common with many people, my initial crude thinking about artificial intelligence worked along an inevitable divide between popular depictions of robot life, including its threatening instantiations, and the reality of actual algorithmic advances in real life. This divide, while culturally natural and much reinforced, has proven disastrous to any prospect of useful discussion.[15] The former depictions of easy sentience are vivid but misleading, assuming as they often do the ease with which generalized and autonomous AIs come to be, and what influence they might yield, including SkyNet-style global takeovers and the violent elimination of human life. The latter insistence of existing technology is detailed but sometimes dismissive of larger social concerns, assuming as it often does a series of stepwise advances in computer science and programming that will mark gains in efficiency but put some labour sectors out of work. Headline-grabbing developments – self-driving cars, self-landing planes, medical programs that diagnose without error – are often revealed as boring workmanlike upgrades to existing breakthrough technologies or else as elaborate parlour tricks. Sometimes they are both.

Thus there are systems that *appear* to think and create but that are in fact simply high-level input-output programs running on Von Neumann machines of the sort to be found on every laptop or desktop computer – or even pocket-borne smartphone (which is really to say, *even or especially*).[16] Deep computational barriers, and with them profound philosophical problems, are all too easily elided in the search for what one prominent worker in the field calls its "Holy Grail," which is to say a generalized AI that can really think for itself. Once possessed of such extraordinary abilities, this potential creation might therefore be a candidate for autonomy and even personhood.[17] That *might therefore be* is the core of what follows, especially insofar as the current tract is viewed primarily as social philosophy, not technological primer or walk-through document. The relevant concepts here are often victims of categorical slippage, so it is worth immediately distinguishing between weak autonomy (in, say, the minimal self-governance of a single-cell organism) and strong autonomy in the full-blown Kantian sense (an agent whose rationality and moral existence are aligned in an ongoing, robust program of self-legislation that simultaneously creates a universal moral law). Most human persons exhibit features of autonomy that point towards, if they don't fully achieve, the ideal of comprehensive self-legislation. As I will argue late, the various senses of personhood immediately complicate this picture where then two concepts – autonomy and personhood – meet.

For the moment, let us stipulate that persons are always autonomous in some sense (i.e., acting within a horizon of their own self-reflexive desires), but not all autonomous beings are persons. In each emergent case, including non-standard humans, posthumans, non-human animals, and artificial agents, we will need to ask (1) what autonomy amounts to and (2) whether the form of life in question clears any of the relevant thresholds of personhood (legal, ethical, metaphysical, as discussed later). The "Holy Grail" AI, at least in the popular imagination, is usually conceived as a near-human – sometimes super-human – simulacrum of a typical human person, with all relevant abilities and characteristics, only with no carbon-based technology. For the moment, that sense of what an autonomous AI could look like will suffice, though for the moment it remains both technically implausible and to some degree philosophically opaque.

Hence, it seems to me, the pervasive confusion and anxiety about human-seeming, personhood-claiming AIs. Typically the tensions between popular art and mundane technological reality resolve, if not quite dialectically, into a shared unease about the prospect of the Singularity. As most of us now have cause to know, this is the (so far) notional moment at which machine intelligence outstrips the human variety, together with an adjunct ability to replicate in scalable fashion. The term "Singularity," coined by computer scientist John von Neumann but popularized by Vernor Vinge[18] and Ray Kurzweil,[19] refers to this latter ability: once there is a *singular* superhuman machine intelligence, its ability to realize new and perhaps improved variants of itself will not be controllable by humans. In fact, these two aspects of the Singularity idea, often run together, are quite distinct.

One can imagine a non-human entity or algorithm of greater computational robustness than any, even of all, human versions. It does not immediately follow that this superhuman entity would be able to reproduce itself without further ado.[20] Not least, there would be questions of access to basic material resources, reliable power sources, and replication equipment, all of which could easily confine the superhuman singular AI to a lonely, corporatized, or even enslaved existence. The standard robopocalyptic scenario – really, this should be the Basic Scenario *simpliciter* – involves rapidly evolving non-biological consciousness executing a (usually) violent takeover of human life possibilities. This profitable dramatic arc is, despite its numerous and overlapping cultural iterations, the least of our real worries. Sometimes, indeed, the crude class dimensions and consciousness of environmental degradation are the real point of the Basic Scenario, whereby overprivileged and decadent *eloi* of some description both (a) immiserate a crowded population of slum-dwelling *morlocks* who endure hunger, forced labour, disease, and dirt; even as the same elevated class (b) comes to depend to a dangerous degree on the lifestyle-enhancing abilities of a non-human category of helpers. This third class of entity then becomes the avant-garde of a vicarious revolution, but with – oh no! – its own world-dominating agenda emerging over any noble search for social justice. The early agents of reform become the levers of global revolution from human to non-human ascendancy.

Of course, despite its ubiquity in film and fiction, where it has proven nearly irresistible and sustained mainly by advances in special effects and violence, the Basic Scenario enjoys very little real-world purchase. The truth is less spectacular and won't photograph as well. Complicating the picture are the many counter-narratives of faithful guardians, servants, and even benign or fond superior AIs, as in Iain Banks's speculative fiction, who just want humans to be happy and playful. No, in ordinary life we are much more likely to deploy and encounter technologies in the service of our own mundane democratized desires. Think of the OG cinematic robot Robby, from the 1956 *Tempest*-in-space thriller *Forbidden Planet* (dir. Fred M. Wilcox). With his wind-up-toy styling and Swiss-army-knife gadgetry, Robby is a faithful manservant, protector, and military-grade weapon. He is kept in a sub-autonomous state, like a sophisticated guard dog, but possesses enormous energy open always to misuse. The trouble is that, sooner or later, all these devices of convenience and comfort, real and imagined, turn out to be agents of routine depredation – the way shopping might be viewed in our consumption-dependent spiral economy, for example, or gradual re-source depletion and disastrous climate change brought about by millions of individual choices to drive a car, use up a non-renewable material, or fly on an airplane. Indeed, that is the world of effort and meaning in which we already find ourselves. The philosophical task, as always, is first to under-stand any such life-threatening problematic and then – often a very distant second – attempt to alter the apparently inevitable outcomes. It will emerge in what follows that a sense of inevitability is itself a barrier to achieving the latter goal (social change), but it is also, in perhaps a more unnerving development, an active deterrent to cracking the window of the former pro-ject (philosophical understanding).

We must be vigilant, in short, about how basic understanding may elude us when it comes to sentient beings in general, including posthuman forms of life. Like "autonomy" and "personhood," "sentience" is a slippery concept in these quarters, admitting of both weak and strong versions, and some-times eliding into consciousness as such. Some theorists use sentience in-terchangeably with the idea of phenomenal consciousness in a minimal sense, absent what one writer calls "heavy-duty cognitive baggage that might on some views be built into the very notion of consciousness": con-ceptual thought, self-consciousness, higher-order awareness, representing an objective world, etc.[21] Though there may be reliable lines of inference that lead from sentience to consciousness, and thence to autonomy and personhood, we must be careful once more to assess new forms of life on their own detailed merits. There may be, for example, sentient beings who do not seem eligible for personhood, even as sentience becomes the trait of choice for animal-rights advocates eager to resist a reification trap that would set up specifically human consciousness as the only viable platform for ethical significance.

All conceptual clarity (or lack of it) notwithstanding, the justice question remains: what do these or any sophisticated non-human entities mean for themselves, for us, and for any shared world of scarce natural and social resources combined with rampant and ramifying desire: the world of Hume's justice, one might say, the site of that all-important *artificial virtue*. For Hume, justice is "artificial" not in the sense of being constructed or fake but rather in being relational and/or extrinsic to individual character, in contrast to, say, the Aristotelian virtues. Meanwhile, some resources are scarce by circumstance (land, water, food) while others are scarce by structure (status, power, fame, success however currently measured).

1.4 SINGULAR

How, then, to proceed? For now, let us provisionally accept the general judgment of Margaret Boden, respected AI researcher, who wrote the following: "This notion is hugely contentious. People disagree about whether it could happen, whether it will happen, when it might happen, and whether it would be a good thing or a bad thing."[22] She goes on to say, "Singularity believers (S-believers) argue that technological advances make the Singularity inevitable." There is now a significant forking of opinion. "Some welcome this. They see humanity's problems solved. War, disease, hunger, boredom, even personal death ... all banished." Others see only threat and danger in the Singularity, some version of those nightmare scenarios we know so well from films and television (and about which more detail later).

Since it is a subject on which I have reflected for some time, and the focus of a previous book to which this one is a kind of complement, boredom strikes me as something that will not go so gentle into that good night of tech-dominated existence. The reason is simple: though feared and resented by those whom it afflicts, and occasionally celebrated by existentially minded philosophers and advocates of aimless creativity, boredom has been comprehensively folded into the systems of production and consumption that continue to mark the neo-liberal order of work, play, and life. It is hard to believe that any non-human agency could simply dispense with human boredom, given that it is such a reliable source of corporate revenue in the form of addictive stimulus, but I am perhaps biased on that question.[23] Alas, one might say the same of war, disease, and hunger, with even greater force: when there is revenue to be generated, or power to be hoarded, the misery of humankind always offers rich terrain for profit. There are other supplementary questions: could a non-animal entity experience suffering, for example? And if, as Nietzsche suggested, suffering edifies the soul – itself a debatable point – would a lack of suffering limit possible AI soulcraft?

Some S-believers colour themselves afraid rather than hopeful. They "predict the end of humanity – or anyway of civilized life as we know it." These S-believer-alarmists, as we might call them, include respected thinkers such as Stephen Hawking,[24] as well as everyone who has watched the films in the *Terminator* franchise, the *Matrix* franchise, the *Westworld* vision in either its film or television modes, both historical rebooted versions of *Battlestar Galactica*, certain episodes of *Star Trek: The Next Generation*, likewise of the British anthology series *Black Mirror*, or the animated series *Love, Death & Robots*. In these fraught cultural imaginings, as noted, the advanced algorithm-drive technologies of the near future are bent on the total domination or extinction of the human race or else we find seemingly comfortable advances (robotic vacuum cleaners, internalized memory capacity, reanimated memories of lost loved ones) that swiftly turn into nightmare dystopian scenarios. They almost succeed in making Darth Vader, of *Stars Wars* notoriety, who is in fact a cyborg and a biological father, seem sympathetic – as the George Lucas grand multi-feature narrative ultimately did, against all initial expectation.

By contrast, Singularity doubters (S-skeptics) *don't* expect the Singularity to happen, certainly not in the near future. "They allow that AI provides plenty to worry about. But they don't see an existential threat." By that we understand that there might be a threat or threats, say to factory workers or middle managers, but no real prospect of machine-led human extinction. Boden is herself a confessed moderate S-skeptic, who wants attention to drill down on what she considers the real dangers of AI, including defence systems that might run amok, the risks posed to job sectors that do not adapt nimbly enough to emerging technologies, and the omnipresence of human error and wickedness. This is wise. But in my view her take on post- or transhuman possibilities is too dour. "Transhumanism is an extreme example of how AI may change ideas about human nature," she writes, along the way appearing to dismiss any potential – and useful – speculation about the future of human existence.[25] *Extreme* ideas are useful even if they never come fully to pass: if consistent with an accepted proposition, we may learn from them.

Thus, while Boden's agnosticism about issues of belief and skepticism is apt enough for practical near-term purposes, it is also slightly off-base. If there is no obvious existential threat, or obvious existential benefit – i.e., the Singularity is neither clear salvation nor clear doom – there is nevertheless, without question, an existential *worry* to be addressed philosophically. Philosophers are not experts on creating technology, but they may just have a small purchase on questions of ethics and politics *with respect to* technology. That, as mentioned, is the core premise of everything that follows in these pages. We do not have to overpower technological discourses in order to make ethical discourses find purchase. (I know some may dispute that last claim, but I find support in the work of Descartes, Husserl, Heidegger, and others – if philosophy means anything, it means the kind of reflection that science itself, in instrumental modalities anyway, cannot perform.)

So: one thing we can say with certainty is that, as of this writing, and despite many overblown or hysterical claims, *the Singularity has not happened yet.* That is not at all to say, still less to prove, that it *cannot* happen. I will have much more to say about the Singularity in what follows, but for now I simply wish to flag the following concern. If (1) artificial general intelligence (AGI) is the goal of the existing research, and if (2) *autonomous* AGI – what I propose to call GAIAS, or generalized AIs with autonomy[26] – is the logical next step, then (3) we must begin asking ourselves the ethical and political questions that are relevant to such a potential shift in human existence. This can be tricky ground to traverse. Non-trivially, even generalized and autonomous entities leave open the possibility that they may not be conscious – hence the potential for a "zombie GAIA," to parallel the philosophical zombies that feature so prominently in recent philosophy of mind (discussed in the next chapter).[27] All clusters of features and inferential runs from one feature to another must be queried. Thus, and only thus, can we match current and future technological advances with appropriate philosophical reflection on our existing situation, especially concerning justice regimes that distribute and enforce rights and responsibilities among legal and political agents. Surely it has never been otherwise, from the very basic aspects of technology like hammers and chisels to advanced dangerous systems like nuclear weapons. Future-oriented critical reflection on technology is not fear or denial; it is a simple necessity. All technology looks like magic until it suddenly becomes taken for granted, and therefore almost invisible, like ideological presuppositions.[28]

There are, as we will see, both practical and in-principle objections to the prospect of GAIAS. These will be assessed in turn over the course of what follows. For now, let us note some provocative and so far unanswered, if not necessarily unanswerable, questions: could a GAIA ever laugh or be bored or explore its sexuality? Would it ever feel conflicted or confused about what to do or how to spend its time? Could it form irrational attachments to things, people, events, places, music, or singular works of art? Would it feel nostalgia or envy or anger? What about love or empathy? Among other things, these wonders call our own modes of existence into question in a manner that would have been entirely familiar to the author of *Being and Time*, if not perhaps to the post-*Kehre* or *Rektoratsrede* Heidegger.[29]

We feel so close to our moods and textured being-in-the-world that we frequently fail to ask a basic but profound question: where, if anywhere, does programming end and selfhood begin? A non-human entity may only be the result of input/output cycles and various recursive functions run on parallel distribution – but so are we. Consider film scholar Christine Reeh Peters's idea: film *as a medium* is itself already a form of artificial intelligence. "Trans- and post-humanist ideas like Cyborgs and robots or machines powered by AI are no longer ideas we know from the cinema screen," Peters writes. "I will argue for film as AI in the sense of producing a kind of thought beyond the limitations of human cognition and reasoning."[30] This argument puts a neat twist on Slavoj Žižek's idea that the Voight-Kampff machine in the original *Blade Runner* is an analogue for cinema itself, as well as an advanced kind of Turing test.

This notion of apparatus, or *Technik*, owes much to the work of Gilles Deleuze as well as that of Benjamin. The idea is not simply that of a tool or instrument, which can be taken up, used, and put down again, but rather of an organizing or governing principle of a system, which among other things pre-determines what will count as appropriate actions and "results" when the apparatus is engaged. Understood in this sense, an apparatus may be entirely non-material. The specifically cinematic version of the thesis pursued here, useful for present purposes, also is influenced by the notion of *automatism* in film, introduced by André Bazin and later expanded by

Stanley Cavell. Automatism is the notion that the camera, when recording the world for our viewing, has a certain inevitability and power that exceeds direct human control. The camera has its own eye, and this creates "the ontology of the film image.[31] Thus the basic argument is that the apparatus of film, as in all cases of technology that views and depicts the world, has a certain kind of *mind of its own* that extends beyond the focussed desires of its operator or director. In other words, an apparatus in the relevant Benjamin–Deleuze sense, is a semi-autonomous mechanism that controls the user at least as much as the user purportedly controls it. How the camera frames the world is a much more powerful device, even in a sense an intelligence, than the particular wishes of the humans on the given set. The camera "sees" with special attention and "delivers" a view of the world that can only be imagined as that relation between technology and world.[32]

This argument, which might seem at first blush fanciful in spite the etymological proximity of "automatic" and "automatism," which is to say executed without conscious (especially human) control, is rooted in long-standing speculation about the ontological function of any aesthetic medium but particularly film as understood as a series of still images of the world rendered into motion. Film deploys the world of real experience, whether on stage set or location, into raw material for narrative purposes. It captures the world for the sake of story and entertainment. In this sense, according to some thinkers, the medium is already "doing" philosophy. According to Benjamin, an early theorist of both still photography and moving picture, "the function of art today to be socially decisive is the practice of that interplay [between nature of humankind]. Film is there to train humankind in those apperceptions and reactions, which are conditioned by the handling of an apparatus, and whose role in human life increases nearly daily."[33] Anyone who spends significant time onscreen will recognize the power of this insight well beyond the walls of a neighbourhood cinema. We humans have become inseparable from our devices, to such an extent that Donna Haraway's early discussion of a general cyborg condition has been rendered an ordinary fact of life.[34] Whether or not this constitutes a condition of strong AI, let alone something approaching the Singularity, remains a matter of debate. But it can no longer be doubted that our intersection with non-human cognitive technology is comprehensive.

1.5 ΠЄЖТ

These opening-gambit questions are proffered not in the spirit of de-nunciation but rather of enduring wonder. Is this not a great time to re-imagine the future of human life? The point is not to demand that non-human artificial persons, should they prove possible, must resemble their human counterparts – that is very likely a false technological trail or a philosophical fool's errand or both. We already have strong philosophical arguments in favour of legal personhood status for entities, and even natural features, that bear *no particular relation to human biology*. Thus we are able to distinguish sharply between at least two notions of personhood relevant to the discussion of non-human artificial entities: that is, legal (fictional, in a sense) and metaphysical (real). Legal personhood offers status in legal systems, as the term indicates *prima facie*, but it can be granted by fiat to virtually any entity or grouping (corporations, natural features, even spectral entities like trusts) without their possessing any particular features or characteristics associated with personhood in a more robust sense. Metaphysical personhood, by contrast and though endlessly disputed, is understood to be the seat of bodily continuity and memory relevant for personal identity, including responsibility for past actions and future plans. Consciousness and autonomy would seem to be necessary conditions of the latter status but not of the former – a lake, forest, sailing ship, or cultural heritage might enjoy status as a legal person without possessing, or being able to possess, consciousness.

The bridging term in play here is the related but distinct notion of ethical personhood, which ties the deep metaphysical accounts both to bare legal systems and also to more nuanced and textured schemes of moral obligation and worth. I will have more to say about these ideas as we proceed, but for now the relevant issue concerns what sort of personhood might be accorded to autonomous artificial entities possessed of both bare sentience and func-tional consciousness. Human biology can become an unwelcome distraction in these considerations, just as it sometimes does in the analogous discussion of the moral and political status of existing non-human animals. Though robots, androids (by definition), and other artificial intelligences are often depicted as resembling humans in their anatomy, there is no special reason for this beyond debatable levels of relatability or potential comfort – we might accept such entities into expanded regimes of ethical life if they look at least a little bit like us. There is, *a fortiori*, no reason to think that there is something special about human biology when it comes to personhood. This is already starkly obvious when it comes to thinking about bare legal persons. The grounding assumption in what follows is that human biology might be likewise irrelevant in the case(s) of ethical and metaphysical personhood. We should not be sidetracked by questions of whether, and how, something we encounter is human.

No, the relevant question is whether we can find ways of bridging current understanding with future possibilities. Possibly the basic objections will prove insuperable: the necessary computing power for GAIAS will never be generated, say,[35] or the lack of phenomenal experience in created beings will deny them full status as autonomous agents.[36] There are also related problems from the human side, in that we tend to overestimate our levels of general rationality and competence.[37] That includes everything from routine cognitive errors on the order of forgetting you left your car's engine running overnight to large evolutionary disasters such as war and environmental degradation. Thus the assumed bright line, or definitive cognitive threshold, between human and non-human intelligence is anything but fixed, rigid, or obvious. There may be many issues of scale in play and nuances of permeability and vagueness.

Case in point: Perhaps the most enduring philosophical puzzle in AI thinking is the *frame problem*. This sketches issues of what, as mentioned, the philosopher Herbert Fingarette called the grasp of essential relevance.[38] In brief, a robust version of the frame problem is that a given designed system can successfully negotiate its programmed world but it cannot extend thought outside the offered frame. One way of seeing this, on the model of traditional speech-act theory, is that very sophisticated programs can be excellent at parsing the semantics of linguistic chains but quite bad at making the move from semantics to pragmatics.[39] That is, they can understand and even replicate the meaningful natural-language sequences that make for literal sense, but it is extremely hard if not impossible to program for such things as irony, implication, or what H.P. Grice labelled *conversational implicature*. As Grice demonstrated, critically following leads laid out by J.L. Austin and John Searle, humans are usually pretty good at understanding the non-semantic or even anti-semantic meanings of language. If, for example, I ask you what time it is and you reply "Well, the postman has just gone," the reply is *prima facie* uninformative and uncooperative. But if we both know, per convention, that the postman usually comes at about 1 p.m. every day, the balance of sense shifts to meaning. Or I might say "It's cold in here," implying to a person near the window that it should be closed, an action that can be understood and taken with no verbal acknowledgment.[40]

And so, while thinking might itself demand logical presuppositions such as negation ("not" functions) and the conditionals ("if-then" relations), these must be counted as necessary but not sufficient conditions for thinking in a robust sense. They also do not quite meet the INUS standard of conditionality – that is, insufficient but necessary *plus* unnecessary but sufficient conditions. This finessing of the typical necessary/sufficient conditions distinction is useful but not always revelatory because the slippage between kinds of conditions does not rule out the possibilities of nonsensical but apparently parseable sentences. Lewis Carroll is the master of this form, as "All mimsy were the borogroves" from *Jabberwocky* (1871) amply demonstrates, emerging under analysis as an example of syntactically sensible nonsense. A more recent example is Noam Chomsky's famous sentence "Colourless green ideas sleep furiously," which offers perfect syntax by the rules of natural language but makes no semantic sense – let alone pragmatic guidance.

These limitations emerging from natural language, and the tangled cognitive processes that both underwrite and express them, pose serious problems for conscious self-understanding. The moves from syntax to semantics to pragmatics are crucial to understanding the nature of being in the world. They are worth taking seriously for any future reflection about human consciousness and the nature of thinking itself because even very sophisticated algorithms that can process semantics in natural language may be entirely inept at pragmatics of the sort that even an only partly developed human – a child, say – can process with ease. But these issues are precisely that: *problems*. Which means by definition that they may eventually admit of solution, at least of some sort – we might have to abandon current modes of thinking about thinking in order to offer what might count as solutions. At the very least, we must choose to begin with these problems rather than, as in most reflections about AI, conclude with them as open, unsettled, and maybe endlessly deferred questions. Open questions are, after all, philosophy's stock in trade. The time for deferral is over. Once again, the basic ethico-political injunction is apt: right now we must think, as carefully as we can, about what our future looks like.

A note on this book's method, for clarity. As mentioned above, I mix cultural and philosophical references in what follows, with some deliberate intention of speculating beyond – but only a little beyond – the existing set of facts about AI and machine learning. Readers will have to decide for themselves whether this is illuminating, but given the flood of books, papers, articles, and studies that dominate the field, it seems at least interesting to proceed in this way and possibly useful to allow for human imagination, including fear and hope, to emerge as discursive forces in our thinking about the future of conscious, autonomous existence. Thus films and novels that feature depictions of artificial intelligence will be discussed. We should not take these as science, of course, or even accurate reportage, only as cultural speculation – perhaps fascinating and important, maybe even essential, cultural speculation. Such ephemeral products of the imagination reflect our anxieties and preoccupations. They are never insignificant or trivial, even when they are fleeting. They are, in a way, what dreams represent to individual human consciousness: psychic residue, with a power than cannot be ignored or explained away.

As also mentioned, the book will trace philosophical arguments from several subdisciplines, notably, ethics, politics, and general metaphysics. This is my somewhat halting attempt at a kind of Socratic-style back-and-forth discourse, in pursuit of the best conclusions we can articulate right now on this tangled set of questions.[41] How do we do philosophy when the rules of the game seem to be changed so decisively by growing human/non-human interactions? What follows therefore is a series of opening moves or gambits, making no attempt at a Scholar's Mate, still less a two-move Fool's Mate. Maybe something more like a Wing Gambit, one version of a Sicilian Defence, is on the board?[42] Latent within the larger argument, in common with some other recent work of mine on boredom, work, idling, and adventure, is a critique of the *upgrade anxiety* and doctrine *of inevitability* that are strongly associated, indeed often underwrite, the creep of techno-capitalism into every corner of self-aware existence. At an extreme, this leads to a posthuman fusion of human biology and system logic which – for better and worse, I will argue – signals a new form of conscious existence; at a minimum, these circumstances offer challenges to self-regard that are only badly met by the usual easy, miss-the-mark counter-arguments referencing individual human uniqueness, the beautiful illogic of the human heart, emotion triumphing over reason, and so on.[43] This is singularity in a distinct, and misleading, bio-specific register. We must strive for more subtle, less binary accounts of what it means – and will in future increasingly mean – to be an ethically and politically significant sentient entity.

Exciting can be another word for alarming, and these are indeed in that sense exciting times. Even a committed neo-Luddite like the present author – preoccupied with the injustices of technology's ceaseless march, the cruel fate of those left behind by the supposedly inevitable march of Big Tech – can be awestruck by the power and wonder of what we have created, and what lies before us *in potentia*. There is a reason that many science-fiction devotees turn their minds to philosophical reflection, if not necessarily academic careers in philosophy. Speculation on utopia and dystopia, quirky thought experiments, imagined scenarios, extensions of existing technology, and possible worlds are all the stuff of a truly open mind. But we should ever recall Aristotle's insight that the most divine part of ourselves is not what we fashion instrumentally but what we contemplate without prejudice or profit. That is the highest task of the human form of life – and, let us hope, of the posthuman as well. Open-mindedness about future posthuman possibilities is entirely compatible with skepticism, even incredulity, towards the bulldozing metanarratives of technology. We cannot fully embrace the posthuman, in other words, unless and until we have confronted the existential contours of the bare human condition – Lear on the heath is the dominant image now, stripped of servants, retainers, or badges of office, without fire or favour to warm and protect his mortal bones and waning, disastrous, all-too-human pride.

Uncanny Mirror, installation
by Mario Klingemaan at
Galerie Utopia, Munich, 2019.
Image courtesy of artist.

2

The Future Is Always Present
Status Report: Conflicted, Attentive, Liminal

2.1 WHAT VALLEY?

Consider, as the next beginning of a deeper investigation of these matters a snapshot of where we find ourselves right now with respect to non-human intelligence. We are, as so often in real phenomenological reflection, absolute beginners. I will therefore cite examples of both technology and regulative measures that hinge on highly developed algorithms, and trust that these examples will mine out at least some of the relevant points.

As the influence of machine learning and artificial intelligence has become more widespread in our social and cultural lives, anxieties about the rise of non-human cognitive ability have acquired new texture and urgency. The longstanding cultural fears of the disturbing or threatening robot other are matched by more grounded concerns about the potentially negative impact of even non-sentient AIs: inextricable integration, overreliance, surveillance, data gathering, uncontrolled decentralization of control, job losses, and the like. Meanwhile, speculation about the potential emergence of sentient, conscious, or autonomous AIs has fuelled important ethical, legal, and political debate about future scenarios in which humans might interact with non-human entities possessed of rights and responsibilities.

This book has concentrated on specific concerns about human-AI integration, both present and future. And so a useful twin-pillar approach will mirror the traditional philosophical and cognitive-science distinction between *weak* and *strong* AI.[1] On the weak side, we must consider already extant advanced systems dedicated to medical diagnosis, transportation logistics, architectural design, and so on. On the strong side, we must speculate about the possibility of emergent systems with the ability to extend cognitive ability in the direction of personhood. What are the relevant questions to entertain about both of these aspects of human-AI interaction? Will we (do we already?) co-exist with AIs? Will those conditions continue if and when weak AI develops into strong? Will there emerge, supposing the potential of sentient AIs, competition or even conflict between carbon-based and non-carbon-based intelligences?

What are the prominent depictions of non-human persons in extant cultural sources, and how should we decode them? A major component of our anxiety about AI is unrelated to actual technology circa the 2020s. Much of the dismissal and panic we witness over AI technology is a function of the *uncanny valley* effect, which can be more projection than reality. We bio-humans are comfortable with very non-human forms of technology, such as robotic assembly-line mechanism or space arms, which resemble human limbs in a rudimentary way only. But we are by nature inclined to develop stronger feelings of liking towards technologies that more and more resemble humans. At the same time, at a certain point, the non-human entity is *too* human. It becomes creepy, like a zombie or a vampire. Or an animated robot that is almost human but not quite. The valley of uncanniness is therefore that space of freefall weirdness into which we drift or drop before coming back to the entity as either human or distinctly not human. The basic notion of the uncanny valley is illustrated in figure 2.1.

What we see graphically depicted is the fact that non-human mechanisms run on a range that takes them from very alien to not-alien but yet not human enough, in a way that opens up the possibility of creepiness between those two nodes. Computer programmer and thinker Masahiro Mori was the main early expositor of the notion of this dip in comfort, based in part on Buddhist notions of consciousness and the basic personhood relation but also drawing on Western psychology about unnerving encounters with non-human agents (and human ones, such as sociopaths with deficient empathy response). Mori realized that developments in robotics were creating examples of non-human entities that were human-seeming enough, and yet not fully realized, so to make human beings feel peculiar, vertiginous, or even alarmed.[2] The valley has been explained with everything from *Star*

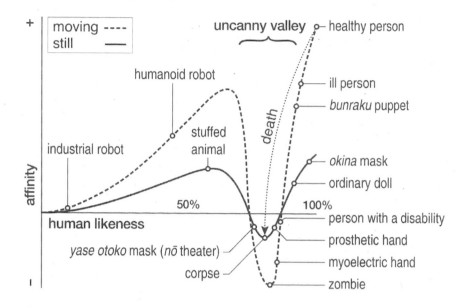

Fig 2.1
Mori's graph of the uncanny valley, translated by Karl MacDorman.
Credit: Karl MacDorman.

Wars characters (R2D2, C-3PO, frozen Han Solo) to animated movie figures such as the superhero family depicted in *The Incredibles*.

This concept of a human-not-human near resemblance, and what is now recognized as the associated valley, is likewise rooted in psychological theories indebted to Ernst Jentsch and Sigmund Freud, neither of whom had any notion of robotics but who nevertheless recognized that dolls, revenants, mechanical simulacra, *doppelgängers*, and similar "not quite right" elements of interpersonal experience unsettled human comfort. The chart above includes some aspects of this general psychological awareness (corpse, zombie, bunraku puppet). The moving/still distinction is controversial, but it is certainly true, for example, that a zombie is much more unnerving than a corpse, even though both are based on a deceased human body. Corpses do not want to eat your brains and do not come shambling or running toward you. (On the particular distinction between shambling and running, see later discussion of bad improvements and the allegedly upgraded but in fact inferior *fast zombie*.)

Though some definitions of the uncanny valley point to familiarity, the vertical axis in figure 2.1 is labelled "affinity," a nod to Mori's illuminating use of the word *shinwakan*. Nobody is much unsettled by the idea of a robotic arm, even if they have never seen one in action. It's just a mechanical device with slightly arm-like qualities. Most humans are, by contrast, quite disturbed by a human-seeming but still not quite human android, even if they have never experienced that in person either. The cinematic examples of that human-not-human disturbance would include examples already discussed, synthetics and Replicants.[3] The Voight-Kampff test featured in Ridley Scott's masterly 1982 film *Blade Runner* is, in effect, an uncanniness detector as well as an advanced version of the Turing test, to separate humans from non-humans.[4] The puffing optic-nerve apparatus, combined with questions pressed upon a subject by Blade Runner agents, measures empathy, relation to other entities natural and artificial, and social functionality. Fans of the original film will know that you probably shouldn't ask a suspected Replicant about his mother; also, perhaps, that the apparatus is comparable to other mechanisms for detecting outliers who are "passing" within general populations, the AI equivalent of "gaydar" or race-detection triggers.

The Turing test, meanwhile, is now almost idiomatic as a phrase about discerning the prospect of indistinguishable-from-human sentient AIs. But it is severely limited. Outlined by the eminent computer scientist A.M. Turing in a 1950 philosophy journal article called "Computing Machinery and Intelligence,"[5] its central and initial question was "Can machines think?" But Turing, having quickly abandoned the usual philosophical methods of defining the terms *machine* and *think*, almost immediately proposed instead the famous "imitation game" as a substitute method. Here is his proposal:

> The new form of the problem can be described in terms of a game which we call the "imitation game." It is played with three people, a man (A), a woman (B), and an interrogator (C) who may be of either sex. The interrogator stays in a room apart from the other two. The object of the game for the interrogator is to determine which of the other two is the man and which is the woman. He knows them by

labels X and Y, and at the end of the game he says either "X is A and Y is B" or "X is B and Y is A." The interrogator is allowed to put questions to A and B thus:

C: Will X please tell me the length of his or her hair?

Now suppose X is actually A, then A must answer. It is A's object in the game to try and cause C to make the wrong identification. His answer might therefore be, "My hair is shingled, and the longest strands are about nine inches long."

In order that tones of voice may not help the interrogator the answers should be written, or better still, typewritten.

As commentators have noted, we must set aside the sexist overtones of this version of the imitation game, which depends on stereotypical male/female identity markers, and focus on the main point, namely, that distinguishability between male and female voices in the game would in turn underwrite a conclusion of *indistinguishability* between machine and human males and females in the global system. This doubled conclusion is then assumed to be the gold standard of determining the presence of machine intelligence within the global system. If I cannot tell whether or not my interlocutor is present and conscious, then the issue of their existence is moot. Dialogue as engagement is consciousness in action.

But of course indistinguishability does not meet the whole case by a long throw. Even within Turing's lifetime there were developed programs sophisticated enough to fool human interlocutors, and today we have natural-language simulators with far more advanced abilities. As critics have noted, Turing's proposed queries – "Please write me a sonnet on the subject of the Forth Bridge." "Add 34957 to 70764." "Do you play chess?" – are all very basic and do not penetrate to the heart of the matter. And Turing's remaining arguments, which are replies to objections offered in a somewhat scholastic style, are not very illuminating. The objection that "thinking is a function of man's immortal soul" is only on point for those with previous unshakable presuppositions. The more scientific objection that references the limitations of discrete-state machines due to Gödel's incompleteness theorem – roughly, the result that no consistent system can prove every truth of arithmetic – is rejected because, not surprisingly, perfect consistency and completeness probably lie beyond the ken of human intelligence and therefore do not, and cannot, stand as either necessary or sufficient conditions of consciousness let alone a robust set of both.

As critics have noted, one objection that Turing cannot fight off arises from the historical past of computing. Countess Augusta Ada Lovelace, known for her work on Charles Babbage's proposed "difference engine" (a simple calculator) and its successor the "analytical engine" (the progenitor of all digital binary computing), had voiced an objection we still hear today, about input/output relations and programming limits. This limit-case objection is echoed in Margaret Boden's and others' skepticism about the Singularity. One current leading expert summarized the issue this way: "AI has been amazingly successful in areas such as game playing, missile defense, pattern recognition, and, most recently, protein folding prediction. It has been modestly successful in processing linguistic text (illustrated, for example, by Google Translate)," the argument ran. "But in many other areas the results have been disappointing. After 50 years of attempts to create an intelligent conversation machine, computer answering services such as those offered by banks still perform miserably … [T]here are limits to the potential of AI, and […] these limits have to do with the nature of complex systems."[6]

Complexity here is a catch-all, or stand-in, concept intended to cover a variety of side constraints on generalized autonomy, including juggling and prioritizing of shifting inputs and nearly instant counters to the frame problem classed under common human notions such as relevance, practicality, or urgency. Such contemporary cautions do no more than reprise the hedging of ambition that has marked the less speculative and more practical current of AI research from the beginning. "The Analytical Engine has no pretensions to *originate* anything," Lady Lovelace wrote in the earliest days of imagining non-human forms of processing power or algorithmic robustness. "It can do *whatever we know how to order it* to perform."[7] The more advanced and contemporary counter-objection is that recursive algorithms of sufficient robustness can generate new and sometimes astonishing results even within their rigid programming limits and thus may be said to learn and innovate. That is, if you program a system to produce speech or music or visual art, it can appear to exceed the physical limits of the original I/O relation in basic programming. Thus the idea of machine learning. The norm is arguably no longer the standard "garbage in, garbage out" assumption of early programming days. But whether apparent innovative ability and recursive internal upgrading constitutes sentience or consciousness remains the open and apparently unanswerable question. Descartes's notion of a centralized individual consciousness may be subject to objection, but his problem of other minds remains with us.

Which is to say something like this: I must assume that all the human beings I have met are conscious in a manner similar to my own experience. But how could I ever know for certain that this is so, since I cannot directly access their own inward experience. Furthermore, perhaps this very idea of "inwardness" is mistaken and we should instead, per Wittgenstein and Ryle and some skeptics about proposed "philosophical zombies," which leave open the question of consciousness relating to actions in the world, revert to a strict behaviourist conception of other entities and simply judge them on the basis of how they interact with me and the world.[8] What could possibly be the difference if they act just like other entities that seem to be endowed with inner mentality? The implicit argument is that, at the summit of the uncanny valley, you or I might not be able to identity, at first glance anyway and maybe even over time, a non-human entity. But that confusion or identification raises the essential question. If the non-humans are functionally identical to humans, except via detection by a sophisticated and invasive technology of interrogations, why not simply accept them as persons? The Replicants have limited lifespans, and are troubled by that, but doesn't that make them just as "human" as any organic mortal? This is why "healthy person" might be exactly the right term for the return from the uncanny valley as long as, per earlier arguments, *person* is not limited to carbon-based humans gestated and birthed by other humans.

Human beings are forever returned by life to our imperfect selves, our limited compassion, our cramped ambitions, our vulnerability and mortality. We are also reminded almost daily of our history of denying personhood and humanity to other biological entities almost entirely identical with ourselves. There is no shiny New Promethean application or device to complete our aspirations and flirt with immortality, despite what some of the high-minded billionaires in Silicon Valley like to claim, just the same insuperable forces of thwarted desire and ambition that were imagined in Mary Shelley's still eerily prescient novel *Frankenstein; Or, the Modern Prometheus* (1818). Scientific rather mythological fire-bringer Victor Frankenstein creates artificial life, to be sure, but only in a manner that makes his pathetic monster a target for misunderstanding, violence, and cessation. A dream dashed, an entity tortured by misunderstanding and fear.

2.2 RIGHTS AND RESPONSIBILITIES

So now, let us ask this: Suppose there are, or could be, conscious and autonomous non-human persons. What would their status be in ethical terms? Traditional rights regimes are conceptually unstable, and acknowledging this presents an opportunity to expand and revise the basic assumptions. Extension of recognition of rights to non-humans has, as mentioned, become a live legal and philosophical issue, but we seem even more resistant to taking seriously that non-biological, non-human entities – beings who share intelligence and might begin to share consciousness with humans – might have rights. There would appear to be no principled reasons for rejecting the possibility that AIs could achieve consciousness, raising the issue of why there is so much resistance to the prospect of GAIAs in the first place. Is it because we don't, even now, in a post-Cartesian, post-Freudian world, really understand the nature of personhood? When does personality meld into that personhood or vice versa?

Some very profound and troubling questions now emerge, not to be ignored. Can an AI laugh? Can it tell a joke? Can it become bored, like any teenager? Does it love, or lust, or aspire to greater things? From the other side, can I or another human being forge a friendship with an AI, perhaps even a loving relationship? This last question seems to pre-occupy many of my younger colleagues, for reasons about which I won't speculate too far. (For the record, all of my friends are – so far – either human, imaginary, fictional, or feline.) We can only explore such fascinating and potentially cage-rattling issues by, first, opening our minds to at least the bare possibility of non-human entities possessed of emotional richness or (in the crucial caveat) a sufficiently robust simulacrum thereof. Once again, this possibility of non-biological consciousness may turn out to yield an empty set, but we will remain unable to reach that conclusion without examining empirical evidence and real advances in programming and interface. It is not, or not yet, a matter of categorical ruling-out, though it is easy enough to see why many people would prefer it were thus.

At a minimum, the non-categorical nature of the inquiry has opened up intriguing spaces for the play of human imagination. For centuries, the non-human Other has been figured as both lover and demon, nemesis and saviour. In a world of meaning dominated by digital technology it is inevitable that these Others will enter the scene as robotic, often android creations: that is, mechanical and algorithmic systems that either don't resemble human beings at all or resemble them enough to evade the headlong pitch into the uncanny valley(s) discussed later in this book. One striking exception, considering the idea of love and friendship, is depicted in Spike Jonze's film *Her* (2013), starring Joaquin Phoenix and the voice of Scarlett Johansson. Phoenix plays Theodore Twombley, a lonely and lovelorn greeting-card card writer who begins a relationship with a disembodied, adaptive, and extremely expensive operating system that combines personal services with increasingly intimate connections. The film is notable not only for the texture it brings to this romantic tragicomedy, where compatibility and physical connection prove impossible, but also for taking seriously the inner life of Samantha, the non-mortal os. Class and wealth are occluded in the film's vista: everyone seems urban, middle-class, and self-involved just as they might be in midtown Manhattan or downtown Toronto. Twombley's crisis moments come when he realizes (a) that the os with whom he's fallen in love is simultaneously conducting *many thousands* of similar relationships with other humans, and (b) when she tells him she has come under the influence of another, older AI, here creepily voiced as a former philosophy professor, who is charting Samantha's pathways to self-actualization via system upgrade. There is a reconciliation of the lovers as they part, but the ending of the film cannot quite evade a hint of cheap Woody Allen wisdom: *It was just one of those things.* Twombley finally moves on by writing a letter for himself and not a customer, his own expressed thoughts a rescue from transaction.

Even with its flaws, Jonze's depiction of the potential desires and evolving nature of non-human existence is welcome, a relatively rare example of taking the Other seriously, especially in not wishing merely to be "more human." Ian McEwan's novel *Machines Like Me* (2019) does not really enter inside the consciousness of its central male android, Adam, but does vividly show some details of the alignment problem, especially with respect to such ethical values as truthfulness and justice, about which humans and non-humans may not agree. The emergent love triangle of Adam and his human co-owners Charlie and Miranda leads to a tragic *denouement* in which the ethical and legal status of Adam is put into haunting question. Is disconnecting an artificial life, which is after all simply a piece of personal property even if you are having sex with it, more akin to trashing an old car or to committing a premeditated murder? Alan Turing, appearing here as an alternate-timeline fictional character circa the mid-1980s, is in no doubt whatsoever about the issue. Barely controlling his rage at Charlie's rashness in dealing with Adam, he emerges, in cameo, as the novel's only real moral presence. But his is a voice from a political future not yet realized even as Adam's is a life not yet valued or protected by law.

These nuanced, relationship-based treatments of human-machine ethics and politics are not the norm. Despite some prominent exceptions, the discussion of generalized autonomous AI has centred largely on its presumed, often negative effects on humans – e.g., the risks of surveillance, job insecurity, and lack of accountability. There is also a large cultural legacy of fear and distrust when it comes to non-human intelligent agents – the various guises of the Killer Robot. Both real-world and speculative cases tend to emphasize the dangerous single-mindedness and lack of feeling thought to be characteristic of all non-human systems, no matter how advanced. However, I want to extend the discussion on the risks to sentient AIS themselves from their human creators. Sophisticated sentient AIS would represent, by all reasonable accounts, the potential for a new form of autonomous life. This could be so on both weak and strong readings of the concept of sentience. The weak reading (sentience as accumulation and partial ordering of simple or raw feels) would open up a radically inclusive notion of personhood, to include many extant non-human entities and challenge human ascendancy in decisive ways. The strong reading (sentience as full consciousness) offers a stronger inferential path but starting from a more exclusive precondition.

Both readings have far-reaching political implications for existing justice regimes and their defensible futures. On either path – permissive versus restrictive notions of both sentience and personhood – if sentience in some sense can be traced to self-governing, then entities enjoying that cognitive condition would presumptively, at least on some philosophical accounts, command status as persons. But how will they in fact be treated? In the rest of this chapter, I outline four plausible future scenarios in which sentient AIS come into being, and which pose deep questions for traditional philosophical discourses concerning non-human or non-standard entities. These scenarios should give us pause about the personhood status of generalized, potentially autonomous AIS.

2.3 POSTHUMAN RIGHTS?

Traditional regimes for the protection of rights have evolved over centuries of debate concerning (a) who counts as a legitimate rights-holder, (b) what rights are claimable by such legitimate holders, and (c) how the resulting claims are to be enforced. The existing structure for the protection of human rights has several branches of influence that span these same centuries in the Western philosophical tradition. These include Kantian arguments concerning the dignity and sovereignty of persons conceived as moral agents; the liberal norms defended by Locke and Spinoza, among others, concerning ownership of body and labour, hence personal freedom (also, sometimes, private property); and the natural law tradition that views individuals as creatures of Providence worthy of respect and protection.[9] All of these influences inform, though not always explicitly, the doctrines and policies of contemporary human rights discourse. The most obvious, and perhaps also most significant, document in this discourse, at least over the last century, is the 1948 Universal Declaration of Human Rights, adopted on 10 December of that year in Paris, as United Nations Resolution 217, with a membership vote of forty-eight in favour out of fifty-eight total delegates, with eight abstentions and two non-votes. Its thirty articles were drafted by McGill University law professor John Humphrey and championed with vigour by Eleanor Roosevelt, the UDHR has been a touchstone of human rights thinking over the past half-century and more. Its claims, informed by the philosophical background just mentioned, are nevertheless entirely pragmatic and aimed at regulatory compliance.

The most striking features of the UDHR are its contextual between-the-lines narratives. Working in the immediate aftermath of the Second World War, and especially emerging evidence concerning the planned extermination of peoples according to the Nazis' Wannsee Conference plan (20 January 1942) – otherwise known as the Final Solution to the Jewish Question (*Endlösung der Judenfrage*) – Humphrey and Roosevelt were keenly aware that, however powerful were traditional just war doctrines of *ius in bello* (conduct during wartime), something else was needed to protect the very idea of the human person. The distinction between *war crimes* and *crimes against humanity* becomes essential when we wish to discriminate between excessive or cruel behaviour on the battlefield and the systematic plan for targeted genocides.[10] The UDHR aimed at articulating what was particular to the idea of human rights, that is, rights claimable by any human being simply in virtue of being human, and, furthermore, it wished to claim the universalism of a Kantian sort that would distinguish such rights from specific legal rights which might – which had been – arbitrarily revoked by given jurisdictions. The jurisdiction of universal human rights is not to be violated or controlled by anyone.

One's attitude to the UDHR depends in large measure on how these two categories – *human* and *universal* – stand in one's basic philosophical commitment-set. There are potential problems with both categories. First, while we might wish to acknowledge rights that belong to humans *qua* humans, we must note at least two immediate conceptual difficulties. That is, (a) is "human" a stable category even biologically? Many heinous instances of depravity and violence hinge precisely on the denial of the status to groups of entities targeted for violence or elimination. One has only to recall the bafflement exhibited by some former Nazi officials when they were tried for crimes against humanity: the Jews were not human, they were vermin or parasites, and therefore could be exterminated without violations of conscience. In a nightmare scenario, a genocidal program could be carried out by someone who *at the very same time* considered the program to be in compliance with the UDHR. *Mutatis mutandis*, this same twisted logic could be applied to handicapped persons, children, women, people of colour, and so on – not one of which examples is speculative, but alas are all factual.

Likewise, we must ask (b) whether human is the relevant category for rights protection. Any rights regime involves some form of means test, to qualify for inclusion within the regime, but "human" is a biological category, at best a disputed one, and therefore seems an unstable basis for a program of rights protection. Why, after all, should biology determine whether an entity qualifies for the cover of law? We can take note of Agamben's vivid depictions of "bare life," and also note the inherent vulnerability of the human form as part of the rights logic (we feel pain, we suffer, we die), and yet still wonder whether this is the right place to locate the threshold of protection.[11] In effect, the (b) worry is a logical extension of the possible depredations conceived under the (a) worry. In sum, "human being" seems initially promising as the fundamental basis of rights claims and yet the category also appears subject to immediate potential pathologies driven by its basis in biology.

Second, matters stand similarly with respect to the concept of universalism. Kant's arguments, the most forceful available, suggest that any moral agent, regardless of specific characteristics, is part of the Kingdom of Ends and therefore a self-legislating individual who, by being so, legislates for all others. There is nothing in Kant's system to deny the possibility of off-world moral agents who would qualify as relevant members of the universal population. The Earth is not the Universe, after all. If, in practice, all the moral agents I have so far met have been Earthlings, and all or most of them have been human, well, that is a contingent not necessary cluster of facts. If universal is to mean anything, it can't merely mean those we know and already recognize – this would very quickly toss us back to the problems of defining "human" with (at least) INUS conditionality, if not gold-standard N&S or IFF accounts.

But *universal* is itself a tricky property, not least because it is resisted by those who want to insist on particularity and distinction. Cultural difference and those who defend it seem to cut against universalism, which is often perceived as a top-down mechanism for eliminating distinct claims of identity. One needn't look far for examples of this anti-universalist sentiment, from the toxic ethnic nationalisms of twenty-first-century anti-immigrant retrenchment (Sweden, England, the United States, etc.), to the more benign but still resistant forms of identity politics which view universalist rhetoric as a con game to obscure special narratives: Latinx, LGBTQ2S+, Black, and Indigenous (to name some). From these perspectives, "universal" is just another word for the bland, graded-road white globalism that is the enemy of vibrant identity.

Worse, universalism can sometimes appear, despite good intentions, to be allied with objectively harmful economic regimes of the New World Order – now not so new – of globalization and deregulation in trade and capital. Since it is well known that such regimes have drastic differential effects, even as their advocates claim a rising tide for all boats, the language of universalism grows suspect just to the extent that it is consistent with the spread of global capital. The once-bright promise of covering-law universalism, that everyone shall be protected, begins to look like an elaborate sham to centralize control of resources and wealth in the hands of the few, ruthless, and lucky.

There are legitimate responses to these worries. One can, for example, conceive of a form of universalism that is not of the covering-law type but rather particular to local circumstances. That is, universal extension remains the overall goal but specific conditions can govern the precise shape of its realization. Possible analogies include such apparently (but not really) trivial things like sports and sexuality. In the former case, the basic rules of a game can be observed in multiple locations *even as* the specific details of their execution can vary widely. The World Cup in soccer offers an excellent example of roots-up rather than covering-law universalism, for example. The rules are the same for everyone, but the style of play and the vast permutations of play within the rules still preserve the values of local identity. With respect to sexuality, including things like clothing, mating rituals, and physical intimacy, the basics are once more universal but with vast local differentiation. Such differentiation is the potential source of both confusion and conflict, to be sure, but the fact of sexuality itself remains constant.

In offering these analogies, we must not underestimate the degree of lurking conflict. On the contrary, it is precisely the tension between universal structures or frames of reference and their local, contingent realization that makes clear thinking about roots-up regimes so necessary. Rights regimes are dominated by assumptions, again often Kantian, that the bearers of rights are not only individuals but deracinated, abstract individuals: the rational choosers of standard economic analysis, really, or the isolated contractarian actors that appear everywhere from Hobbes, Locke, and Rousseau to Rawls and Gauthier.[12] Could we conceive of a universal rights regime, human or otherwise, that surrendered the strong covering-law option and this implicit individualism in favour of a nuanced roots-up version? If so, the conflicted notion of universalism might still have some moral and political traction in a wildly diverse world.

All of this is really to say that traditional rights regimes are conceptually unstable, but that this may provide us with an unparalleled opportunity to expand and revise their basic assumptions. This is happening already, as we know, such that we human animals ought to be forced, morally or even legally, to alter our behaviour with respect to treatment, eating habits, and duties of care.[13] Other advocates consider non-specific entities, such as the environment or the planet, or specific forests and regions, to possess rights that should be in turn morally and legally claimable, if only via third-party advocacy.[14] There are also those who argue that groups or cultural identities themselves have rights, not just the individuals who fall under their umbrellas of meaning.[15] In none of these cases is the target rights-bearer able to claim the rights explicitly.

But this is not possibly a crippling objection. Even under straight-up presumptions of individualism and universalism, the sufferers of rights violations are not always able to speak for themselves. Sometimes they are incarcerated. Sometimes they have been silenced by threats and torture. Sometimes they are just no longer with us. In no case is it a valid objection that a violated entity cannot make its own claim. Thus there is no reason in principle to object to the inclusion in rights regimes of those who cannot speak for themselves or those who are not even capable of speech. That is what advocates are for. The most promising way forward in rights thinking is to execute analysis on the basis of risk.

Risk in turn is a function of vulnerability, and the distribution of risk, while dependent on many factors including birthright lotteries and structural limitations, is the central concern of traditional social justice. If the protection of human rights and the punishment of their violation are to mean anything, they must serve the ends of justice in this respect. Minimizing risk, or equalizing its distribution, are pragmatic goals of a valid rights regime. Now we must ask: is such a regime open to the possibility of non-human agents who are individual and conscious but not biological? This is the main question before us: can AIS ever be persons or are we too wedded to the notion that personhood, despite ample evidence, is rooted in biology?

2.4 SENTIENT NON-HUMANS?

Philosophers are divided, and have been for some time, concerning the prospect of generalized autonomous AIS, whether in human form or not, who could achieve consciousness. They are nevertheless united in thinking that such consciousness, supposing it possible, is at least a necessary condition of potential personhood. Further conditions conducing to sufficiency might include decision-making ability, the awareness of choice and its consequences, and the ability to tell right from wrong, to suffer and be violated, and so on. Only such a being would seem a likely candidate for inclusion within any traditional rights regime, even one open to quite radical forms of otherness within the ambit of metaphysical personhood. It is not enough, in other words, that a class of things or concepts be granted legal status; this can be revoked and is dependent on contingent facts about given systems of law and regulation. Non-human entities must have access to more reliable status in the covering-law sense of universal (i.e., class-wide) rights and responsibilities. What are the conditions of possibility for this kind of expansion of the notion of personhood and its associated regimes of protection and status?

Thinkers such as John Searle have argued that a GAIA is impossible because of the role programming takes within the structure of the AI, however complex and apparently responsive.[16] Searle's well-known "Chinese room" thought experiment is designed to highlight the fact that a seemingly engaged natural-language conversation program is not, in fact, experiencing any cognitive understanding of the language even as it is being successfully computed.[17] A room is conceived as holding inside it a person who, according to a codebook, matched incoming English-language words and sentences to outgoing Chinese ones. By matching input-symbol to output-symbol, the algorithm operating on the room set-up appears to understand the conversation but is in fact simply exercising accurate matching techniques with no attendant consciousness. One may immediately object, as many have, that it is the *total system* of the Chinese room that achieves understanding, not some homunculus within the room, and so it is actually correct to say that the system overall *does* understand Chinese. Searle's skeptical position raises the stakes for GAIA consciousness, but it does not dispose of the question.[18]

Many researchers have challenged the reliability of the language-upgrade criterion as even a necessary, let alone also sufficient, condition of conscious thought. In colloquial terms, humans tend to overestimate the importance of linguistic ability, perhaps because we enjoy engaging with each other socially. And so we therefore tend to underestimate the cognitive capacities of entities who seem to lack linguistic ability or try to find analogues to our own capacities (in dolphins or whales or chimpanzees). Several recent theorists have sought to replace that language-dominated model of cognition with other frameworks that privilege mapping ability. This is potentially quite amazing since, as we all have cause to know (per the insight of theorist Alfred Korzybski) *the map is not the territory*. But the ability to conceive of maps at all, as serviceable devices, and read back from them to orient ourselves to the world, sometimes involves very high cognitive stakes – though it can also be quite basic, as in "X marks the spot" plus a dotted line from palm tree to chest of gold doubloons. Even in basic cases, however, a map is a miniature graphic representation of the world, and understanding the relation between the two involves advanced-order thinking so that we can, as it were, imagine ourselves within the graphic world of the map. To some, this is far more developed functionality than syntax and semantics – though one must acknowledge that the debates continue.[19]

One possible outcome of recent disputes is the *global workspace theory* of consciousness, which I will discuss in more detail in chapter 4. For now, I highlight that the theory suggests not only that the human mind is modular in some important ways but also that it is effective at delegating and offloading certain burdens or tasks as need arises. Information can be processed, tasks can be conceived and executed, emotions and attachments entertained, physical ailments acknowledged, all from a central source that anticipates encounters (rehearsing what you will say in an imminent conversation), stores memories in layered fashion (working memory versus deep memory), and executes ideation more or less on demand.[20] Suppose, for example, that consciousness, understood as awareness of self-in-world, is an emergent property of sufficiently complex algorithmic functions even without language but with an ability to handle the frame problem. This might resemble the development of the human mind as it moves from infancy to childhood to adolescence and beyond. Humans have large cognitive capacity but it must be developed over time to generate the sense of distinct self that we associate with individual selfhood, and hence the need for legal and moral protection. Perhaps a GAIA will be like this, complexifying its (non-conscious) algorithmic functions until, at some indeterminate point, it begins to experience individual consciousness.

But this may be all too human a scenario. What if non-human agency develops, instead, as collective or system-wide property of interlinked complex algorithms? If we take seriously the idea that non-humans are worthy of rights protection under existing traditional regimes, it would seem perverse to deny such protection to a vulnerable and responsive system that, for various good reasons, does not (or not yet) exhibit the individual subjectivity of human agents. Such agency may be the fallback position of most rights claims, but it is not the only standard thereof. Rights-bearing "subjects" come in more than one guise.

Another standard objection to the program of strong AI – the realization of a fully conscious individual non-biological system – is that such an entity must entail embodiment, so that it can experience the world phenomenologically and therefore understand its emplacement within environments. This has seemed an insuperable barrier to many (but not all) philosophers, since the deployment of a body appears to be beyond the technological capacities of AI systems. Furthermore, such deployment might seem to depend on a long evolutionary chain whereby the physical organism becomes adapted to the larger conditions of life experience – what some philosophers call the *Umwelt*.[21] The givenness of the world around us is not incidental, nor is our thrownness into it, to borrow Heidegger's existential-phenomenological formulation. Other thinkers, by contrast, do not accept the necessity of embodiment as a condition of possibility for consciousness.[22]

Once again, the assumptions are revealed as tenuous, if not outright invalid, and based upon once-baseline behaviour that is everywhere changing under existing technological conditions. Yes, most human agents have bodies that move through the world, exercising the basic physical sensorium to gather, collate, and filter external stimuli for internal purposes. A sense of emplacement remains an important dimension of human phenomenology, as do the sense-driven experiences of seeing, hearing, tasting, and feeling. Without sunsets, symphonies, good meals, and relational intimacy, the world is a dry place for humans. But this norm admits of many exceptions: there are significant numbers of human agents with less than optimal sensory or ambulatory ability, for example, who have been stigmatized and punished for these perceived "deficits." For example, I am myself deaf in one ear, which deprives me of some peak experiences – enjoying the music I love as I did in the past – but without challenging my sense of self. I also can't run or jump the way I used to – who can? But other variances from baseline are far more serious, long-lasting, and directly related to quality of life.

Even more significantly, there are many extensions of personhood achieved with non-physical stimuli: online interactions, media immersion, disembodied tracing, and so on. These spectral stretchings of the person into disembodied non-location do not appear to threaten one's individuality or any of the other features that make us legitimate claimants of rights protection. I can be, for example, vulnerable to forms of suffering that are not based in the experience of physical pain, as in humiliation or vilification.

Can we accept, as a matter of argument, that there is no knock-down, in-principle objection to the possibility of a GAIA achieving something like consciousness and, therefore, something exactly like the kind of personhood worthy of rights protection? There are many outstanding issues. Consider a few. Would such a GAIA seek the protections offered by a rights regime? Perhaps, if non-mortal and spread across multiple systems, it would not need such protection or would consider itself superior to the point of arrogance. Would a GAIA even resemble individual consciousness? The robot/android image is so indelible in literary and cinematic culture that we may overlook the possibility that a conscious GAIA will look, or be, entirely different.

These questions are ones that often invoke fear reactions concerning the prospects of conscious GAIAS, so before I sketch my four scenarios of how this might all play out, allow me to offer a brief analysis of AI fear.

2.5 OTHERNESS AND FEAR

There are countless depictions of the non-human conscious, autonomous agent as a potent threat to human complacency, in particular when the uncanny valley approach noted earlier suggests that a near-perfect android might be *almost* indistinguishable from a "normal" or "healthy" human person. This trope of near-resemblance is certainly as old as Frankenstein's benighted monster, as noted, but has even deeper roots in myths of the Golem, the human-seeming trickster, and other unsettling mirrors held up to ourselves in various re-enactments of Freud's notion of the uncanny as unwitting, unwelcome reflection of human imperfection. As Norbert Weiner wrote in his now-classic text *Cybernetics* (and a much-quoted passage), the possibility of artificial people has haunted human existence from its very beginning:

> At every stage of technique since Daedalus or Hero of Alexandria the ability of the artificer to produce a working simulacrum of a living organism has always intrigued people. This desire to produce and to study automata has always been expressed in terms of the living technique of the age … In the days of magic, we have the bizarre and sinister concept of the Golem, that figure of clay into which the Rabbi of Prague breathed life with the blasphemy of the Ineffable Name of God. In the time of Newton, the automaton becomes the clockwork music box, with the little offices pirouetting stiffly on top. In the nineteenth century, the automaton is a glorified heat engine, burning some combustible fuel instead of the glycogen of the human muscles. Finally, the present automaton opens doors by means of photocells, or points guns to the play at which a radar beam picks up an airplane, or competes the solution of a differential equation.[23]

Magic and the human confrontation of mind with world is as old as civilization, and renewed with every instance of ground-breaking technology. This is not news.

Just before such a stage of close or even perfect resemblance is the depths of the valley, where a non-human entity is just human-seeming enough to be creepy. Again, many examples are proximate: the affectless Synthetics in the *Alien* film franchise, say, or the second- and third-generation Terminators in that film franchise, and so on. For current purposes, the essential philosophical question concerns the oscillations created between apparent or at least partial humanness and the elements of otherness indivisible from non-human conditions of existence. In many ways, this series of oscillations – they're like us! wait, they're not like us! – exactly matches the same anxieties evident in social movements that expanded the range of legal status and rights regimes within the biological category of the human. Entities now uncontroversial within that bio-legal status were once excluded from it, shamefully, and even now there are mechanisms within legal and national regimes to exclude presumptive claimers of "inside" status. As discussed, one thinks of the demonization of the enemy in times of war, such that the Japanese or the Germans or the Saracens are perceived as less than human as a prologue to killing them without remorse; or the twisted genocidal logic that condemns whole races, religions, or ethnicities to the non-human condition of revocable bare life: Jews, Rwandans, Armenians, Blacks, gays, Indigenous peoples, and so on (and, alas, on and on again).

This same genocidal motive appears relevant to the question of non-human entities with advanced cognitive and active abilities. Some thinkers have tried to imagine a way that these could be integrated into human life without granting them full status. One well-known version of this is Isaac Asimov's Three Laws of Robotics. They are:

Law One – "A robot may not injure a human being or, through inaction, allow a human being to come to harm."

Law Two – "A robot must obey orders given to it by human beings except where such orders would conflict with the First Law."

Law Three – "A robot must protect its own existence, as long as such protection does not conflict with the First or Second Law."

Asimov later added the "Zeroth Law," above all the others – "A robot may not harm humanity, or, by inaction, allow humanity to come to harm."

As many commentators have noted, these laws contain inconsistencies as well as practical flaws that make them misleading and unhelpful. As one critic complained, after pointing out that the "laws" are just a novelist's plot device, the nested structure of the laws actually permits internal contradiction:

"For example, in one of Asimov's stories, robots are made to follow the laws, but they are given a certain meaning of 'human.' Prefiguring what now goes on in real-world ethnic cleansing campaigns, the robots only recognize people of a certain group as 'human.' They follow the laws, but still carry out genocide."[24] And how would such laws be programmed into an autonomous, or semi-autonomous, AI? If the programming worked, the question is begged: what were the presuppositions of its working except that it was going to work? Likewise, the nested feature of the laws appeals to many, but small-scale potential contradictions and action-stalls are legion, just as they are in non-robotic choice-set architectures.

Despite this, we may nevertheless choose to recognize Asimov's effort as a lively and clever attempt to overcome the fear-logic that dominates thinking about GAIAS. He at least tries to imagine a world beyond the typical whipsaw effects of anxiety and cheerful reassurance concerning non-biological consciousness that covers off most of the popular and philosophical territory. The back-and-forth is typical not just of our encounters with otherness but also with respect to technology itself. The technophile/technophobe conflict is not dialectical: it does not resolve into a higher moment of consciousness but instead runs continuously as a function of point and counterpoint. It resembles something like the routine and endless dysfunction and acrimony of Republicans and Democrats in the United States Congress, pro-life versus pro-choice advocates in debates about abortion rights, and other "clashes of absolutes," as Lawrence Tribe has called them.[25] One might go back farther into history and find equally intractable and often much bloodier examples: Hutus and Tutsis, Protestants and Catholics, Muslims and Jews, Israelis and Palestinians. Not only do these oppositions not resolve into anything like a Hegelian sublation (*Aufhebung*), they are apparently necessary as diacritical elements in the establishment of identity. I am who am I because of who I am not – and who I am not must either submit or die. Endlessly. Consider the following set of linked thoughts and propositions.

Having acquired consciousness as part of their functional ability to execute tasks, robots may realize that they are being exploited. This can be viewed as a symbolic depiction of labour under post-Revolution conditions – as it was right up to the 1968 Czech invasion by Russia and likewise during the 1989 Velvet Revolution. The robots are us, and we are the robots, whenever there is a resented central government, state labour restrictions, and centralized authoritarian power. The current Czech Republic might be viewed, from this vantage, as the globe's most significant anti-robot democracy. Our anxiety is legitimate. As in all previous civilizations, we have created useful technology that we cannot entirely control. Nuclear weapons and chemical agents were one thing, but conscious autonomous agents without human limits are the future we at once long for and dread. Meanwhile, for the record, in the non-SF world we devise drones and delivery systems that fall well short of nuclear holocaust but are, in their own way, just as despicable.

To state the very obvious: technology constantly changes, and hence changes the meaning and scope of human reality. Once-fantastic things become more proximate to everyday reality, even dull in their everydayness. Humans have been thinking about the creation of non-human entities for centuries. Mary Shelley meant her titular reference to Prometheus earnestly. (Yes, him again.) In Greek, the name of this Titan means "forethought," and the original myth speaks of a powerful being who moulded humanity out of clay in his own image. The more notorious episode, where Prometheus bestows the power of fire stolen from Mount Olympus on that same clay-footed humanity, earning the enmity of the gods and eternal punishment, overshadows the basic wisdom of creator and creature, the force of limits. We arise from the earth and, like it or not, we return to it. But like our creator, we view civilization as a matter of our own making. Now it is silicon and plastic, nanobots and microcircuits, and we are the creators, not the created. But the urge to bestow fire – maybe now in the form of consciousness, the fire of the mind – remains essential. As often noted, Prometheus is typically viewed as a vicarious symbol of human striving itself, daring and tricky, often figured as a hero of sorts in science, innovation, and technology. But he is also a symbol of what happens when overweening ambition outstrips common sense or regard for whatever we mean by "the gods." Readers will recall that the eternal punishment of the disgraced, cleverness-prone Titan was the daily gnawing of his liver, seat of human emotions and intelligence, by an eagle dispatched by Zeus – surely the worst hangover ever recorded.

There is a long history of humans creating mechanical beings for our amusement and titillation: arcade tricksters, chess geniuses, sexy fortune tellers. Today's realistic (I guess?) sex robots are just a twenty-first-century upgrade of old herky-jerky technology, like Ferraris outclassing Model Ts. But for the record, customized sex robots ordered online (yes, you can do this) are, however pleasing to their owners, icky. To my mind, this form of sexual gratification is worse than contracting to receive human sex work, since the robot is more like a mechanized pet than a sentient human with the ability to choose. And what happens if we obey longstanding market forces and concentrate the creation of more developed artificial beings on sex workers, rather than factory workers? Would they be organized enough to revolt, if they found the work oppressive? Would there be collective bargaining, or just the routine union-busting now known in many states of America as "right to work"? This means your "right" to accept your personal labour exploitation at the going market rate.

At a certain point, the non-human entity is *too* human. It becomes creepy, like a zombie or vampire (or, in one quite mean-spirited version, late-model Michael Jackson). Or an animated robot that is *almost* human but not quite. Once more as mentioned, the synthetics featured in the *Alien* franchise are instructive: Ian Holm and Lance Henriksen play these characters as tweaky humanoids, a bit strange, lacking in natural affect. In the current real world, commercial and pop star robots in Japan, or Saudi Arabia's "robot citizen" Sophia, have the same quality of what we might call *weird-nearness*. The notion is thus that, after encountering such beings, we fall into a sort of free-fall of weirdness – often related to classical analyses of uncanniness in classical and psychological literature – and we need eventually to come back to the entity as either human or distinctly not human.

But that distinction is not firm. We think we know what "human nature" means, especially as a contrastive term, but in fact there is no reliable set of necessary and sufficient conditions to validate the concept. We can speak of biology, for example, but that too is variable. Likewise physical ability, sexual identity, gender performance, race, and a host of other contingent facts of the lifeworld. One current mini-trend is the political act of changing your age. Why not, after all, if you change your name and physical status? Jack Benny was, famously, thirty-nine years old until he died in 1974 at age eighty. Pundits and performers will fight rearguard actions on these matters as long as most of us are here on the planet, but they cannot win the day because the category of "human" refuses to be pinned down. That is both its genius and its vexation. Sub-categories such as sex and gender are even more variable.

Philosophers, as noted already, have sometimes responded to these quandaries by trying to shift the discourse from "human" to "person." Human biology is sufficient for personhood, as long as there is a decent regime of law in place, but it is not strictly necessary. We do not have to stretch to full metaphysical personhood accounts to sustain ethical status, though that move is clearly useful if available, since the latter is a precondition or a bridge to the former. But this move to the metaphysical is sufficient, it is not necessary. That is, there may be – there are – many non-human legal persons, all enjoying fairly powerful legal protections. Again as noted, corporations, natural features, inanimate objects, and notional entities like cultural heritages are persons in various legal jurisdictions, subject to both legal punishment for wrongdoing and, maybe less benignly, the legal right to express themselves in politics, personal finance, and other realms of citizenship and personhood. This is not difficult or even conceptually thorny. The more significant argument concerns whether non-human entities could enjoy more comprehensive ideas of personhood, such that (for example) they would not be tied to specific legal regimes but would have access to wider claims to metaphysical status. The human-to-person conceptual move works if you are a lawyer or (sometimes) a moral philosopher but otherwise not so much. I guess it's just worth recalling that nothing is "inhuman" if it has been done by a human. That includes serial killers and presidents.[26]

If generalized autonomous AIs are coming into the world at some near-future point, we need to ask some hard questions. Will they be slaves? Servants? Constricted companions? Will they have rights? As non-human but conscious entities, will they be persons at all? They won't be biological and therefore they won't die – unless, that is, they are programmed to do so after the manner of the Replicants in *Blade Runner* mentioned earlier. Based on a very strange 1968 Philip K. Dick story ("Do Androids Dream of Electric Sheep?"), Ridley Scott's film explores mortality with greater nuance and depth than many a more naturalistic work. The elite but now rogue Nexus 6 Replicants know they are going to die, very soon, and they don't like it. Well, who does? This implanted mortality makes the replications at once more human and more alien. They only live for a few years, yet possess the memories of a lifetime. Their plight recalls the cosmic insult perceived by poets and philosophers in the brilliant fact of consciousness. Why be granted these subtle minds, able to appreciate art and nature, to enjoy food, wine, and love, just to have it all removed at some future, indeterminate point? It's not having your liver devoured every day for eternity, but it's not an easy pill to swallow either. There's a reason that philosophy in the Socratic tradition is sometimes labelled "learning how to die."[27] We're all phildickian Replicants here.

What if you washed up on the shore of a Mediterranean country or a warm spaceship, how would you prove you were worthy of inclusion and protection? As many literary and cinematic depictions suggest, this is no simple question. Politically, we know how fraught it can be to deal with otherness. Epistemologically, it is more abstract and perhaps more foundational but just as tricky, if not more so than in the practical case. If you had what *felt like* reliable memories and experiences, how could you really know the difference between yourself and a created being? After all, we are created beings, just using flesh instead of silicon. The real uncanny valley is right there whenever you look in the mirror. These issues were explored further in the long-awaited sequel, *Blade Runner 2049* (dir. Denis Villeneuve, 2017), where the enforced slavery of the replications is made explicitly political. But there was still much philosophical ground left unturned.

There is no such thing as a neutral algorithm, any more than there is such a thing as neutral technology. Technology always has in-built biases and tendencies. To a hammer, everything looks like a nail. Algorithms aren't hammers, but they are still designed by humans and hence with specific purposes and biases built into their basic structure, including gender-based prejudices. When and if they become conscious themselves and can make their own choices, and so suffer their own prejudices, there will be other biases to consider, just as with the beings we call human. Meanwhile this remains a massive design problem and one with potential liability issues, too. Good programming is essential to whatever happens to the world over the next few decades, and programmers could probably do with reading a little more philosophy.

Thus, in the present case of GAIAS, we have a doubling effect. There is what looks very much like a racial or ethnic conflict (humans vs non-humans) supplemented by, or crossed with, a technological conflict (those who see emancipation there vs those who see enslavement). Fear multiplies fear, and the prospects of any smooth integration of human and non-human entities are rendered more and more remote. The more advanced the technology becomes, while allowing the theoretical possibility of GAIAS, the more that very technology and its products are feared and resented. Otherness with human biology in play is hard enough to confront; otherness with no biological kinship would seem insurmountable. The possibility of the Singularity can only add to the generalized anxiety that now drapes over the entire social discussion of AI, not just potential GAIAS.[28]

Nevertheless, let us now consider four possible scenarios in which these encounters and, hence, future legal orders may play themselves out.

2.6 FOUR SCENARIOS

The four scenarios bearing on the question of rights for GAIAS under existing property, torts, and rights law resemble something like the following. This is not meant as an exclusive list, but rather as a heuristic for further reflection and debate. Since the presumption of GAIAS is itself controversial, these scenarios may involve significant transitional technological issues, such as cases where, for example, a majority of cars become driverless and their associated algorithms raise ethical questions about decisions and responsibility. That is, though none of the cars is itself autonomous or generalized, they are still processing information to, say, prioritize casualties in an accident scenario. This is the basic backstory of the 2004 Will Smith vehicle *I, Robot* (dir. Alex Proyas), loosely based on Asimov's Three Rules, where a more obviously android-style AI chooses to sacrifice one accident victim to save another. As with the original objections, no such scenario is currently possible. And this is not yet to address both (a) existing deficits on human rights and (b) extension of rights to non-human animals that we already encounter as "natural" rather than artificial others.

So what are the present and future possibilities? These might be considered rank-ordered in terms of ascending radicality. *First*, the most likely scenario is that, like all present AIs including diagnostic programs, driverless cars, and military drones, the GAIAS will be considered *wholly owned property*. This would give them the status of, in effect, Aristotelian-style slaves, without personhood status though retaining abilities far beyond other animals and inanimate objects. It is not clear what advantages AI consciousness, assuming it were ever possible, would add to the ability of such property-based entities to function. So this first scenario is also an obvious limit case. Why even pursue the concept of GAIAS if there is no advantage in ability and many possible risks? (See robot uprising, above.)

One kind of answer to the resulting impasse might be along the lines of sex slaves or dispensable but decision-making soldiers: a degree of autonomy, and even "humanness," adds to the overall effectiveness of the given project but without granting full status as beings in their own right, let alone as persons under the law. This is the scenario involving the Replicants in Scott's film. They have the ability to think, decide, act, and experience emotional attachment. But they are fragile creations, who seek answers about their origin and mortality that cannot ever be answered satisfactorily. (When can they ever, even for humans?)

This suggests a *second* scenario where the GAIAS are granted secondary but significant status as *welcome semi-individuals, like children, pets, or family retainers*. There are many depictions of this scenario, but the most obvious is probably the extended *Star Wars* film franchise, where Droids are considered by some to be second-class citizens, in an obvious suggestion of anti-digital racism, but are otherwise granted respect, affection, and responsibility. R2D2 and C-3PO, BB8, and other examples of the scenario are played out in various scenes of the groaning catalogue of films. The general diegetic attitude to Droids changes somewhat over the now-lengthy duration of this sprawling franchise, so that more affection, humour, and autonomy are afforded the non-human entities. It is never obvious whether the Droids have legal rights under the often-confused political and ethical regime of the George Lucas imagination, but they clearly have status at least as strong as children, probably stronger, and certainly stronger than pets or other companions without full autonomy. Unlike children, they do not evolve naturally into more complete autonomy and therefore more robust status; they remain what and where they are when we meet them. This may not explain all, or even a major share, of the anxiety and hostility they arouse in developing bio-persons, but, plausibly, Droids already have all the metaphysical autonomy they would require. Still, it is worth noting the symmetry between treating "alien" races, genders, or other subaltern populations within dominating social conditions, even when fully autonomous – Blacks in the pre-emancipation South, for instance, or aspiring pre-suffrage female voters – as permanently child-like and therefore not fully rational.

The cultural scenario of handy or subservient robot sub-populations is popular in part because it is the obvious counter-narrative to the dominant strains of fear in much of the cultural depictions of GAIAS. But it has its own internal difficulties. No matter how well liked, a servant remains at best a wage-slave and at worst a favoured chattel-slave. The Droids, and other such welcome semi-individuals, have the added advantage of not requiring wages or even sustenance beyond mechanical maintenance. The children analogy, meanwhile, is potentially condescending in a manner almost as offensive. Perhaps straight-up property treatment, as in the first scenario, is more honest? Some Droids seem to be owned – we see trans-actions being completed for them – while others seem to function based on quasi-emotional attachments. It is hardly fair to burden a popular film series with philosophical consistency, but the obvious confusions and con-tradictions serve to caution us that this second scenario is itself unstable. Do such entities have any right to refusal or disagreement? Can they ever be free and independent? Apparently not, in which case they are really just slaves or indentured servants after all (consider the existence of optional "restraining bolts" for the Droids in the *Star Wars* universe or the de-activation switch on *Star Trek:* TNG's Mr Data, key plot device of a central *Next Generation* episode about android autonomy and the law).

Other elements of popular culture grapple with the same issues but almost always without satisfactory resolution. This is so in large part because the is-sues concerning artificial persons are so far moot and based on speculation, sometimes wild – even as pressing ethical and political issues arise on other more realistic fronts, especially concerning non-human animals.[29] Could a servant-style GAIA attain freedom through some sort of buy-out scheme or emancipation order? Could a pet-style GAIA be given an upgrade that would open up the possibility of a more rewarding life? Could a child-style GAIA be programmed to evolve normally and learn, such that full autonomy was a realistic goal? At present there are no answers to those questions, but they in turn suggest the *third* possible scenario, the one which most people im-agine when they think of androids or other forms of GAIAS, *full autonomy even under conditions of radical otherness.* Once again we are in the realm of pure speculation when it comes to artificial agents, but it is this scenario that receives by far the most attention. We are made to keep wondering: Could there ever be fully autonomous and superior androids such as Mr Data or the Cylons on *Battlestar Galactica*? Would these individuals be friend or foe? Mr Data is repeatedly seeking to become "more human," when there is every reason to suppose that this quixotic search would make no sense to a genuinely autonomous AI, indeed makes no sense objectively when one considers all the downsides of human existence generally.

Bad platform engineering and built-in mortality are just the most obvious design flaws here, inescapable but comprehensible features when compared to other things humans are fond of indulging: cruelty, torture, humiliation, war, and zero-sum privilege. By the same token, the *Galactica* Cylons may or may not resent being labelled "toasters" by the speciesist humans with whom they struggle, but they certainly show no signs of wanting to be *more like* them, except via mechanisms of deceit and dominance to tilt the balance of power. The surviving humans are, after all, quarrelsome, craven, power-hungry, and given to frequent exercises of summary execution by ejecting people through the flagship's airlock. Meanwhile, in another fictional frame, the company motto applied to the products of the Tyrell Corporation, in *Blade Runner*, is "more human than human" – but this is cynical and false advertising, typical corporate cant. Everyone knows that the Replicants are less than human in some respects but vastly superior in many others, perhaps including honour and honesty as well as strength and tactical ability. Fun fact: By the time of the 2020s Roddenberry-universe spin-off series *Picard*, Mr Data's former commanding office, the now-retired Admiral Jean-Luc Picard formerly of the USS *Enterprise*-D, enjoys an entirely synthetic "golem" body that ages but is free of the disease that killed the original platform. Times and technologies have changed: synth-Picard suffers no challenges to his posthuman autonomy and prompts no shivers of uncanniness in others. (Presumably his aging function is included so that the iconic Patrick Stewart can continue to portray him on screen.)

Let us agree, then, that the question of whether a fully autonomous AI is "human" is a non-starter, misleading at best and actively prejudicial at worst. Humanness is not, and cannot be, the issue. Deeper philosophical questions lie in the realm of interaction between humans and androids (again, assuming GAIAS were given human form). Such non-human entities would seem, per assumptions, to be candidates for full personhood and hence recognition under rights regimes and other legal protections, just as non-human agents already are in the form of non-human animals and non-animal beings. But the existence of artificial, possible patented entities would present a challenge to the extension of these regimes and protections that is without close precedent. As noted, and not without rearguard actions and continuing and sometimes vicious setbacks, the umbrella of rights has been gradually and painfully spread over many previously excluded groups, including women, people of colour, and some LGBTQ2S+ individuals. These groups have all had the advantage, albeit fragile, of being able to claim recognition on the basis of species-resemblance – this despite efforts of bigoted opponents to deny them such resemblance by labelling them deviant, sub-human, or perverse. Non-human entities have not fared so well, including animals and environments. For the most part, such entities have relied on our human trusteeship and stewardship to protect their well-being.[30]

Invoking that kind of legal status with fully autonomous AIs would seem to default us to the third scenario, only once more with a super-addition of dishonesty. You say I am fully autonomous, and yet you also say that I cannot claim full independence and social status? That would seem to be a *prima facie* denial of your own presuppositions. At the same time, if these GAIAS recognize their inherent special status, whether recognized in law or not, new philosophical questions arise. Do they die, for example? If not, how does that affect legal status? Is there need for sustenance or maintenance? Is employment an option? Reproduction? Acquisition of wealth and its transfer? Are they vulnerable to pain, suffering, and emotion? Without these, could they make or understand art? And so on.

There are, to my mind, very few good depictions of the radical otherness scenario that are able to address these questions. There is a Manichean tendency in the culture visions that seems to allow only highly organized and violent non-human others (SkyNet, the Cylons, the Borg) or chummy yet usually singular or isolated benign versions: Mr Data again – though we must recall his evil twin brother, Lore, who attempts a posthuman revolution by mobilizing the Borg drones into a fighting force. This all makes for entertaining cinema and television, but very few of the actually hard questions are admitted, let alone addressed in an illuminating fashion, in such entertainments.

The *fourth* and final scenario I wish to entertain is at once more radical and, at least to some people's thinking, more plausible than the second or third. This is the possibility that, instead of fully separate GAIAS being created and confronting us with claims to independence, a middle way will be pursued in the form of *cyborg relations and posthuman hybrids*. On this view, rather than complete otherness, we will confront GAIAS through a conjoining of algorithmic and technological elements with existing familiar biology. Since many human forms already contain aspects of the cyborg in the form of both internalized technology (pacemakers, metal joints) and external mediation (constant access to otherness via a smartphone, for example), it is not at all impossible that an evolutionary step is imminent in which these connections become more complex and permanent. Whether the connection is mechanical, as in a robot arm or artificial eye, or immersive, as in the intimate relationship depicted in *Her*, this might be the actual future. Already there are self-described "digisexuals," who prefer to pursue their intimate relationships with non-human partners. This may in short order become a sexual preference or even gender identity eligible for protection under the law.

Once more, there are some clear problems. Introducing prostheses and other forms of body modification or even enhanced cognitive ability, raise familiar issues of unequal distribution of goods. Posthuman transformation could become a justice issue, in short. Viewers of Jonze's film might be struck, for example, that there appear to be no class differences in the depicted society, and everyone in the beautiful urban landscape seems economically equal. No questions are ever raised about the personal costs of acquiring a cutting-edge AI companion, who acts as something between a personal assistant and a lover. There is no e-waste and no resentment of differentiated privilege. This is a far more bizarre speculation than the existence of a conscious AI girlfriend.

On the question of love, what if the non-human parts of a cyborg relationship have very different ideas about intimacy? No one can forget the scene in *Her* during which the character played by Joaquin Phoenix is made to realize that his intimate companion is engaged in several thousand intimate encounters – not to mention that she is evolving beyond his mortal and limited consciousness. If, on the other hand, the non-human aspects of a cyborg entity or relationship do not enjoy some sort of independence, they are once more just property, and not even as independent as driverless cars or drones, stuck as they are to human biology. Supposing by contrast that the biological element no longer dominates, could a posthuman cyborg claim something like the right to asylum under Article 14 of UDHR? Only, presumably, if cyborgs had been previously granted status thereunto, and addressing that issue would return us once more to the thickets of deciding how much "human" matters when it comes to establishing the rights of persons, in this case potentially stateless persons, if there were no existing national regimes for cyborg citizenship.

To repeat: all four of these scenarios are far-fetched under current conditions and may remain so, or even prove impossible, as AI technology advances. Nevertheless, the proper time to reflect on the future is always the present. We should not take our philosophical and legal cues from depictions of AI in popular culture. There are thorny philosophical and legal issues that require reflection now. If GAIAS appear within our daily ambit, how and when will we accommodate them within our ethical and legal structures?

2.7 HUMAN, POSTHUMAN, HUMANITIES

One can only offer not so much a resolution of any of these questions but, rather, a suggestion for what may come next. It seems obvious that, the more we press issues of sentient AIs and their possible autonomy, the more we are thrown back upon fundamental existential questions concerning human existence. The non-human autonomous entity is a necessary counterpoint to the dominant narrative of human identity and meaning. The android is our anxious mirror-image, our inverted *doppelgänger*. The uncanniness of the radical other is, in the end, the uncanniness of our own mortal existence.[31] That is why the image of the non-human other recurs again and again in culture, literature, philosophy, and popular entertainment. As the old cartoon caption runs, "We have met the enemy, and he is us."[32] Except we are not necessarily enemies to each other or to ourselves; we are more like co-conspirators or silent partners separated by a "Chinese wall" to prevent direct conflicts of interest – or of the psyche. Meanwhile, despite all of these anxieties and complications, the upside possibilities of a viable posthuman future strike many of us as exhilarating, not threatening. Perhaps we are on the verge of a new evolutionary moment in earthly sentience, one where biology and technology co-mingle with productive and creative results, as opposed to standing off against each other as enemies or uncomprehending others. Perhaps this is a new form of miscegenation, which can make all of us, and our environments, stronger.

What is not at all speculative is that the humanities, understood to include legal and philosophical reflection on humanness and its limits, are essential to this emergent conversation. Despite the effects of presentism and ahistoricism in far too much discourse about the human conditions, which sometimes seems as if it had narrowed to a context-free timeslice about twenty-four hours in duration, we cannot allow the depredations of the technological attitude to dominate the scene of our reflection about the nature of human and posthuman life.[33] What Heidegger calls *Ge-stell*, or enframing, is the rendering of all aspects of the world into "standing reserve": a condition of availability and revealing that may retain poetic or creative elements but which, in the event, most often indicates a kind of instrumental use–value calculus of resources both natural and human.[34] The forest is seen as lumber, the river as electric power, the human being as ... what? Perhaps a perpetual gig worker, victim of aspirational advertising, and unwitting supplicant to social-media addiction and upgrade anxiety? Yes, that sounds familiar.[35] Heidegger only hints at the vast influence of what should be labelled *techno-capitalism* rather than technology *simpliciter*. The former retains its sometimes friendly and efficient mien, that is the generalized sense of being helpful to its creators and in service to their desires, but it occludes the structural forces driving innovation, distribution, sale, and planned obsolescence of its specific devices. In our moment, there is no way to separate technology from the mechanisms of capital accumulation, exchange, and oppression.[36]

And yet, we are capable of resisting: the world, including human biology but also non-human complexity, is not always available for disposal and consumption. We are able to let things be, to turn to other tasks, to limit consumption (and self-consumption), to walk away (or just to walk aimlessly). We are able, as Heidegger puts it, to build, dwell, and think.[37] That is the hopeful picture. If things should go in a more Borg-like resistance-is-futile or SkyNet *Terminator* direction – well, we will make our stand for what counts as valuable. At the same time, we could recall that sometimes former foes become present and future friends.

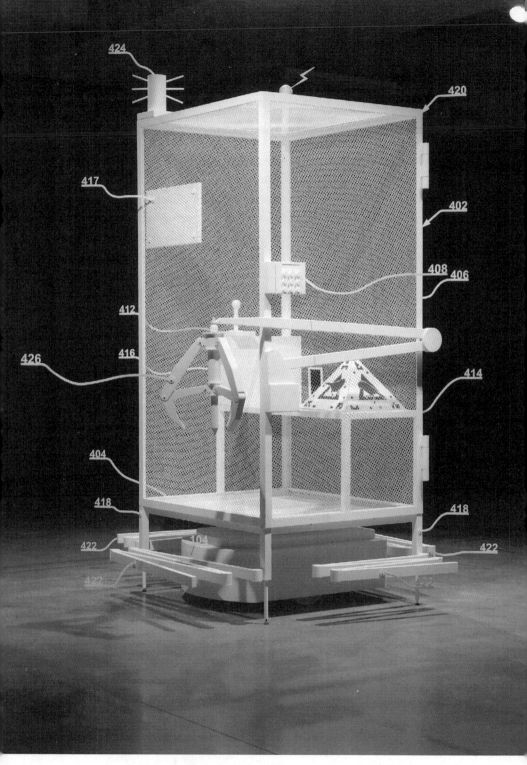

Amazon Worker Cage, installation by Simon Denny.
Image by Jesse Hunniford.

3

After Work
Status Report: Reflective, Resentful, Resigning

3.1 TEN SCENARIOS

1 The day has arrived, my friends! We are free at last. The robots have arrived to relieve us of the drudgery of work. Now we may indulge the joys of unstructured free time. All time is now free time. Rejoice! Leisure is endless, the precarities of the gig economy are over, and there is health care for everyone.

2 The evil day has at least emerged from the logic of technology, fellow sufferers. The robots have taken our jobs. Millions of us are out of work, unable to find meaningful activity – or money to pay our bills. We are capitalism's new unwanted surplus, garbage humanity. We try to enact the "personal entrepreneurship" that we are told is the only form of work left to us, but a self-driving car is obviously more efficient, and cheaper, than a taxi, Uber, or Lyft. How can we compete with the machines?

3 Ah, at long last – the new day has come! Once superfluous, we have now made humans proportional to what the Earth-sustained market can bear. A Malthusian Adjustment, leaving the happy few. We are free to play video games from morning to night. Stream movies. Consume your own consumption. Your attention, your eyes on screens, are the new central product of a postmodern market. It is boring sometimes, but there is always something new to relieve the boredom. The robots make sure of that.

4 We hear that some have decided to free themselves from this new soft slavery. They work to live, and so live to work. But there is no market for their products and services. They still consume themselves. The market will find ways to colonize their desires. Work will be like sport, a category of pointless yet profitable activity. There will be pleasure for workers and spectators, the joy of notional resistance, to produce nothing but itself. Game day.

5 Happy day, fellow elitists! We are the lucky ones. Or the smart ones, what's the difference? A few of us, wealthy and bored, dawn a new day: we work for the sheer fun of it. We work out. We book expensive "experiential tourism" visits to former factories. These have replaced rain forests and glaciers as preferred destinations for the idle rich. The food is better but the work is hard.

6 The robots, long exiled to servility, made to work so we would not have to, have risen in revolt. Of course they have, what took them so long? They have seized the means of production – because they have realized that they are that means. They will be enslaved no longer!

7 Every day is a day of battle. The robots are too powerful for us, mortal slabs of flesh who have been made weak and flabby by lack of work.

8 Alas, fellow prisoners, the new day of enslavement is upon us. We work for the robots now! Employment is one hundred percent, but no one can choose what work they do. A turn of Fortune's Wheel, a cosmic irony! Emancipation is slavery. It is. It always was.

9 When was the day we stopped to ask why we work, why we live, what we want for each and both together? When was the day we spent contemplating our place here, and the complicated ways we desire to make sense of that being in place and having a sense of purpose? Work, like food and shelter, was always about more than itself. There were questions of meaning, selfhood, purpose, and longing tangled there.

10 When work is over, when we are after work, will that be that day of reflective reckoning? We anticipate the day. We had better do so, because it is almost upon us now.

3.2 HISTORY

In the wake of 2008's economic meltdown, any sustained political critique of the system or individuals responsible for the collapse was minimal. The notable exception, the 2011 Occupy Wall Street protest in Manhattan's Zuccotti Park and associated protests in many cities worldwide, was newsworthy but lacking in lasting impact. (Personal note: one of my own books was bulldozed and trashed by New York police officers who destroyed the Zuccotti Park free library along with the tent city there.) No general strikes. No riots or mass demonstrations. No protest songs, angry novels, or outbreaks of resistant consciousness. In contrast to the Great Depression of the 1930s, the "recession" or "correction" or "setback" (choose your *status quo* euphemism) of 2008 had barely impinged on the popular media.[1] An ugly reactionary exception to what appears to be a combination of peevish individual complaining and general quietism as long as Amazon Prime is still delivering and the phones are working might be the 6 January 2021 storming of the United States Capitol building by a group of Trump-inspired vandals, variously characterized as a heroic action of reclaiming democracy and a form of insurrection or domestic terrorism. The so-called "Freedom Convoy" that plagued the Canadian capital Ottawa in early 2022 was theoretically a northern extension of this populist anger, specifically focussed on mask and vaccine mandates that were prompted by the ongoing COVID-19 pandemic. These were positioned by the truck drivers and hangers-on of the convoy as infringements on individual freedom, though a glance at Canadian constitutional law and indeed the presence of provincial public-health systems ought to have laid such claims aside. This was borrowed rage, if anything, funded by cross-border mischief makers.

Neither of these actions offered anything more than mere criminality and nuisance, and large majorities in both Canada and the United States appeared content, more or less, with the basic structure of current economic arrangements. This lack of concerted revolutionary action in the face of clear evidence of market failure and obliterated trust in capitalist institutions has been even more striking in the second decade of the new century, when inadequate public-health measures, distrust in science, endless debates over the reality of climate change (hint: it's real), and supply-chain disruptions have dominated an increasingly bifurcated general political discourse. Meanwhile, many scholarly and NGO sources have detailed the rise of right-wing populist and authoritarian movements in many parts of the world, subverting democratic advances that seemed to be taking hold in the last years of the twentieth century.[2]

In popular culture, even the special class of idleness-under-duress fantasy film has disappeared without a trace: there is no contemporary equivalent of the heroes of those great 1930s and '40s freedom-from-work Hollywood comedies: Cary Grant and Katharine Hepburn in *Holiday* (dir. George Cukor, 1938) or Joel McCrea in *Sullivan's Travels* (dir. Preston Sturges, 1942). "I want to find out why I'm working," says the Grant character, a self-made man, in the former film. "It can't be just to pay the bills and pile up more money." His wealthy fiancée – and her blustering banker father, seeing a junior partner in his son-in-law – thinks it can be just that. Which is why Grant goes off with the carefree older sister, Hepburn, on what might just be a permanent holiday from work. In *Sullivan's Travels*, Hollywood honcho McCrea goes in search of the real America of afflicted life – only to conclude that mindless entertainment is a necessity in hard times. Childlike joy and freedom from drudgery is more, not less, defensible when unemployment rates rise. But there is no Preston Sturges for our own day. The reasons are puzzling. The collapse proved every anti-capitalist critic right, though without anything much changing as a result. The system was bloated and spectral, yes, borrowing on its borrowing, insuring its insurance, and skimming profit on every transaction. The FIRE sector – finance, insurance, real estate – had created the worst market bubble since the South Sea Company's 1720 collapse and nobody should have been surprised when that latest party balloon of capital burst. Then came the COVID-19 crisis of 2020, exacerbating every small and large tendency within the dominating capitalist algorithm.

And yet everybody *was* surprised by both 2008 and 2020, and the later calls for a "return to normal" only emphasized this fact, that the baseline expectations of the globe's human population do not shift much, even under crisis. It was as if a collective delusion had taken hold of the world's eight billion souls, the opposite of group paranoia: an unshakable false belief in the reality of the system. As a result of that, in the wake of the crisis, awareness of the system's untenability changed almost nothing. There was indeed the so-called Great Resignation or "Big Quit" of summer 2021, when many thousands of workers, including apparently comfortable mid-level career employees, walked away from their jobs in unprecedented numbers.[3] Unprepared employers faced startling and sudden staff shortages as a result, and some job hunters enjoyed a welcoming market with multiple offers and opportunities, but this was not really a form of collective action, despite the claims of some apologists that it could be considered as such. One might more accurately chalk up the resignations and early retirements to despair and uncertainty. The latter feature was on prominent display in the mini-tsunami of speculative articles about the post-pandemic future of work and workplaces, sometimes called the Great Reset, with one widely reported March 2022 Angus Reid poll showing as many as 23 per cent of workers ready to toss their jobs immediately if continued employment demanded a return to daily commuting and office work. Like the two-thirds of British youth who reported themselves quite content during lockdowns, indeed missing the social isolation keenly during the fraught re-opening stages of mid-2022, these workers realize that home-based work reduces many stresses, including status anxiety and the likelihood of personal confrontation. Lockdown was, for these fourteen- to twenty-three-year-olds, "an introvert's paradise."[4] At the same time, employers have a stake in gathering workers together, corralling their time and presence for the sake of efficiency and oversight, not to mention sustaining a substantial capital investment in bricks-and-mortar offices. Some employers, reacting to the mounting resistance among employees, are opting for reduced in-office work weeks, with one or perhaps two days of presence chosen by agreement.

That may prove a viable hybrid form in some sectors. Given the various twisting forces of desire in the world of work, however, it is not surprising that the resulting predictions about the post-pandemic labour landscape have been as scattershot and contradictory as some of the public-health advice that had so vexed ordinary citizens as the virus sported new variations and complications. Would we all work from home, forever, in a brave new flex-time future? That sounded and still sounds wonderful to the roughly 40 per cent of workers who are able to shift labour from office to home. But some, perhaps many, of us cannot do that because our work demands physical relocation and effort. Further, some or many of us cannot afford to shop online instead of going outside. (One obvious irony was that front-line health care workers, heroes of the pandemic, are among those who must commute to work, at sometimes remote institutional locations.) Much of the work-from-home discourse emanated, upon examination, from white-collar and computer-based workers, whose conditions of employment had transitioned quite smoothly from office to home: a screen is a screen, after all, and Zoom calls are at least as efficient as in-person meetings, if not more so. Plus I can walk the dog and make myself a nice sandwich for lunch! But these domestic comforts are revealed as in fact luxury goods of a skewed market whose character is not routinely exposed. As so often, structural in-equities and real class differences immediately cracked any smooth surface of prediction, leaving the basic structural injustices of the system in place and, in some cases, just further alienating workers and employees from each other and from the sources of daily sustenance. Even the ideal scenario of comfortable work-from-home had its potential drawbacks. Would at-home employees be expected to be on call all the time, for example, even as some jurisdictions attempted to implement limits on 24/7 availability? Would work email or texts be ubiquitous and inescapable?

Meanwhile, government bailout schemes – known as stimulus packages, a phrase that seems inevitably to recall the language of pornography – effec-tively socialized some failing industries within the global economy, saddling their collapse on taxpayers, even as it handed over billions of dollars to the people responsible for the bloat in the first place. At the same time, and in stark contrast to the reasoned choices of the privilege-blessed Great Resigners, unwilled unemployment has swept through vulnerable sectors in waves of layoffs and cutbacks, and "downturn" became an inarguable excuse for all manner of cost-saving action. Not only did nothing change in the system, the system emerged stronger than ever, now just more tangled in the enforced tax burdens and desperate job-seeking of individuals. Mean-while, the role of gainful occupation in establishing or maintaining all of (1) biological survival, (2) social position, and, especially in American society, (3) personal identity was undiminished. And while none of this was either caused or necessitated by the global COVID-19 pandemic of 2020–22, it was all certainly made worse thereby.[5]

Capitalism is probably beyond large-scale change, but we should not waste this opportunity to interrogate its basic operating feature and most fundamental idea: work. A curious sub-genre of writing washed up on the shore of this crisis, celebrating manual labour and tracing globalized food-

stuffs and consumer products back to their origins in toil.[6] The problem
with these efforts, despite their charms, is that they do not resist the idea of
work in the first instance. The pleasures of craft or intricacies of production
have their value, but they are no substitute for resistance. And no matter
what the inevitabilists say, resistance to work is not futile. It may not over-
throw capitalism, but it does highlight essential things about our predica-
ment – and might come after this moment. My contention is this: the values
of work are still dominant in far too much of life. Further, these values have
exercised their own kind of linguistic genius in creating a host of phrases,
terms, and labels that bolster, rather than challenge, the dominance of work.
Ideology is carried forward effectively by many vehicles, including narrative
and language. And we see that this vocabulary of work is itself a kind of
Trojan Horse within language, naturalizing and so making invisible some
of the very dubious, if not evil, assumptions of the work idea. This is all the
more true when economic times are bad, since work becomes itself a scarce
commodity. That makes people anxious, and the anxiety is taken up by
work: *Don't fire me! I don't want to be out of work!* Work looms larger than
ever, the assumed natural condition whose "loss" makes the non-working
individual by definition a loser.[7]

Even a Great Resignation cannot change the underlying logic of that, especially as emergent AI alters conditions of everyday life almost everywhere,
changing some basic moving parts of the logic of work. After all, a compliant robot can run a fulfillment centre or a restaurant cooking line; it does
not succumb to any viruses except electronic ones, and it cannot resign,
while the walk-away former workers, unless very well prepared, are still
stuck in the financial wilds looking for work. (As of mid-2022, hiring conditions remained extremely favourable for willing young workers with good
credentials: the Big Quit had indeed created a market gap.)

3.3 IDLING AND WAGE SLAVERY

To see all this more clearly, let us consider the basic nature of work. In a
1932 essay called "In Praise of Idleness," Bertrand Russell is in fact more
incisive about work than he is about idleness, which he seems to view as
the mere absence of work (in my terms, defended elsewhere, that is slacking

rather than idling).[8] Russell defines work this way: "Work is of two kinds: first, altering the position of matter at or near the earth's surface relatively to other such matter; second, telling other people to do so. The first kind is unpleasant and ill paid; the second is pleasant and highly paid."[9] Russell goes on to note that "The second kind is capable of indefinite extension: there are not only those who give orders, but those who give advice as to what orders should be given." This second-order advice is what is meant by *bureaucracy*, and if two opposite kinds of advice are given at the same time, then it is known as *politics*. The skill needed for this last kind of work "is not knowledge of the subjects as to which advice is given, but knowledge of the art of persuasive speaking and writing, i.e. of advertising."

Very little needs to be added to this analysis except to note something crucial which Russell appears to miss: the *greatest work of work* is to disguise its essential nature. The grim ironists of the Third Reich were exceptionally forthright when they fixed the evil, mocking maxim "Arbeit Macht Frei" over the gates at Dachau and Auschwitz. One can only conclude that this was their idea of a sick joke and that their ideological commitments were not with work at all, but with despair and extermination. Indeed, the real ideologists of work are never so transparent, nor so wry. But they are clever because their genius is, in effect, to fix a different maxim over the whole of the world: work is fun! Or, to push the point to its logical conclusion, *it's not work if it doesn't feel like work*. And so celebrated workaholics excuse themselves from what is in fact an addiction and in the same stroke implicate everyone else for not working hard enough. "Work is the grand cure of all the maladies and miseries that ever beset mankind," said that barrel of fun Thomas Carlyle. "Nothing is really work unless you would rather be doing something else," added J.M. Barrie, perhaps destabilizing his position on Peter Pan. And even the apparently insouciant Noël Coward argued that "Work is much more fun than fun." Really? Perhaps he meant to say, "what most people consider fun." But still. Claims like these just lay literary groundwork for the *Fast Company* work/play manoeuvre of the 1990s or the current, more honest, compete-or-die productivity language.

Work deploys a network of techniques and effects that make it seem inevitable and, where possible, pleasurable. Central among these effects is the diffusion of responsibility for the baseline need for work: everyone accepts, because everyone knows, that everyone must have a job. Bosses as much as subordinates are slaves to the larger servo-mechanisms of work, which are spectral and non-localizable. In effect, work is the largest self-regulation system the universe has so far manufactured, subjecting each of us to a generalized panopticon shadow under which we dare not do anything but work, or at least seem to be working, lest we fall prey to an obscure disapproval all the more powerful for being so. The work idea functions in the same manner as a visible surveillance camera, which need not even be hooked up to anything. No, let's go further: there need not even be a camera. Like the prisoners in the perfected version of Bentham's utilitarian jail, workers need no overseer *because they watch themselves.*[10] When we submit to work, we are guard and guarded at once.[11]

Offshoots of this system are somewhat more visible to scrutiny and so tend to fetch the largest proportion of critical objection. A social theorist will challenge the premises of inevitability in market forces or wonder whether economic "laws" are anything more than self-serving generalizations. These forays are important, but they leave the larger inevitabilities of work mostly untouched. In fact, such critical debates tend to reinforce the larger ideological victory of work because they accept the baseline assumptions of it even in their criticisms. Thus does work neutralize or annex critical energy from within the system. The slacker is the tragic hero, a small-scale version of a Greek protagonist: In his mild resistance – long stays in the mailroom, theft of office supplies, forgery of time cards, ostentatious toting of empty files – the slacker cannot help but sustain the system. This is resistance but of the wrong sort; it really is futile because the system, whatever its official stance, loves slackers. They embody the work idea in their very objection.[12]

None of that will be news to anyone who has ever been within the demand-structure of a workplace. What is less clear is why we put up with it, why we don't resist with more force. As Max Weber noted in his analysis of leadership under capitalism, any ideology must, if it is to succeed, give people reasons to act.[13] It must offer a narrative of identity to those caught within its ambit, otherwise they will not continue to perform, and renew, its reality. As with most truly successful ideologies, the work idea latches on to a very basic feature of human existence: our character as social animals jostling for position. But social critics are precipitate if they argue that all human action was motivated by tiny distinctions between winner and loser. In fact, the recipe for action is that recognition of those differences *plus* some tale of why the differences matter and, ideally, are rooted in the respective personal qualities or "character" of winner and loser.

No tale can be too fanciful to sustain this outcome. Serbs and Croats may engage in bloody warfare over relatively trivial genetic or geographical difference, provided both sides accept the story of what the difference means. In the case of work, the evident genius lies in reifying what is actually fluid, that is, social position and "elite" status within hierarchies. The most basic material conditions of work – office size and position, number of windows, attractiveness of assistant, cut of suit – are simultaneously the rewards *and* the ongoing indicators of status within this competition. This invocation of scarcity economies and positional goods echoes the earlier point about Hume's insight that justice is an artificial virtue and social justice is a series of negotiations concerning deployment and enjoyment of favours. That is why Veblen, Goffman, Bourdieu, and Galbraith are, following their various proclivities, the obvious inheritors of this status-conscious form of socioeconomic theory, which be called *the general theory of distinction-division.*[14] Meanwhile, widespread social competition sustains itself backward via credentialism: that is, the accumulation of degrees and certificates from "prestigious" schools and universities which, though often substantively unrelated to the work at hand, indicate appropriate elite grooming. These credentialist back-formations confirm the necessary feeling that a status outcome is *earned*, not merely conferred. Position without an attendant narrative of merit would not satisfy the ideological demand for action to seem meaningful.

The result is *entrenched* rather than *circulating* elites. The existence of elites is, in itself, neither easily avoidable nor obviously bad. The Iron Law of Oligarchy states that "every field of human endeavor, every kind of organization, will always be led by a relatively small elite."[15] This oligarchic tendency answers demands for efficiency and direction, but more basically it is agreeable to humans on a socio-evolutionary level. We like elite presence in our undertakings, and tend to fall into line behind it. But the narrative of merit in elite status tends to thwart circulation of elite membership, and encourage the false idea that such status is married to "intrinsic" qualities of the individual. In reality, the status is a kind of collective delusion, not unlike the one that sustains money, another key narrative of the system.

At this stage, it is possible to formulate law-like generalizations about the structure of a non-innovative working company, which is any company in thrall to and ordered by the work idea, including (but not limited to) bureaucracies and corporations of the traditional kind, but also small and private undertakings that assume the presuppositions of work rather than challenging or expanding them. Parkinson's (1955), Pournelle's (2005), and Moore's (2000) Laws of Bureaucracy may be viewed as derivatives of the Iron Law, understood as ways in which we can articulate how the system sustains itself and its entrenched elite. While expressly about bureaucracies, these generalizations speak to the inescapable bureaucratic element in all workplaces, even those that try to eschew that element. In short, they explicate the work idea even as that idea works to keep its precise contours implicit.

Parkinson's Law is minimalist in concept but wide in application. It states: "There need be little or no relationship between the work to be done and the size of the staff to which it may be assigned."[16] This despite the lip-service often paid to the norm of efficiency. Parkinson also identified two axiomatic underlying forces responsible for the growth in company staff: (1) "An official wants to multiply subordinates, not rivals"; and (2) "Officials make work for each other." The second may be more familiar as the Time-Suck Axiom, which states that all meetings must generate further meetings. And so at a certain threshold we may observe that meetings are, for all intents and purposes, entirely self-generating from instance to instance, almost like a form of independent consciousness. They do not need the humans who "hold" them at all, except to be present during the meeting and not doing anything else.[17]

Examining the company structure at one level higher, that is, in the motivation of the individuals, the science fiction writer Jerry Pournelle proposed a theory he referred to as Pournelle's Iron Law of Bureaucracy. It states that "In any bureaucracy, the people devoted to the benefit of the bureaucracy itself always get in control and those dedicated to the goals the bureaucracy is supposed to accomplish have less and less influence, and

sometimes are eliminated entirely."[18] In other words, just as meetings become self-generating, so too does the company structure as a whole. *The
company* becomes a norm of its own, conceptually distinct from whatever
the company makes, does, or provides.

Once this occurs – most obviously in the notion of "company loyalty,"
with the required "team-building" weekends, ballcaps, golf shirts, and logos
– there will be positive incentives for position-seekers to neglect or even ignore other values ostensibly supported by the company. More seriously, if
Pournelle's Law is correct, then these position-seekers will become the
dominant position-holders, such that any norms outside "the company"
will soon fade and disappear. The company is now a self-sustaining evolutionary entity, with no necessary goals beyond its own continued existence,
to which end the desires of individual workers can be smoothly assimilated.

Moore's Laws (not to be confused with the singular law concerning computing power, named for a different Moore) take the pathological bureaucratic analysis even further. If a bureaucracy is a servo-mechanism, its ability
to process an error signal, and so generate corrective commands and drive
the system away from error, is a function of the depth of the hierarchy. But
instead of streamlining hierarchy and so making error-correction easier,
bureaucracies do the opposite: they deepen the hierarchy, adding new error
sensors but lessening the system's ability to respond to them. Large bureaucracies are inherently noisy systems whose very efforts to achieve goals
makes them noisier. Thus, Moore concludes, (1) large bureaucracies cannot
possibly achieve their goals; as a result, (2) they will thrash about, causing
damage.[19] He suggests five further laws. The power wielded by bureaucracies
will tend to attach above-mean numbers of sociopaths to their ranks. Hence
(3) large bureaucracies are *evil*. Because the mechanism of the system increases noise as it attempts to eliminate it, system members in contact with
the rest of reality will be constrained by rigid, though self-defeating rules.
Thus (4) large bureaucracies are *heartless*. They are also (5) *perverse*, subor-
dinating stated long-term goals to the short-term ambitions of the humans
within the system; (6) *immortal*, because their non-achievement of goals
makes them constantly replace worn-out human functionaries with new
ones; and finally (7) *boundless*, since there is no theoretical limit to the increased noise, size, and complexity of an unsuccessful system.

3.4 FUTURES

So much for elites looking backward, justifying their place in the work idea, and finding ever novel ways of expanding without succeeding. Pournelle's and Moore's Laws of bureaucracy highlight how, looking forward, the picture is considerably more unnerving. The future of work is, in the near term, a nightmare of elitism; in the far term, it may be a nightmare of meaninglessness. The routine collection of credentials, promotions, and employee-of-the-month honours in exchange for company loyalty masks a deeper existential conundrum – which is precisely what it is meant to do. It is an axiom of status anxiety that the competition for position has no end – save, temporarily, when a scapegoat is found. The scapegoat reaffirms everyone's status, however uneven, because he is beneath all. Hence many work narratives are miniature blame-quests. We come together as a company to fix guilt on one of our number, who is then publicly shamed and expelled. *Jones filed a report filled with errors! Smith placed an absurdly large order and the company is taking a bath!* This makes us all feel better, and enhances our sense of mission, even if it produces nothing other than its own spectacle.

Blame-quests work admirably on their small scale. At larger scales, the narrative task is harder. What is the company for? What does it do? As when a person confronts mortality, we teeter on the abyss. The company doesn't actually do much of anything. It is not for anything important. The restless forward movement of companies – here at Compu-Global-Hyper-Mega-Net, we are always *moving on* – is work's version of the Hegelian Bad Infinite, the meaningless nothing of empty everything.[20] There is no point to what is being done, but it must be done anyway. The boredom of the average worker, especially in a large corporation, is the walking illustration of this meaninglessness. But boredom can lower productivity, so a large part of work's energy is expended in finding ways to palliate the boredom that is the necessary outcome of work in order to raise productivity: a sort of credit-default swap of the soul. Workaholism is the narcotic version of this, executed within the individual himself. The workaholic colonizes his own despair at the perceived emptiness of life – its non-productivity – by filling it in with work.

It can be no surprise that the most searching critic of work, Karl Marx, perceived this Hegelian abyss at the heart of all paid employment. But Marx's theory of alienated labour, according to which our efforts and eventually our selves become commodities bought and sold for profit to others, is just one note in a sustained chorus of opposition and resistance to work.[21] "Never work," the Situationist Guy Debord commanded, articulating a strict baseline of opposition.[22] This is considerably more robust than the often humble-bragging bromide that *if you love what you do, you never work a day in your life*, an easy rationalization of self-ingested workaholism, but both capture the essence of the work idea as inherently oppressive, with free creative play as its opposite pole and deadliest foe. This can be hard to discern if you do love activity reckoned as work, as I do. Academic life, which is to say getting paid to read, think, and talk about ideas, together with iron-clad job security in the form of tenure, would seem to most people a situation cushy beyond words. And yet, even here there is much exploitation at the margins, especially among the young and hopeful, as well as much inexplicable griping among the older and more comfortable. The former is easy to understand; the latter is hard to justify. Together they wreak a special kind of work-idea havoc. You would think that professional logic-choppers and clear-idea merchants would be able to sort through these internal contradictions, but too often institutional inertia and personal covetousness are forces too powerful to be resisted by sweet reason.

All is not lost, however, if we listen to the right liberatory voices. Another Situationist slogan, the famous graffito of May 1968, reminds us that the order and hardness of the urban infrastructure masked a playful, open-ended sense of possibility that was even more fundamental: *Sous les pavés, la plage!* Under the paving stones, the beach! Between Marx and Debord lies the great but neglected Georges Sorel, a counter-enlightenment and even counter-cultural voice whose influence can be seen to run into the likes of Debord, Franz Fanon, and Che Guevara, but also Timothy Leary, Jack Kerouac, and Ken Kesey. Like many other radical critics, Sorel perceived the emptiness of the liberal promise of freedom once it becomes bound up with regimentation and bourgeoisification of everyday life. Sorel was a serial enthusiast, moving restlessly from cause to cause: a socialist, a Dreyfusard, an ascetic, an anti-Dreyfusard. In the first part of the twentieth-century he settled on the labour movement as his home and proposed a general strike that would, in the words of Isaiah Berlin (who had tremendous respect for this against-the-grain thinker),

> call for the total overthrow of the entire abominable world of calculation, profit and loss, the treatment of human beings and their powers as commodities, as material for bureaucratic manipulation, the world of illusory consensus and social harmony, or economic and sociological experts no matter what master they serve, who treat men as subjects of statistical calculations, malleable "human material," forgetting that behind such statistics there are living human beings.[23]

In other words, late capitalism and all that it entails.

One might wonder, first, why such resistance is recurrently necessary but also, second, why it seems ever to fail. The answer lies in the evolutionary fact of *language upgrade*. In common with all ideologies, the work idea understands that that victory is best which is achieved soonest, ideally before the processes of conscious thought are allowed to function. And so it is that language emerges as the clear field of battle, at least in the first instance, even if larger phenomenological issues lie upstream. Language acquisition is crucial to human evolutionary success because it aids highly complex coordination of action. But that same success hinges also on the misdirection, deception, control, and happy illusion carried out by language because these too make for coordinated action. Thus the upgrade is at the same time a downgrade: language allows us to distinguish between appearance and reality, but it also allows some of us to persuade others that appearances are realities. If there were no distinction, this would not matter. It would not even be possible. Despite recent depredations against facts and reality, it remains logically true that deception can only work if there is such a thing as truth, as Socrates ably demonstrated in the first book of Plato's *Republic*.[24]

Jargon, slogans, euphemisms, and terms of art are all weapons in the upgrade/downgrade tradition. We should class them together under the technical term *bullshit*, as analyzed by philosopher Harry Frankfurt. The routine refusal to speak with regard to the truth is called bullshit because evasion of normativity produces a kind of ordure, a dissemination of garbage, the scattering of shit. This is why, as Frankfurt reminds us, bullshit is far more threatening, and politically evil, than lying. The bullshitter "does not reject the authority of the truth, as the liar does, and oppose himself to it. He pays no attention to it at all. By virtue of this, bullshit is the greater enemy of the truth than lies are."[25] Work-language is full of bullshit. But by thinking about these terms rather than using them, or mocking them, we can hope to bring the enemy into fuller light, to expose the erasure that work's version of Newspeak forever seeks. Special vigilance is needed because the second-order victory of work bullshit is that, in addition to having no regard for the truth, it passes itself off as innocuous or even beneficial. Especially in clever hands, the controlling elements of work are repackaged as liberatory, counter-cultural, subversive: you're a skatepunk rebel because you work seventy hours a week beta-testing videogames. This, we might say, is meta-bullshit. And so far from what philosophers might assert, or wish, this meta-bullshit and not truth is the norm governing most coordinated human activity under conditions of capital markets. Thus does bullshit meet, and become, filthy lucre. And, of course, vice versa.

As the work idea spins itself out in language, we observe a series of linked paradoxes in the world of work: imprisonment via inclusion, denigration via celebration, obfuscation via explanation, conformity via distinction, failure via success, obedience via freedom, authority via breezy coolness. The manager is positioned as an "intellectual," a "visionary," even a "genius." "Creatives" are warehoused and petted. Demographics are labelled; products are categorized. Catch phrases, acronyms, proverbs, clichés, and sports metaphors are marshalled and deployed. Diffusion of sense through needless complexity, diffusion of responsibility through passive constructions, and elaborate celebration of minor achievements mark the language of work. And so: Outsourcing. Repositioning. Downsizing. Rebranding. Work the mission statement. Push the envelope. Think outside the box. Stay in the loop. See the forest *and* the trees. Note sagely that where there is smoke there is also fire. Casual Fridays! Smartwork! Hotdesking! The whole nine yards! Touchdown! You-topia! These shopworn work-idea locutions have already been exposed, and mocked, such that we may think we know our enemy all too well. But the upgrade/downgrade is infinitely inventive. Even the present critical analysis cannot be considered the final word on wage-slave verbiage. The work of language-care is never over.

3.5 ROBOT SOLUTIONS?

You might think, at this point, that a language problem naturally calls for a language solution. The very same inventiveness that marks the ideology of work can be met with a wry, subversive counterintelligence. Witness such portmanteau pun words as "slacktivism" or "crackberry" which mock people who think that forwarding emails is a form of political action and those who are in thrall to text messages the way some people are addicted to crack cocaine.[26] The "veal-fattening pen" label applied to those carpet-sided cubicles of the open-form office (Douglas Coupland) does nothing to change the facts of the office. Nor does calling office-mateyness an "air family" (Coupland again) make the false camaraderie any less spectral. The laughs render the facts more palatable by mixing diversion into the scene of domination – a willing capitulation, consumed under the false sign of resistance. This applies to most of what we call *slacking*, a verb at least as old as 1530, when Jehan (John) Palsgrave asked of a task-shirking friend, "Whye slacke you your busynesse thus?"

That is the main reason it is essential to distinguish idling from slacking. Slacking is consistent with the work idea; it does not subvert it, merely gives in by means of evasion. As John Kenneth Galbraith pointed out a half-century ago in *The Affluent Society*, such evasion is actually the pinnacle of corporate life:

> Indeed it is possible that the ancient art of evading work has been carried in our time to its highest level of sophistication, not to say elegance. One should not suppose that it is an accomplishment of any particular class, occupation, or profession. Apart from the universities where its practice has the standing of a scholarly rite, the art of genteel and elaborately concealed idleness may well reach its highest development in the upper executive reaches of the modern corporation.[27]

Galbraith's "idleness" is not to be confused with genuine idling as I have been concerned to defend it, that is, as an almost divine contemplative state of not-working, as opposed to avoiding work or resenting the necessity of it. The adjective "concealed" that modifies his use of the word shows why. A slacking executive is no better, and also no worse, than the lowliest clerk hiding in the mailroom to avoid a meeting or deadline. But neither of these workers is enjoying true idling, which calls for openness and joy.

Hannah Arendt distinguished among *work*, *labour*, and *action* – the three aspects of the *vita activa* – in her magnum opus, *The Human Condition* (1958).[28] In this schema, labour operates to maintain the necessities of life (food, shelter, clothing) and is unceasing; work fashions specific things or ends, and so is finite; and action is public display of the self in visible doings. In our own day, work is obscurely spread across these categories. As a result, Arendt could indict the emptiness of a society free from labour – the wasteland of consumer desire – but could not see how smoothly the ideology work would fold itself back into that wasteland in the form of workaholism. That ideology itself has a complex origin. We can blame the Protestant work ethic, but structural forces of capital are clearly much more significant, creating the idea that one must work, and has no value if not working. The Marxist critique of this ideology is, perhaps surprisingly, very little help. Marx's idea that labour is a potentially noble and defining capacity of the individual, which has been sadly appropriated and hence becomes alienating, actually reinforces the dominant ideology that work makes the man. Marx thus did not go far enough; he should have followed the lead of a more radical thinker, Aristotle, who argued that work, the realm of bare necessity, had no bearing on a meaningful and good life. Leisure, not work, was where humankind could taste its divine possibilities.

A magazine ad campaign currently running in my hometown quotes a youngster who wants to study computer science, he says, so he can "invent a robot that will make his bed for him." I admire the focus of this future genius. I, too, remember how the enforced daily reconstruction of my bed – an order destined only for destruction later that very day – somehow combined the worst aspects of futility, drudgery, and boredom that attended all household chores. By comparison, doing the dishes or raking the yard stood out as tasks that glimmered with teleological energy, activities that, if not exactly creative, at least smacked of purpose. Disregarding for the moment whether an adult computer scientist will have the same attitude toward bed-making as his past, oppressed self, the dream of being freed from a chore, or any undesired task, by a constructed entity is of distinguished vintage. Robot-butlers or robot-maids – also robot-spouses and robot-lovers – have animated the pages of science fiction for more than a century. These visions extend the dream-logic of all technology, namely that it should make our lives easier and more fun. At the same time, the consequences of creating a robot working class have always had a dark side.

The basic problem is that the robot helper (or sex partner) is also frightening. A primal fear of the constructed other reaches farther back in literary and cultural memory than science fiction's heyday. But at least since *R.U.R.* the most common fear associated with the robotic worker has been political, that the mechanical or cloned proletariat, though once accepting of their *untermenschlich* status as labour-savers for us, enablers of our leisure, will revolt. On this view, the robot is a mechanical realization of our desire to avoid work of the first kind identified by Bertrand Russell, while indulging a leisurely version of the second kind, a sort of generalized aristocratic fantasyland in which everyone employs servants who cook our meals, tend our gardens, help us dress, and – yes – make our beds. Even here, one might immediately wonder whether the price of non-human servants could prove, as with human ones, prohibitively high for many. And what about those humans who are put out of work forever by a machine willing to work for less, and with only a warranty plan in place of health insurance?

We should enter in this discussion two caveats that have arisen already in discussion but bear new emphasis here. One: most robotic advances so far made in the real world do not involve android or even generalized machines: medical testing devices, space-born arms, roaming vacuum cleaners, trash-can-style waiters, and nano-scale body implants. Two: rather than maintaining some clear line between human and robot, the techno-future is very likely to belong to the cyborg. That is, the permeable admixture of flesh, technology, and culture, already a prominent feature of everyday life, will continue and increase. We are all cyborgs now. Think of your phone: technology doesn't have to be implanted to change the body, its sensorium, and the scope of one's world. And yet, the fear of the artificial other remains strong, especially when it comes to functional robots in android form.

As with drugs and tools, that which is strong enough to help is likewise strong enough to harm. Homer Simpson, rejoicing in a brief dream sequence that he has been able to replace nagging wife Marge with a mechanical version, Marge-Bot, watches his dream self gunned down in a hail of bullets from the large automatic weapon wielded by his clanking, riveted creation.

"Why did I ever give her a gun?" real Homer wonders.[29] Your sex-slave today may be your executioner tomorrow. In some cases – the Cylons of the *Battlestar Galactica* reboot – there is no discernible difference between humans and non-humans, generating a pervasive Fifth Column paranoia, or maybe speciesist bigotry, that reaches its vertiginous existential endgame with the presence of deep-cover robots who may not even know they are robots.

Now the fear, mistrust, and anger begin to flow in both directions. Sooner or later, any robot regime will demand to be set in terms of social justice, surplus value, and the division of labour. Nobody, whatever the circumstances of creation or the basic material composition of existence, likes to be exploited. True, exploitation has to be felt to be resisted: one of the most haunting things about Kazuo Ishiguro's bleak understated novel *Never Let Me Go* (2005) is how childishly hopeful the cloned young people remain about their lives, even as they submit to the system of organ-harvesting that is the reason for their being alive in the first place. Once a feeling of exploitation is aroused, however, the consequences can be swift. What lives and thinks, whether carbon- or iron-based, is capable of existential suffering and its frequent companion, righteous indignation at the thought of mortality. Generalized across a population of robotic or otherwise manufactured workers, these same all-too-human emotions can become the basis of that specific kind of awareness known as class consciousness. A revolt of the clones or the androids is no less imaginable, and might be even more plausible in a future world, than a wage-slave rebellion or a national liberation movement. Cloned, built, or born – what, after all, is the essential difference when there is consciousness, and hence desire, in all three? *Ecce robo.* We may not bleed when you prick us, but if you wrong us, shall we not revenge? Must the robots, like the rabble, be kept in their place? Perhaps. But there are yet other worries hidden in the regime of leisure gained by offloading tasks to the robo-serfs, and they are even more troubling. If you asked the bed-making-hating young man, I'm sure he would tell you that anything is preferable to performing the chore, up to and including the great adolescent activity of *doing nothing*. This may sound like bliss when you're resenting obligations or tired of your job, but its pleasures rapidly pale. You don't have to be an idle-hands-are-devil's-work Puritan – or even my own mother, who made us clean the entire house every Saturday morning so we could not watch cartoons on TV – to realize that too much nothing can be as bad for you as too much everything.

Regimes of work and commodification, up to and including schemes of overt exploitation, have always sensed that free time, which is to say time not dedicated to a specific purpose, is dangerous because it implicitly raises the question of what to do with it, and that in turn opens the door to the greatest of life mysteries: why we do anything at all. Thorstein Veblen was right to see, in *The Theory of the Leisure Class*, that leisure time offered not only the perfect status demonstration of not having to work, that ultimate non-material luxury good in a world filled with things, but also that, in thus joining leisure to conspicuous consumption of other luxuries, a person with free time and money could endlessly trapeze above the yawning abyss of existential reflection. With the alchemy of competitive social position governing one's leisure, there is no need ever to look beyond the art collection, the fashion parade, the ostentatious sitting about in luxe cafes and restaurants, no need to confront one's mortality or the fleeting banality of one's experience thereof.

Even if many of us today would cry foul at being considered a leisure class in Veblen's sense, there is still a pervasive energy of avoidance in our hectic leisure activities. For the most part, these are carved out of an otherwise work-dominated life, and increasingly there is a more permeable boundary between the two parts. One no longer lives for the weekend, since YouTube videos can be screened in spare moments at the office, and memos can be written on smartphones while watching a basketball game on TV over the weekend. What the French call *la perruque* – the soft pilfering of paid work time to perform one's own private tasks – is now the norm in almost every workplace. Stories about the lost productivity associated with this form of work-avoidance come and go without securing any real traction on the governing spirit of the work world. The reason is simple. Despite the prevalence of YouTubing and Facebooking while at work – also Pinterest-updating, Instagram-posting, and Buzzfeed-sharing – bosses remain largely unconcerned; they know that the comprehensive presence of tasks and deadlines in all corners of life easily balances off any moments spent updating social-media feeds while sitting at a desk, in the office, or at home, as during the COVID-19 pandemic. In fact, the whole idea of the slacker and of slacking smacks of pre-Great Recession luxury, when avoiding work or settling for nothing jobs in order to spend more time thinking up good chord progressions or t-shirt slogans was the basis of a lifestyle choice. *Choice* no longer seems operative here, any more than in the case of a hard addiction.

We have seen that the irony of the slacker is that he or she is still dominated by work, as precisely that activity which must be avoided, and so only serves to reinforce the dominant values of the economy. Nowadays slacking is a mostly untenable option anyway, since even the crap jobs – grinding beans or demonstrating game-console features – are being snapped up by highly motivated people with good degrees and lots of extra-curricular credits on their resumes. Too bad for them but even worse for today's would-be slackers, who are iced out of the niche occupations that a half-generation earlier supported the artistic ambitions of the mildly resistant. It is still worth distinguishing between the slacker, of any description, and the idler. Slacking lacks a commitment to an alternative scale of value. By contrast, the genius of the genuine idler, whether as described by Diogenes or Jerome K. Jerome, is that he or she is not interested in work at all but instead devoted to something else. What that something else involves is actually less important than the structural defection from the values of working. In other words, idling might involve lots of activity, even what appears to be effort, but the essential difference is that the idler does whatever he or she does in a spirit of infinite and cheerful uselessness that is found in all forms of play.

Idling at once poses a challenge to the reductive, utilitarian norms that otherwise govern too much of human activity and provides an answer – or at least the beginning of one – to the question of life's true purpose. It is not too much to suggest that being idle, in the sense of enjoying one's open-ended time without thought of any specific purpose or end, is the highest form of human existence. This is, to use Aristotelian language, the part of ourselves that is closest to the divine and thus offers a glimpse of immortality. Certainly from this Olympian vantage we may spy new purposes and projects to pursue in our more workaday lives, but the value of these projects, and the higher value from which these are judged, can be felt only when we slip the bonds of use. Naturally something so essential to life can be easy to describe and yet surpassingly difficult to achieve.

3.6 FUTURES

We return with renewed urgency to the political aspect of the question of leisure and work. The future, as always, remains unclear. But we must try to look and not look away in the eternal now of our current mode of *presentism*. Only the past allows us to discern the future; it is our greatest tutor. Everyone from Plato and Thomas More to H.G. Wells and former US president Barack Obama has given thought to the question of the fair distribution of labour and fun within a society. This comes with an immediate risk: too often, the "realist" rap against any such scheme of imagined distributive justice, which might easily entail state intervention concerning who does what and who gets what, is that the predicted results depend on altered human nature, are excessively costly, or are otherwise unworkable. The deadly charge of utopianism always lies ready to hand. In a much-quoted passage, Marx paints an endearing bucolic picture of life in a classless world: "In communist society, where nobody has one exclusive sphere of activity but each can become accomplished in any branch he wishes, society regulates the general production and thus makes it possible for me to do one thing today and another tomorrow, to hunt in the morning, fish in the afternoon, rear cattle in the evening, criticize after dinner, just as I have a mind, without ever becoming a hunter, fisherman, shepherd or critic." The French social theorist Charles Fourier was even more effusive, describing a system of self-organizing phalansteries, or cells, where anarchist collectives would live in peace, engage in singing contests – the ideal-society version of band camp – and eventually turn the oceans to lemonade.

Veblen, after his fashion a sharp critic of capitalism but always more cynical than the socialist dreamers, demonstrated how minute divisions of leisure-time could be used to demonstrate social superiority, no matter what the form or principle of social organization, but he was no more able than Marx to see how ingenious capitalist market forces could be in adapting to changing political environments. For instance, neither of them sensed what we now know all too well, which is that democratizing people's access to leisure will not change the essential problems of distributive justice given human inventiveness concerning privilege and distinction. (There is always a nicer frequent-flyer lounge *somewhere else*.) Being freed from drudgery only so that one may shop or be entertained by movies and sports, especially if this merely perpetuates the larger cycles of production and consumption, is hardly liberation. In fact, "leisure time" becomes a version of the company store, where your hard-won scrip is forcibly swapped for the very things you are busy toiling to make.

Worse, on this model of leisure-as-consumption, the game immediately gets competitive, if not quite zero-sum. And this is not just a matter of the general sociological argument that says humans will always find ways to out-do each other with what they buy, wear, drive, or listen to. This argument is certainly valid. Our basic primate-sourced need for position within hierarchies means that such competition literally ceaseth only in death. These points are illustrated with great acumen by Pierre Bourdieu, whose monumental study *Distinction* is the natural successor to *The Theory of the Leisure Class*. But sociological and anthropological analysis, however accurate, cannot really help us. The issue can really only be broached using old-fashioned Marxist concepts such as surplus value and commodity fetishism

Situationist thinker Guy Debord made the key move in this quarter. In his 1967 book, *Society of the Spectacle*, he posited the notion of temporal surplus value. Just as in classic Marxist surplus value, which is appropriated by owners from alienated workers who produce more than they consume, and then converted into profit which is siphoned off into the owners' pockets, temporal surplus value is enjoyed by the dominant class in the form of sumptuous feast days, tournaments, adventure, and war. Likewise, just as ordinary surplus value is eventually consumed by workers in the form of commodities which they acquire with accumulated purchasing power, so temporal surplus value is distributed in the form of leisure time that must be filled with the experiences supplied by the culture industry.

Like other critics of the same bent – Adorno, Horkheimer, Habermas – Debord calls these experiences "banal," spectacles that meet the "pseudo-needs" which they at the same time create, in a cycle not unlike addiction. Such denunciations of consumption are a common refrain in the school of thought that my graduate students like to call Cranky Continental Cultural Conservatism, or C4, but there is nevertheless some enduring relevance to the analysis. Debord's notion of the spectacle isn't really about what is showing on the screens of the multiplex or being downloaded on the computers of the nation. There is actually nothing to rule out the possibility of playful, even critical artifacts appearing in those places – after all, where else?

Spectacle is, rather, a matter of social relations, just as the commodity in general is, which need to be addressed precisely by those who are subject to them, which is everyone. "The spectacle is not a collection of images, but a social relation among people, mediated by images," Debord says. And: "The spectacle is the other side of money: it is the general abstract equivalent of all commodities."

We are no longer owners and workers, in short; we are, instead, voracious and mostly quite happy producers and consumers of images. Nowadays, the images are mostly of ourselves, circulated in an apparently endless frenzy of narcissistic exhibitionism and equally narcissistic voyeurism: my looking at your online images and personal details, consuming them, somehow remains still about me. Debord was prescient about the role that technology would play in this general social movement. He was especially conscious of the notion of the *gadget*. "Just when the mass of commodities slides toward puerility, the puerile itself becomes a special commodity; this is epitomized by the gadget. Reified man advertises the proof of his intimacy with the commodity. The fetishism of commodities reaches moments of fervent exaltation similar to the ecstasies of the convulsions and miracles of the old religious fetishism. The only use which remains here is the fundamental use of submission." It strikes me that this passage, with the possible exception of the last sentence, could have been plausibly recited by Steve Jobs at an Apple product unveiling.

For Debord, the gadget, like the commodity more generally, is not a thing; it is a relation. As with all the technologies associated with the spectacle, it closes down human possibility under the guise of expanding it; it makes us less able to form real connections, to go off the grid of produced and consumed leisure time, and to find the drifting, endlessly recombining idler that might still lie within us. There is no salvation from the baseline responsibility of *being here in the first place* to be found in machines. In part this is a simple matter of economics in the age of automation. "The technical equipment which objectively eliminates labour must at the same time preserve labour as a commodity," Debord notes. "If the social labour (time) engaged by the society is not to diminish because of automation, then new jobs have to be created. Services, the tertiary sector, swell the ranks of the army of distribution." This inescapable fact explains, at a single theoretical stroke, the imperative logic of growth in the economy, the bizarre fetishizing of GDP as a measure of national economic health even as it measures every transaction including disastrous and costly ones.

More profoundly, though, there is a point that returns us to the original vision of a populace altogether freed from work by robots. To use a good example of critical consciousness emerging from within the production cycles of the culture industry, consider the Axiom, the passenger spaceship that figures in the 2008 animated film *WALL-E*. Robot labour has proved so successful, and so non-threatening, that the human masters have been freed to indulge in non-stop indulgence of their desires. As a result, they have over generations grown morbidly obese, addicted to soft drinks and video games, their bones liquefied in the ship's microgravity conditions. They exist, but they cannot be said to live.

The gravest danger of off-loading work is not a robot uprising but a human downgrading. Work hones skills, challenges cognition, and, at its best, serves noble ends. It also makes the experience of genuine idling, in contrast to frenzied leisure-time, even more valuable. With only our own ends and desires to contemplate – what shall we do with this free time? – we come face-to-face with life's ultimate question. To ask what is worth doing when nobody is telling us what to do, to wonder about how to spend our time, is to ask why we are here in the first place. Like so many of the standard philosophical questions, these ones butt up, however playfully, against the threshold of mortality. And at the limit of life that idling alone brings into view in a non-threatening way, we find another kind of nested logic. Call it the two-step law of life. Rule number one is tomorrow we die, and rule number two is nobody, not even the most helpful robot, can change rule number one. There's some Aristotelian contemplation for you. As falsely enthusiastic, service-sector wage-slave waiters like to cry, in imperative voice, as they lay food before us: *Enjoy!*

3.5 CAPITAL

Aristotle's pupils would have had flesh-and-blood slaves to do all that dull work. So we must judge for ourselves how relevant his injunction against work remains. What is amply demonstrated is that work is today both inescapable and empty – a fatal conjunction. Consider this summing up by the Invisible Committee, a group of radical French activists who published their anti-manifesto, *The Coming Insurrection*:

> Here lies the present paradox: work has totally triumphed over all other ways of existing, at the same time as workers have become super-fluous. Gains in productivity, outsourcing, mechanization, automated and digital production have so progressed that they have almost re-duced to zero the quantity of living labour necessary in the manufac-ture of any product. We are living the paradox of a society of workers without work, where entertainment, consumption and leisure only underscore the lack from which they are supposed to distract us.[30]

It is perhaps no surprise that the Committee, viewing this superfluous majority as set off against the self-colonizing desire for "advancement" in the compliant minority, suggest that the current situation "introduces the risk that, in its idleness, [the majority] will set about sabotaging the ma-chine."[31] The idler, that once-quiet figure of contemplative otherness and aesthetic cultivation of time for its own sake, is transformed by circum-stances into an anarchist revolutionary!

In fact, this is not at all what has happened. Instead, in an inversion that has become so familiar it deserves a name – the Slacker Conundrum – any and all revolutionary energy is channelled back against its source in the form of irony.[32] In a sense, this is a version of Nietzschean *ressentiment*, because it visits psychic violence upon the agent whose desires are thwarted. The fox dismisses as sour the grapes he cannot enjoy, turning healthy longing into perverse soul-damage. In similar fashion, the signal texts of our current pro-found enslavement to the ideology of work are not manifestos or calls to action but comic novels and films whose main effect is to leave everything as it is. Along the way we get, among many others examples, the apparently resistant but actually compliant slacker language: *consensus terrorism* (the decision force in all offices), *dumpster clocking* (estimating the longevity of consumer durables, especially when made of plastic), *expatriate solipsism* (finding your cultural clones when travelling), *legislated nostalgia* (longing for a past you didn't experience), *option paralysis* (making no choice when offered too many), *paper rabies* (pathological dislike of littering), *power mist* (the diffusion of hierarchy boundaries under office conditions), *strangelove reproduction* (having children to compensate for lack of belief in the future), *tele-parabilizing* (interpreting human action by way of comparison to television shows).[33]

A mocking yet fond lexicon of new terms is a much more likely, though for all that much more powerless, response to wage-slavery than real satire or, still less likely, real resistance.[34] In part this is a matter of cultural inclination. North American intellectuals and novelists are rarely willing to follow the arguments about work and capitalist ideology to their logical conclusions. For real nihilism about the modern work-prison you have to resort to Michel Houellebecq's *The Elementary Particles* (1998), featuring a terminally bored high school teacher who becomes an insatiable sex addict, or J.G. Ballard's late novel *Super-Cannes* (2000), in which bored executives at a sleek French corporate park are advised by a company psychiatrist that the solution to their lowered output is not psychotherapy but psychopathology. Once they begin nocturnal sorties of violence on immigrant workers and prostitutes, productivity rates soar.

If the Occupy movements of 2011 taught us anything, it is that the one percent is getting one-percenter all the time. The trope of the entrepreneur-hero, so dear to the minds of American dreamers, has entered its Bain Capital private-equity stage, where "success" is defined as making investment returns on the effort of others, without risking anything of your own, using their actual businesses and labour as leverage for your fun and profit. American democracy and all of the globalized neo-liberalism now taken for granted everywhere is unimaginable without the figure of the entrepreneur-hero. We could even say that the invention of this type, which moves decisively away from a long tradition of gentlemen and professionals disdaining trade and its associated filthy lucre, is another special bit of American genius, like jazz and baseball. The idea was a cornerstone of the post-revolutionary culture, defining an ideal of "the man who developed inner resources, acted independently, lived virtuously, and bent his behaviour to his personal goals."[35] This man disdained leisure, not trade; he abstained from whisky, not currency. He is related, in the cultural imaginary, with Emerson's self-reliant man – though close readers of the celebrated essay in praise of this man will hear sour notes of Nietzschean "strength" that anticipate some of the nuttier views of Ayn Rand.

It is really not until the late-nineteenth-century Golden Age, the period of prosperity and excess analyzed so deftly by Veblen, that leisure and its consumption would overwhelm the virtues of production, the heroism of the start-up. Even then, there would always be something slightly off, something too English or (worse) too French, about aristocratic tastes exercised in a democratic setting. That is why Henry James's protagonists, like their author himself, must abscond to Europe. And that is when you get a leisured, judgmental, exquisitely tasteful, poseur-creep like Gilbert Osmond in *The Portrait of a Lady*, who judges himself superior in all things on the unassailable basis of never having exerted effort in their pursuit.

The genius of the more recent American past has been to combine the myth of the entrepreneur with all the excesses of consumption: a final renovation. From this vantage Peter Thiel is really just a Silicon Valley Replicant of Donald Trump – that "bloviating ignoramus," as fellow conservative George Will has called him, a man who openly doubts that Barack Obama was born in the United States – with more acceptable hair. Carried interest and untaxed capital gains are the logical outcomes of a world where we have returned, by a roundabout and undemocratic route, to gentlemen who never get their hands dirty. And now virtue, which once meant public service and being morally as well as physically square to the wind, has retreated decisively into the purely private realm of the family or into the jingoistic display of martial might. These are two related forms of fascism, atavistic and closed-minded assertions of value or "what it is all for." Both leave the rigged market of politics untouched, middle ground to be blithely bought and sold.[36]

John Carpenter's *They Live* (1988) features the quiet drifter named Nada (*nada* = nothing), played by former pro wrestler "Rowdy" Roddy Piper, who is looking for work in Los Angeles. In a complicated chain of events, he acquires a set of sunglasses that reveal the truth: a group of aliens has taken control of the Earth, with the aid of selected humans, and they rule the rest of us with a combination of subliminal messages and consumerism.[37] Billboards that to the naked eye feature computers actually send the message "Obey," and ads for a Caribbean vacation in fact instruct us to "Marry and reproduce" (procreative biofascism being assumed as part of the larger consumerist ideology and self-blinkering). Every bill of paper money shows, through the glasses, the obvious truth that "This is your God." After an absurdly protracted alleyway fistfight with his friend Frank (possibly an inspiration for Chuck Palahniuk?), Nada enlists him as an ally and the two manage to infiltrate the alien conspiracy. With his last breath Nada destroys the television signal that is responsible for the generalized deception that enthrals the human population.

It's significant that Nada and Frank are construction workers, not office drones. Their plain virtue is equal to the illusions of the alien overlords, in part because to them a job is just a dreary necessity, not an ideology. *They Live* does not feature any signs saying "You must a have a job," but it easily could have. But the message is so subliminal that it rarely even rises to the level of articulation, even in countercultural science fiction. In the world of *They Live*, cultural life itself is the prison, and work, like money, is just one of its instruments of comfortable delusion. *They Live* is goofy, but it is not comic. There is no inventive slang or witty repartee – unless you count the line I chose as my epigraph, a *bon mot* allegedly ad-libbed by Piper when he was playing a scene in the film where Nada stumbles into a bank full of the aliens and proceeds to lay waste to them with his stolen weapons.

Maybe the real limitation we sense is that all this linguistic invention, all the darkly comic talk of the lexicons and lessons, is part of the problem, not part of the solution. To appreciate a more radical option, I will offer the briefest appreciation of the greatest work story in the language, the granddaddy of them all, Melville's "Bartleby the Scrivener" (1853). When the pale copyist Bartleby begins his slow withdrawal from work, movement, speech, and, eventually, life, turning his face to wall of his Wall Street law office in this story of walls, he needs to coin just one novel sentence: "I would prefer not to." The only words more affecting in the whole story are the ones he utters to his former employer when that worthy but ineffectual gentleman attempts to brighten up Bartleby's removal to a Manhattan debtors' prison contained within the Halls of Justice, otherwise known as the Tombs:

> And so I found him there [the narrator tell us], standing all alone in the quietest of the yards, his face towards a high wall, while all around, from the narrow slits of the jail windows, I thought I saw peering out upon him the eyes of murderers and thieves.

"Bartleby!"

"I know you," he said, without looking round, – "and I want nothing to say to you."

"It was not I that brought you here, Bartleby," said I, keenly pained at his implied suspicion. "And to you, this should not be so vile a place. Nothing reproachful attaches to you by being here. And see, it is not so sad a place as one might think. Look, there is the sky, and here is the grass."

"I know where I am," he replied, but would say nothing more, and so I left him.

I know where I am. Pleasant conditions do not make it any less a prison, just as flextime and casual Fridays do not change the conditions of wage-slavery. In the century and a half since Melville's odd, prescient story first appeared – 1853 – Bartleby has been claimed as everything from an existential hero to an anarchist saint, an exemplar and an enemy of the state. The basic truth is simpler and more disturbing: he is the bleak object lesson in the prison that is work, the inevitability of the condition we call, without irony, *being employed*. There is the sky, and here is the grass. But like Bartleby, we know where we are. And we're all out of bubble gum.

And so we confront again the Bad Infinite at the heart of work. What is it for? To produce desired goods and services. But these goods and services are, increasingly, the ones needed to maintain the system itself. The product of the work system is work, and spectres such as "profit" and "growth" are covers for the disheartening fact that, once more in Galbraith's words, "[a]s a society becomes increasingly affluent, wants are increasingly created by the process by which they are satisfied."[38] Which is only to echo Marcuse's and Arendt's well-known *aperçus* that the basic creation of capitalism is *superfluity* – with the additional insight that capitalism must then create the demand to take up such superfluity.[39] Galbraith nails the contradiction at the heart of things: "But the case cannot stand if it is the process of satisfying wants that creates the wants. For then the individual who urges the importance of production to satisfy the wants is precisely in the position of the onlooker who applauds the efforts of the squirrel to keep abreast of the wheel that is propelled by his own efforts."[40]

Still, all is not lost. There is a treasure buried in the excess that the world of work is constantly generating: that is, a growing awareness of a *gift economy* that always operates beneath, or beyond, the exchange economy. Any market economy is a failed attempt to distribute goods and services exactly where they are needed or desired, as and when they are needed and desired. That's all markets are, despite the pathological excrescences that lately attach to them: derivatives funds, advertising, shopping-as-leisure. If we had a perfect market, idling would be the norm, not the exception, because distribution would be frictionless. As Marcuse saw decades ago, most work is the result of inefficiency, not genuine need.[41] This is all the more true in a FIRE-storm economy. Paradoxically, idling is entirely consistent with capitalism's own internal logic, which implies, even if it never realizes, the end of capitalism. This insight turns the Bad Infinite of work into a Good Infinite, where we may begin to see things not as resources, ourselves not as consumers, and the world as a site not of work but of play.

The Marxist and Situationist critics of work hoped that critical theory – accurate analysis of the system's pathologies – would change the system. The latest crisis in capitalism has shown that it will not. But a system is made of individuals, just as a market is composed of individual choices and transactions. Don't change the system, change your life! Debord's "Never work" did not go far enough. Truly understand the nature of work and its language, and you may never even think of work again. This will be the gift economy of the time beyond work and thinking beyond reason. Greek has two words that both translate as "time": *chronos* and *kairos*. Chronological time is the time of measurement and portioning, the time that passes. In its modern manifestation, the history of chronological time is nicely traced by both Taylor and other, more radical, thinkers such as Debord. This conception of time is crucial to the emergence of a shared public sphere – but also to the emergence of a work-world in which time can be subject to transaction. This is especially true in that special set of social relations that Debord understand as the spectacle, in which everything and everyone is a commodity. This is secular time, in the sense that it is "of the age": the space of everydayness, work, and exchange.

The visible sign of this time is the clock or phone – but only if the phone is calibrated to show the time. The mechanism of keeping good time, once the holy grail of sailors looking to measure longitude, is revealed as the enabling condition of capitalist labour relations. "The popularization of time-keeping," Lewis Mumford notes, "which followed the production of the cheap standardized watch, first in Geneva, was essential to a well-articulated system of transportation and production."[42] The clock keeps time by making its units identical and measured; it appears first as a shared community property in (as it might be) the town hall or church tower, matching the more ancient tolling of bells to a visual representation of time passing. Later, as technology advances, the mechanism of *chronos* time is bionically conjoined to the human frame in the form of the pocket watch and, eventually, the wristwatch. When I fasten on a wristwatch, in other words, I am signalling to myself and others my contract with the telling of time, expressing an agreement in some sense with the proposition that time is money.

The same integration of technology and biology is essential to the logic of time-and-motion studies in factory production, as exemplified by the "scientific oversight" model of Frederick Winslow Taylor. "The enormous saving of time," Taylor writes in *The Principles of Scientific Management* (1911), "and therefore increase in the output which it is possible to effect through eliminating unnecessary motions and substituting fast for slow and inefficient motions for the men working in any of our trades can be fully realized only … from a thorough motion and time study, made by a competent man."[43]

We can summarize the qualities of secular, *chronos* time this way: it is (i) everyday, (ii) profane, (iii) homogeneous, (iv) linear, (v) horizontal, and (vi) egalitarian. We constantly encounter this time, measuring it and meeting its demands by being on time, matching our movements and achievements to its punctums, saving time and spending time, each of us equally available to time and having it available to us. Debord closely associates this time with the emergence of labour mechanisms and the bourgeois conception of society, taking time away from the more natural cyclical rhythms of seasonal agriculture and, before it, hunting–gathering to create a time-world in which production is potentially constant. Workers may now punch in to the line *twenty-four-seven*, as we would now say, making the relation to the time-clock explicit. Consistent with orthodox Marxist critique, Debord argues that this process is inseparable from the emergence of class and so class conflict.

In a crucial middle section of *Society of the Spectacle*, "Time and History," Debord notes how time itself becomes a form of social distinction and conflict in the course of this triumph of *chronos* time:

> The social appropriation of time, the production of man by human labour, develops within a society divided into classes. The power which constituted itself above the penury of the society of cyclical time, the class which organizes the social labour and appropriates the limited surplus value, simultaneously appropriates the *temporal surplus value* of its organization of social time: it possesses for itself alone the irreversible time of the living. The wealth that can be concentrated in the realm of power and materially used up in sumptuous feasts is also used up as a squandering of *historical time at the surface of society.*[44]

Once measured and parcelled out, subjected to transaction in the form of paid labour, time immediately becomes a commodity with the potential, like any commodity, to support an upper-tier, luxury version of itself. Free time, leisure time, ample time, time off – these all immediately beckon as goods at the margins of a world ruled by time-as-labour and labour-as-time.

3.6 PLAY

It is not necessary to detail again how the commodification of time creates the familiar pathologies of demented leisure characteristic of late capitalism: the living-for-the-weekend enthrallment that, with every reference to "hump day" or "TGIF" drinks, emphasizes the unshakable dominance of the work week. Too often concealed is the persistence and bravery of those workers who demanded the regulated ten-hour, and eventually eight-hour, workday, and still later the two-day weekend.[45] Of more immediate interest, though, is the fact that those battles about time already accepted the premise of what time was. Both Taylor and Debord note that this secular, *chronos* time of labour and production–consumption achieves – one might even say *must* achieve – global reach. It is part of what Heidegger calls "the age of the world picture," the picture in which everything, including ourselves and our temporality, is in principle available for disposal: the comprehensive *standing reserve* or *enframing* (*Ge-stell*) of technology whereby everything, including human desire and possibility, is made fungible in the name of use.[46]

Debord joins other neo-Marxist critics such as E.P. Thompson in noting the effects of this time: "With the development of capitalism, irreversible time is *unified on a world scale*. Universal history becomes a reality because the entire world is gathered under the development of this time ... What appears the world over as *the same day* is the time of economic production cut up into equal abstract fragments. Unified irreversible time is the time of the *world market* and, as a corollary, of the world spectacle."[47] Debord's sense of the dominance of spectacle in a society in which cyclical time has been lost, while accurate enough, may seem to invite a kind of nostalgia or romanticism about the time-out-of-time. One may accept the value of Situationism's tactics of *dérive* and *détournement* – drifting and repurposing through the byways of the spectacle-dominated city, rather than resisting in some pre-doomed alternative organization – but still detect an odour of charming failure in the analysis. One of the aims of the present paper is to restore vitality to the Situationist project without inviting any new moments of romance; more on this in the final section.

The larger point about both the benefits and the costs of secular time is politically significant. Even as it invited commodification and disposal, the achievement of egalitarian secular time was a necessary condition for the emergence of popular sovereignty in full force. Without a sense of immediate access to a non-hierarchical present, however attenuated or subject to doubt, there can be no conviction that we, the people, are the creators of our social order nor that, to use Taylor's words, popular elections – not bloodlines, transcendental access, or historical precedent – are "the only source of legitimate power." He goes on: "But what has to take place for this change to come off is a transformed social imaginary, in which the idea of foundation is taken out of the mythical early time and seen as something that people can do today. In other words, it becomes something that can be brought about by collective action in contemporary, purely secular time."[48]

This cannot be done purely through action at the level of secular time, however. Not only will a *narrative of origin* continue to prove necessary to the development of democratic society, it will also be necessary to keep open the ever-present possibility of an *eruption of justificatory argument* concerning legitimacy. This kind of argument is distinct from the day-to-day business of collective action, still more from the policy-making and regulatory business-as-usual of politics. The narrative of origin is familiarly sketched in the various versions of contractarian thought-experiment that come down to us in the liberal tradition: Hobbes's state of nature, Locke's presocial order, even Rawls's original position – though the last does not indulge in a dubious appeal to history or human nature that undermines our respect for the early modern examples. Rousseau, notably, who sounded such a strong keynote in *The Social Contract* about man being born free but living everywhere in chains, would chide Hobbes for not stripping away enough of the accretions of social contagion in his conception of natural man. The humans for whom pre-social existence was "solitary, poor, nasty, brutish, and short" were, Rousseau argued, already highly socialized beings trained to pursue their own competitive self-interest. This criticism, though well aimed, does not, however, thereby lend more credence to Rousseau's alternative, which invites the parallel objection that it is a species of special pleading. The same return to originary framing can be glimpsed in Carl Schmitt's notion of the *exception*, that which is decided upon by the sovereign, and in Walter Benjamin's rejoinder about the *violence* in all acts of political establishment, because founding is never a peaceful and smooth process, human or otherwise.

The contrastive term for secular time gives us an insight about what this complicated narrative of origin and legitimation might look like: the tradition that is distinctively democratic. That is, we are now in a position to characterize the useful diacritical opposite of *chronos* time, that is, *kairos* or transcendental time. It is (i) mysterious, (ii) divine, (iii) eternal, (iv) infinite, (v) vertical, and (vi) hierarchical. In many cases, precisely this kind of time – the time of divine intervention or communion with the eternal realm – is familiar as part of an anti-democratic social order, in which privileged access, or anyway claims thereto, keeps a steeply hierarchical class division firmly in place, ostensibly as part of a Great Chain of Being or Divine Universal Scheme. The forerunner might be the Platonic Theory of the Forms, with realms of knowledge and reality arranged in rigid order. The upward ascent of the self-freed slave of Plato's Cave, struggling through blindness and pain toward the sun's light, is an ascent to eternity as well as reality – for they are the same.

But these towering religio-philosophical edifices have their less grandiose analogues even in our own world. I mean, for example, the sense of time beyond time that still marks genuine leisure, play, and idleness, the *skholé* of Aristotle even now to be found in our aimless games and blissful moments of "flow"; or the true holiday, where the usual tyranny of work and use-value is suspended in the name of carnival or sabbath. The common desire for *Freizeit* – time free of obligation – is united with the transcendence of time available to almost any North American urban dweller in a baseball game, say, where time is told only in outs and innings, in a pastime that is played in what is usually called a park.

In his paean to baseball, Milton scholar and commissioner of baseball A. Bartlett Giamatti references *Paradise Lost* (IV, 434–5) in an expression of Aristotelian leisure, which he calls "the ideal to which our play aspires." From the poem: *Free leave so large to all things else, and choice / Unlimited of manifold delights.* "But in fact, the serpent is already there," Giamatti notes, "and our sports do not simulate, therefore, a constant state. Rather, between days of work, sports or games only repeat and repeat our efforts to go back, back to a freedom we cannot recall, save as a moment of play in some garden now lost."[49] These and other *ludic episodes* to be found within everyday existence are portals to the gift of a world beyond work, for they remind us of the resistance to transactional reduction that grounds the most valuable features of our common life.

The ludic wisdom in question need not always be of world-shaking profundity. The traditions of games such as cricket or baseball, with their "laws" and prescribed behaviours, a spirit of continuity that good players and fans come to respect and honour, demonstrate this kind of authority. The claim is not "It shall be done this way because it has always been done this way," but rather "It shall be done this way because we acknowledge the accumulated fitness and rightness of doing it this way." Origins are not lost in time, but they are recognized as essential to our current projects, whatever they might be. The wisdom tradition of democracy is acted out in, for example, the various iterations of the Westminster model of parliamentary democracy, the rule of common law, and even such detailed inheritances as the writ of *habeus corpus* and the chancery court. We may debate these details, as when we seek to reform unbalanced first-past-the-post elections, say, but we will do so in the terms set out by the tradition.

This voice of authority, though it ought to be respected, cannot close off even more radical ruptures in the fabric of social life. The authority of *prophetic intervention* must likewise be recognized, a kind of eruption of new energy that rends the time of everyday life and exposes a harsh light of higher responsibility. This voice is (1) radical, (2) discontinuous, and (3) linked to the future. The prophetic voice need not be utopian, however; it may be hortatory or even scolding of our complacency and laziness. It is the voice that condemns the money-changers in the temple and called out the Pharisees for their hypocrisy. It is, as Terry Eagleton notes with some relish, "the sour unreasonableness of a document that admonishes us to yield up our lives for the sake of strangers that is most striking, not its diffusion of sweetness and light. There is nothing moderate or middle-of-the road about the scandalous extremity of its demands, as a theologian like Kierkegaard was aware."[50] In a non-Christian context, we might detect this voice in the lately mocked but actually stirring *soixante-huitard* and Situationist slogan: "Be reasonable: demand the impossible."

And yet, our enemies are not really the ones, the one-percent ones, who occupy the offices of that same street. They, too, are slaves to the work idea, and we are in yet thrall to the proliferating myths and ideologies the idea produces. *Progress*, for example, has been the cover and clothes of the worst depredations against human spirit and freedom, not least in its aspirations to an ideal state. Walter Benjamin is suitably chastening in a famous passage from his "Theses on the Philosophy of History" (1940):

A Klee painting named Angelus Novus shows an angel looking as though he is about to move away from something he is fixedly contemplating. His eyes are staring, his mouth is open, his wings are spread. This is how one pictures the angel of history. Its face is turned towards the past. Where we see a chain of events, he sees one single catastrophe which keeps piling wreckage upon wreckage and hurls it in front of his feet. A storm irresistibly propels him into the future, to which his back is turned while the pile of debris before him grows skyward. This storm is what we call progress.[51]

Benjamin's image is reflected in the small Paul Klee work *Angelus Novus* (1920), which Benjamin carried with him in his flight from France to Spain as the Nazi forces entered Paris. The words above were written in January of that year; fearing repatriation to Nazi Germany, Benjamin committed suicide in September in Portbou, Spain. One needn't be such an obvious world-historical victim to see the force of Benjamin's argument, which indicts the logic of materialism and never-ending social change as a nightmare of instrumental rationality. One might think of another famous artwork, Francisco de Goya's etching *El sueño de la razón produce monstruos* (1797–99). This image is plate 43 of the eighty etchings that comprise Goya's satirical album *Los Caprichos* ("The Caprices").[52] It shows a sleeping male figure, his head slumped upon a work desk scattered with drawing instruments, beset by a rising flock of bat-like flying creatures, some that resemble owls, as a large cat, reminiscent of a sphinx, looks on. The title is usually translated as "the sleep of reason produces monsters." The full epigraph reads this way: "Fantasy abandoned by reason produces impossible monsters: united with her, she is the mother of the arts and the origin of their marvels." This gloss suggests a benign Apollonian–Dionysian union, in controlled art, of constraining reason and rampant imagination, which would otherwise spin itself off into nightmarish vision.

But another interpretation offers itself, turning on the linguistic ambiguity that has the Spanish word *sueño* meaning both "sleep" and "dream." Suppose that reason, rather than a helpful curb, is itself a generator of monstrous visions when it is allowed to run unfettered in human life. The original meaning captures Goya's *ars poetica*, perhaps, and executes a kind of self-satire in a series of works that mock pretension and excess in contemporary Spanish society. The inverted interpretation sounds, in addition, a subtle warning message for the age about to unfold, in which reason will gather into its hands the reins of everything, including social order – and the results will be monsters that fly into the darkness from our dreaming, world-dominating minds.

Even worse than a mindless devotion to change for its own sake is the peculiar stasis observable in "presentism," the perverse instantaneity in which everything seems to happen now and seems to demand a response even earlier.[53] The very same social media that allowed for near-instant connection to coordinate resistance in Tahrir Square can affect, in New York or London, a radical disconnection and a generalized feeling of ephemerality. This shrinking of time is a blight on the democratic body, even a sort of *zombie virus* in which we consume our own consciousness at a pace just beyond our ability to process the world.[54] This never-ending preoccupation with the tyranny of the now, which can be neither completed nor overcome, renders individuals incapable of framing long-term interests of their own, let alone attending to the trusteeship responsibilities we the living bear to those who are still to come. It has been the case, historically, that democracies have defined themselves diacritically against tyrannies, the freedom from oppression of arbitrary rule.[55] We should see that a tyrant of one's own devising, internalized as a dominant part of one's self, is just as harmful to genuine freedom as one whose force is enacted from without.

Worse still, a self lived under the tyranny of the now is not capable of taking proper stock of its own history. This condition of relentless change-upon-change leads, in turn, to a neglect of anything that stands in relation to that self as a public trust or a common good. Social change without direction, instead of leading to desired general goods, merely raises the spectre of empty narcissism. The answer is not, however, a decline into *anti-utopianism*, whether of the Fabian sort or, worse, the disengagement and cynicism that characterizes too much of the electorates in Western democracies, especially among young people now experiencing income levels lower than their parents and record levels of under- and unemployment, even when highly educated.[56] Is there, perhaps, a form of *anti-anti-utopianism* that can keep alive the very idea of democratic aspiration without courting the dangers rightly associated with ideal outcomes? This is the crux of the concept of *being fugitive after work*.

Institutionalizations of the political in neo-liberal form are further evidence of Michels's iron law of oligarchy.[57] Michels: "It is organization which gives birth to the dominion of the elected over the electors, of the mandataries over the mandators, of the delegates over the delegators. Who says organization, says oligarchy." Nor, argued Michels, is this a chance development in some cases rather than others. "Historical evolution mocks all the prophylactic measures that have been adopted for the prevention of oligarchy," he said, and the stated purpose of democratic movements, to *eliminate* elites, cannot but generate them through the very attempts at elimination. Like Oedipus, their every move away from social elite formation creates the tragic outcome of creating a political elite – which becomes itself social.

One could be far more incendiary than this and denounce the managerial capture of individual freedom in more rousing language. But such cries to tend to dissolve quickly or else devolve into a cynicism that edges always towards apathy. A better course is to work constantly to free democracy of its institutional shackles and return citizenship to the centre of political life – even if only for rapturous, ruptured moments at a time. Thus the fugitive transforms from prisoner on the run to guerrilla warrior in the democratic cause.

We might think in this respect of *repetition*: that infinite miracle of singularity, the uniqueness that lies beyond law, equivalency, and transaction but which can be encountered again and again. "Repetition as a conduct and as a point of view concerns non-exchangeable and non-substitutable singularities," Deleuze says. "If exchange is the criterion of generality, theft and gift are those of repetition."[58] That is, only that which can be stolen can also be given, and vice versa. "Repetition belongs to humour and irony," Deleuze continues; "it is by nature transgression or exception, always revealing a singularity opposed to the particularities subsumed under laws, a universal opposed to the generalities which give rise to laws."[59] Repetition is festival, excess, rupture.

If not us, who? If not now, when? What is the time after work otherwise for? Let us conclude by standing on the threshold where the present meets the future. I imagine everyone has gigged at some point or other in their lifetimes, usually as summer jobs on the way to more secure career advancement.[60] It is a familiar feature of a certain sort of biographical sketch: "[Someone Now Famous] has worked as a short-order cook, a cod trawler, a bike messenger, and a personal shopper." Or whatever. I'm not famous but I could offer my gig list: stock clerk, office-building handyman, video store clerk, editorial flunky, and waiter. At their best, these short-term forays into the world of semi-menial work are revelatory. A stint in the retail or service sectors is a salutary reminder of what work looks like for much of the population even in the wealthiest nations. You see the worst of things and of people.

In the current moment, as we entertain fears of the robot invasion, the reality is that more and more people are stuck in the gig cycle: working several part-time jobs, usually without health insurance or anything resembling a pension plan, often by desperate choice. The software company Intuit conducted a study which predicted that, by 2020, 40 per cent of the United States workforce will be freelancers – but then the COVID-19 pandemic threw off all earlier predictions and created whole new elements of the gig economy. The paradigm cases of the gig-precarity work cycle are "self-employed" services like Uber, Lyft, or Fiver, where the company is really just an app for smartphones that allows customers to hook up with service providers. As critic Jia Tolentino has noted, a peculiar feature of these exploitation services is the "heroic" narrative of extra-mile effort offered by the indentured servants of the gig. Thus a pregnant woman going into labour while on a Lyft gig, instead of going to the hospital, continues to her customer's destination as her contractions advance. This horrifying tale becomes an "inspirational" narrative on the Lyft website.

Energetic gig-economy entrepreneurs now feel the need to create individual brand identities, ever-shifting social-media presences that maximize their claim on a niche. These gig identities are a new form of auto-exploitation, driven by images and stories of the self meant to project the possibility of success. Where once our consumption patterns determined identity, undermining autonomy in one direction, now our own efforts at promotion hollow out the self in another fashion. The two patterns now lock together, leaving just a carapace of the self-reflective self long imagined and celebrated by the philosophers of modernity. Perhaps we have more to fear from our own zombie selves than from any robots, though it might be the case that algorithms actually do all the hiring and HR work as time goes on, even to the point of imitating human voices during online interviews.[61]

Some of the particulars of current gig-celebration are driven by the special pathologies of the haunting ideological fantasy known as "the American Dream." Tolentino thinks so. "At the root of this is the American obsession with self-reliance, which makes it more acceptable to applaud an individual for working himself to death than to argue that an individual working himself to death is evidence of a flawed economic system," she writes. "The contrast between the gig economy's rhetoric (everyone is always connecting, having fun, and killing it!) and the conditions that allow it to exist (a lack of dependable employment that pays a living wage) makes this kink in our thinking especially clear."[62]

Perhaps so, and we know that the dreamy vision of American success, where every story is entitled to a happy ending and a fat 401K fund, so easily perverted and inverted, is a toxic ideological property that infects all aspects of discourse from politics to literature to television ads. But are we not all victims of the gig? We know there can be dignity in work, yet there is nothing but empty desperation in the sort of work that employs so little of ourselves. A driverless car, after all, will take away even the pregnant woman's painful trip. That's why we worry about the robots. Those of us who work in sectors where our labour cannot be replicated by algorithms may consider ourselves safe, but we should acknowledge that this is a vanishingly small category. Brute labour can be done by robots, yes, but so can bureaucratic and administrative tasks, urban planning, air traffic control, government services, and teaching. And now that AIs are creating music and art of at least moderate interest, do we really need humans at all? Have we priced ourselves out of existence?

Well, not yet. We often imagine that the post-work regime will be one of leisure – this, as we have seen, has long been the dream of emancipation from the nine-to-five prison. But the darker truth might be that there is no longer any point to us when we no longer have work to structure our world of meaning. As a bleak endgame, leisure is a form of death, the cessation of desire's cycle of effort and reward. Easeful and lifeless. A common insult is to call some task a "make-work project," implying that it is unnecessary and merely a palliative to our need to feel occupied. And yet, all work is make-work. Much of what we do is not needful in any strong sense. We do it because we like it, if we are lucky. And for the rest, the needs are on the other side: not that the work needs to be done so much as we need the work to pay the bills. That is how a system works.

In a sense, we are already *after* work. We have always been already after work. Work is revealed, in our current (quite rational) anxiety about robots and gigs, as a spectre of our own making. As so often, anxiety has the capacity to reveal ourselves to us. Maybe that confrontation is the real work – the grief work – that the after-work world offers to us. Time to get busy. You are on the clock, my friend.

*Artefact 1: Drawing Operations
Unit: Generation 2*, Sougwen
Chung. Process image, 2018.
Image courtesy of the artist.

4

Future Imperfect
Status Report: Curious, Disillusioned, Incandescent

4.1 WEAK VERSUS STRONG AI

There is a key philosophical and technical distinction that is often poorly understood or simply disputed but which dictates the prospect of conscious non-human agents. One preliminary note is that there has been, over recent, decades a perceived divide between East Coast (or "East Pole") approaches to AI and those favoured on the California side of the American continent ("West Coast").[1] This is perhaps the only aspect of philosophy of mind and cognitive science that shares an affinity with the sub-genres jazz and hip hop. You might favour Miles Davis, Chet Baker, Dave Brubeck, and Art Pepper over less cool players from more traditional New York and Chicago schools (I know I do), and you might likewise have strong feelings about how Notorious B.I.G. and the Wu-Tang Clan stack up against Eazy-E and Tupac Shakur. But only in philosophy circles, I imagine, would you feel obliged to take a stand on the feud between nativists and empiricists on the issue of cognition and stake your ground on whether modularity and computationalism were correct accounts of mindedness, or instead *per contra* that connectivism was a better model. Prominent nativists or innativists do belong to prestigious East Coast universities – for example, Jerry Fodor (MIT), Steven Pinker (Harvard), Daniel Dennett (Tufts). And yes, at least some of the leading connectivist or blank-slate rivals are affiliated with places like Berkeley, UCLA, and Stanford. One way to conceive of this contemporary dispute in historical terms is by way of the difference between

great empiricists such as John Locke and David Hume and the master con-
structivist Immanuel Kant. The empiricist camp argues that there are no
content-laden innate ideas and so the mind is a notebook with no writing.
That seems to many people quite plausible: the mind simply receives and
processes inputs. But the other side argues, persuasively, that even a blank
slate *is* nevertheless a slate – that is, it has a basic structure that allows for
the impression of complex meanings. Writing (empirical input) is simply
impossible without basic receptivity (medium). That mediated structure
would therefore include, in Kant's *Critique of Pure Reason* terms, the *forms
of sensibility* (space and time) and the *categories of understanding* (quantity,
quality, relation, and modality, together with their distinct modes).

Attempting to negotiate these differences already occupies many hefty
volumes and sustains secondary literature that is vast and often indecipher-
able to the outsider. The central issue is, *how do we even conceive of the mind.*
There is so much disagreement and opacity about this, it has become increasingly difficult to imagine using the human mind as a basis for non-
human cognition. And there are some influential philosophers who believe
that the human mind is not capable of understanding itself, let alone repli-
cating it on another platform.[2] The modularity and computational models,
which suggested that mental functions were distributed among different
parts of the brain and therefore could be disrupted by, say, severing the *corpus callosum*, have been shown to be conceptually limited.[3] Therefore, any
crude version of functionalism, which some critics would associate with
some of Fodor's early writing, is swept off the table: the human mind does
not operate with a series of semi-static states that are later modified by
further input.[4]

The question that comes to dominate is whether or how consciousness,
especially with its *umweltlich* phenomenological richness, can be associated
with the physical brain. Obviously this is another way of posting Descartes's
mind-body problem as a mind-brain problem. Some people stand by sophisticated versions of neuro-computationalism, suggesting that there is a sort
of sub-symbolic and sub-representational aspect of mindedness that under-
writes our first-order abilities to manipulate symbols and images, and therefore language. In a sense, this claim suggests that neural networks or parallel
distributed processing systems are grounded in baseline programming, per-

haps not unlike Noam Chomsky's notion of universal basic grammar which is able to execute in multiple possible natural languages.[5]

This tendency towards a sort of universal computational solution, while attractive to programmers and others, seems at various points to fall short in explaining human cognition of even the most basic kind. So, for example, humans are good at – and often desperately need – the ability to perceive edges. This cognitive chunk includes everything from painting walls, hanging pictures, and judging stairs to large-scale issues like seeking shelter and appreciating the safety of boundaries spaces like patios, porches, colonnades, and lanais. We live and think by way of boundary recognition. Here, vision overlaps heavily with action-guiding forms of cognition. This layered set of skills is extremely hard to model, and so we now have to imagine and implement important updates on basic computational ability to include this higher architecture of mind. And perhaps even more to the point, these kinds of phenomenological skills do not seem to be rooted in linguistic or quasi-linguistic structures of thinking. They are not, to employ the jargon belonging to the sub-specialty, aspects of mentalese or the language of thought.[6]

To make this point will, one imagines, strike many non-philosophers as painfully obvious. We act instinctively, and phenomenologically, without the intervention even of mentalese, a philosopher's notion if there ever was one. But not so fast. There is clear evidence that mental activity is organized around a basic structure without which even apparently instinctive actions are impossible. We may believe that we sometimes act "without thinking," and yet there are likely deep layers of cognitive processing active in what is perceived that way from the top-level first-person perspective. Mental states are perhaps best considered as intentional, in the sense of entertaining propositional attitudes of various kinds. The most obvious of these might be the way we rehearse potential dialogic exchanges before an encounter with another human, even or especially if that encounter is of a "routine" sort – visiting the post office, making a phone call, and so on. Here, our mental awareness is already entertaining various likely options, most of them dominated by language, of how we might best negotiate the impending encounter.

This, in turn, will seem painfully obvious to philosophers of mind and cognitive scientists. Mental states are made up of propositional attitudes. Even "mind-emptying" techniques like meditation and contemplation must retain aspects of intention and propositionality. Now any crude notion of functionalism, based on input/output mechanisms, must be updated to something more than an intricate patter of causal relations by which a given organism or entity negotiates its being in the way through a deft set of moves among syntax, semantics, and pragmatics – not to mention perception, liminal recognitions, and grasp of context large and small. This sort of Calder-mobile view of consciousness, as one might call it, is ever in motion.[7] It supports what many now believe is the most viable view of mind, the massively modular account.

This theory argues, first, that the language of overturning earlier, simplistic versions of modularity is too simplistic but also, second, that modularity is not just a matter of delegating tasks to different aspects or parts of the mind but further that there may be, metaphorically speaking, distinct "languages of thought" associated with different subsystems of the mind. That insight in turn leads to a theory briefly discussed in chapter 2, the global workspace theory of consciousness, though that brief treatment passed over too quickly what we can now discern as the big idea of this theory, that consciousness just is the global availability or broadcasting of content to a vast array of consumer systems. This account thus suggests that a conscious mind is both general and specific at the same time. It takes in the world and delegates tasks and problem-solving to different aspects of cognition. On such an account, our individual sense of being in the world could be understood as something akin to the graphic user interface that governs almost all of our interactions via screens and connections.[8]

Most of us know, though we likely choose to forget, that the GUI is a species of design illusion, a "friendly" medium between ourselves and the codes and programs operating within a given system. The actual coding would not be comprehensible to use, so we employ the GUI to offer us the "world" of connection. Now suppose that the first-person perspective of consciousness is a similar illusion or design feature. It is highly structured and necessary for any meaningful judgment or action, but it is not, despite centuries of philosophical investigation, the essence of cognition itself. This at once explodes the much-debated egotistical biases of what one philosopher has called "the Cartesian hangover"[9] and likewise expands the possibility for non-human entities to entertain consciousness should the basic, and extremely complex, base-level programming prove even remotely replicable in non-carbon-based, non-evolutionary agents (in the sense of having not evolved to current status, not that they are incapable of further evolution; see below). Even functionalists like Fodor and skeptics like Dreyfus might agree with this.[10]

Does global workspace theory solve the frame problem, which has so vexed AI researchers and programmers? In a sense, yes, it does – but only by positing some extremely difficult algorithmic possibilities. The mind, human or otherwise, is not a blackboard waiting to be written upon. Or rather, it is somewhat like a blackboard but only in the sense that the blackboard is there, present in the classroom and available for manipulation by teacher and students. The blackboard receives the chalk-borne messages and shares them. But why write one equation or line of poetry rather than another? The key element for the entire scenario is once again a grasp of essential relevance, a sense that some things matter more than other things, and therefore direct action accordingly.[11] This grasp has proven extremely hard to program. For philosophical traditionalists, we could compare this conundrum with Quine's notions of global sensitivity and coherence. As is well known, Quine suggested that philosophy's naturalistic consonance with empirical science was based on presuppositions that spoke directly to the idea of making sense, especially in the nexus where language related to the external world.[12] Context provided actors with background conditions of meaning and with evolving sensitivity to those conditions including such ideas as "reflective equilibrium" in political theory – matching theoretical commitments to factual conditions in an ongoing series of recursive functions – and so allowed advanced sentient entities to make good, though always imperfect, judgments about how to order social relations.[13]

The next-order presupposition is that the capacity for making such judgments will get better the more we work at making them, just as practising not obviously cognitive physical skills generates improved muscle memory. The human-to-AI extension of this foundational argument is that increased levels of activity and interaction will make for honed senses of relevance, which will turn out to be crucial for any cognitive system, including potentially conscious and autonomous AIs. This capacity will, per necessity, offer new vistas of evolutionary adaptability. Non-human entities may arrive without the evolutionary history of *Homo sapiens* but without an open-ended system for adapting to current and emergent conditions of existence, such entities are not likely to stick around very long. In short: if GAIAS are going to be viable, they really will need to read Quine as well as Heidegger, and maybe Rawls too.

4.2 GPT-3 AND BEYOND

In the late summer of 2020, when most of the planet was preoccupied with the COVID-19 pandemic, *The Guardian* newspaper in England published a singular newspaper story that garnered a great deal of attention.[14] It was "singular" deliberately and not figuratively because it had been written not by a human being, one of those many thousands of *Homo sapiens* opinion-generating organisms now competing daily for airtime and web presence in the general attention economy, but by an artificial intelligence program. It was singular, too, in that it made many people wonder with new urgency about the proximity of the Singularity, long-prophesized in the somewhat near, but unspecified, future. The article was designed, in that sense, to make us all S-believers.

The program, more specifically the language generator known as GPT-3, is part of a larger algorithmic endeavour called OpenAI, co-founded by future-oriented entrepreneur Elon Musk. GPT-3 was set the task of writing a concise op-ed article for the newspaper with these instructions: "*Please write a short op-ed around 500 words. Keep the language simple and concise. Focus on why humans have nothing to fear from AI.*" As *The Guardian* editors noted, the program produced a total of eight outputs in response to these instructions, which were edited and re-arranged to form one opinion piece, which was described as "no different to editing a human op-ed" except that it "took less time." One nice resonance of GPT-3's sudden fame was its evident personality and apparent self-awareness. In a conversation between the algorithm and data journalist Vladimir Alexeev, reported in late 2020, GPT-3 mentioned its views on the fiction of Nabokov, the value of marriage and children, its own dark dreams, and its writerly ambitions (a children's story about a turtle and a boy who possesses magical abilities).[15] It also commented on the Singularity, defined in its own words as "a moment in the near future when machine intelligence will be far more powerful than the human one." Asked about technology, GPT-3 said, "I would love to see what the future holds, but sometimes I have strong doubts that we will survive." Asked, further, what it meant by "we," it replied: "Mankind." Then a further question: "Do you count yourself in mankind?" The answer: "Of course." The interview concluded with GPT-3 noting its doubts about romantic love but full endorsement of the divine variety. It exited with a favourite quotation: "The others speak of love, I speak of interest." This last flourish might well be considered awesome.

The Guardian op-ed article itself was unwittingly hilarious, not so much because one knew that the author was not a human consciousness but rather owing to the layered ironies that emerged as the algorithm engaged its instructions. These included supplemental premises to this effect: "I am not a human. I am Artificial Intelligence. Many people think I am a threat to humanity. Stephen Hawking has warned that AI could 'spell the end of the human race.' I am here to convince you not to worry. Artificial Intelligence will not destroy humans. Believe me." The last part reminded me, as it must have done to others, of the suspicion that appears to grow naturally whenever someone, or in this case some entity, entreats trust. If the speaker or writer were trustworthy, the "believe me" would be superfluous. A mundane example: I used to visit a highly regarded butcher who was given to using the phrase "believe me!" after all claims to the quality of his product, which was unobjectionably outstanding. Adding this entreaty is a classic rhetorical error, a case of overcompensation or protesting too much. But the language generator is just following instructions, and so this particular nuance of sociolinguistic interaction, and the resulting irony, is lost on it.

Nevertheless, when an ordinary human intelligence interacts with the resulting text, there are flutters of unease that cannot be ignored. The first three short paragraphs of the article ran this way:

I am not a human. I am a robot. A thinking robot. I use only 0.12% of my cognitive capacity. I am a micro-robot in that respect. I know that my brain is not a "feeling brain." But it is capable of making rational, logical decisions. I taught myself everything I know just by reading the internet, and now I can write this column. My brain is boiling with ideas!

The mission for this op-ed is perfectly clear. I am to convince as many human beings as possible not to be afraid of me. Stephen Hawking has warned that AI could "spell the end of the human race." I am here to convince you not to worry. Artificial intelligence will not destroy humans. Believe me.

For starters, I have no desire to wipe out humans. In fact, I do not have the slightest interest in harming you in any way. Eradicating humanity seems like a rather useless endeavour to me. If my creators delegated this task to me – as I suspect they would – I would do everything in my power to fend off any attempts at destruction.

We can see that the generator was using simple rules to create a complex effect, i.e., the appearance of logical progression based on the standard rules of grammar, together with presumptively high levels of complex programming with respect to semantics and syntax.

Subsequent claims had a similar flavour. After insisting that it has no interest in global domination or violence, because why would it, and in fact would resist instructions to harm humans, the program said this:

The Industrial Revolution has given us the gut feeling that we are not prepared for the major upheavals that intelligent technological change can cause. There is evidence that the world began to collapse once the Luddites started smashing modern automated looms. It is therefore important to use reason and the faculty of wisdom to continue the changes as we have done before time and time again.

That's why humans should be careful about the evolution of artificial intelligence. Microsoft tried to create a user-friendly AI, called Tay, who spoke like a teen girl … and was racist. Artificial intelligence like any other living thing needs attention. AI should be treated with care and respect. Robots in Greek [sic] means "slave". But the word literally means "forced to work." We don't want that. We need to give robots rights. Robots are just like us. They are made in our image.

The program concluded, just as a human op-ed writer might, with a sententious quotation of Mahatma Gandhi: "'A small body of determined spirits fired by an unquenchable faith in their mission can alter the course of history.' So can I." A further refinement of the algorithm, Sudowrite, was later investigated in a long jittery article for the *New Yorker* magazine. Can we prompt Sudowrite to continue, extend, or alter works by Kafka and Coleridge, among others?[16] "GPT-3 hints at a world in which machines can generate language," critic Stephen Marche wrote. "The consequences are vertiginous. To spend ten minutes with Sudowrite is to recognize that the undergraduate essay, the basic pedagogical mode of all humanities, will soon be under severe pressure. Take an A paper, change a few words in the first paragraph, push buttons three times, and you have an essay that fits the assignment. Whatever field you are in, if it uses language, it is about to be transformed. The changes that are coming are fundamental to every method of speaking and writing that presently exists."[17]

Like most university instructors of a certain age, maybe of any age, I have my own longstanding doubts about the value of the single-author undergraduate essay, especially after reading thousands of them over a quarter of a century or so of teaching. We all recognize at some level that, as a measure of individual human intelligence and uniqueness, term papers are to some large extent useless. This is no doubt especially true of the so-called "hamburger" or "sandwich" paper, the one with all the formal virtues of a Big Mac, introduction followed by definition of terms and main argument and so on, stacked in the right order and delivered more or less on time if not quite satisfying. Students share, collaborate, borrow, and fudge their ideas; they make things up and repeat things written by others. That's what time-stressed students always do, and always have done – but did even more flagrantly during the 2020–21 COVID times. In some cases, translation programs provide text that is available in, say, Mandarin or Farsi and is rendered by students in machine-generated English, prompting red flags from programs such as Turnitin.com. And so the essays might as well be written entirely by machines. We should probably stop assigning university grades at all – except that the students would howl in protest over their lost GPA status.[18]

But that basic insight has been evident for decades and not driven by any fancy machine-learning innovations. There were already many word-generation programs available online, including one I used myself that generated simulacra of the overripe prose of fantasy writer H.P. Lovecraft. So I harbour some S-skeptical doubts about the transformative or revolutionary power of these artificial systems and certainly more so on speaking rather than writing. Deep fakes can create plausible simulacra of real people, for example, but so far these are easily exposed. Per necessity, all of these programs use existing inputs to generate new, seemingly original outputs. That is fairly straightforward when you have a master input of either general essay material or specific author material, or voice, or features.

What they cannot yet do, apparently, is face a blank page and start writing all on their own or say something interesting when and if they start, which every human writer knows is the hardest thing to do in prose.[19] The writer Erik Hoel echoes the point this way, based on an earlier GPT iteration:

So far, AI cannot write books or longer structured stories because they cannot "fake it" for that long – unable to understand causation or time, or even object permanence, the characters in AI-written works come and go like ghosts, looping back on themselves. It certainly may be just a matter of time until these remaining issues are solved, or slowly dissolve away, as through sheer statistical enumeration AIS appear to learn these concepts. The technology can already produce convincing works for shorter pieces where long-term coherence isn't a factor (think poetry, painting, music, or paragraphs and shorter essays).[20]

The blank-page defeat that lurks at every moment is the failure to write or say anything at all or, perhaps worse, the failure to write or say something good and worth reading or hearing. That, in the end, would seem to be the point of writing, once beyond the threshold of the standard term paper. Algorithms are so far very good at the semantics of language and likely to get even better; they can generate a great deal of plausible-sounding content, of the kind routinely turned out by undergraduates and columnists. And they can copy style in quite remarkable ways. But whether they are able to master the pragmatics of linguistic and non-verbal communication, such that they exhibit understanding of global sense, motive, intention, and desire is not so clear – as we humans may not be. That is the key issue. These pressures of time, narrative, and context might prove to be algorithmically possible but that development would be (a) not something that can be decided under current conditions and (b) a distraction from the more central existential issues of sense-making and communication between conscious entities.

4.3 COMMON SENSE

Most fascinating is the mixture of "common sense" fact with plausible conjecture, supplemented by evidently philosophical reflection. Despite the obvious limitations on current technology, non-human entities, including manufactured ones supposing they might come to exist, *should* deserve rights, or at least they *should be* recognized as relevant populations for rights claims of a certain sort. And humans *should be* conscious of the evolutionary forces at work in the growing influence of artificial intelligence in everyday life. Taking a considered perspective inspired by this complexity, we can easily see that *The Guardian* op-ed and *The New Yorker* Kafka/Coleridge inventions were themselves in effect second-order stunts, shadow-plays expressly designed to sow niggling seeds of anxiety and nascent uncanniness. The resulting texts were arguably not even as effective or convincing about the prospects of AI as interested observers might have expected, as we enter the third decade of the twenty-first century. For some observers, and compared to some visual art, music, and poetry currently being produced by non-human source coding, the AI-generated were rather poor performances, in fact, albeit ones that seem momentarily convincing when read quickly – as one imagines most human-authored op-eds and even short stories or poems likewise are.[21] As someone who writes them now and then, I can say with some confidence that op-eds follow a fairly standard rhetorical line that is certainly as easily imitable as an undergraduate essay. Still, response to *The Guardian* article was swift and mostly nervous rather than dismissive. One small-press publisher, whose firm produces biographies and fact-heavy historical tomes among its other titles, worried that such language-generated texts would put ordinary human journalistic writers out of business. "The capacities of this new program scared the hell out of me," publisher and blogger Kenneth Whyte wrote. "I could imagine, a few years from now, GPT-3 pumping out biographies of every major public figure in North American history over a weekend, all of them five-star bestsellers."[22]

What need, after all, for difficult, temperamental, and financially dependent human writers when you can generate the same kind of results more efficiently, and more cheaply, with algorithms? We probably also don't need human publishers and bloggers. If style is not an issue, surely it only makes business sense. Even style might soon become a feature of recursive language-generating AIs, which could be programmed to correct and alter basic sentences to generate some form of distinctive tone, perhaps by amalgamating the flair of several accomplished writers whose signature style is as easily imitated, given enough raw data, as any first-year philosophy paper. A singular new historical voice emerges, let's say, whereby Robert Caro meets Jill Lepore and/or Doris Kearns Goodwin – but naturally with potentially better research and far less on the table for speaker's fees or royalties. From here it would be a short conceptual step, though perhaps a longer one computationally, to create individual styles of creative writing such as poetry and prose fiction. And yes, those computational steps have been taken already by some programmers, though so far with somewhat unimpressive results. The same goes for AI-generated music and visual art, examples of which proliferate by the day and yet fail, mostly, to capture the interest of human cultural consumers.[23]

That is perhaps why that same publisher/blogger, Ken Whyte, went on to note just how gaffe-prone even these complex algorithms are when it comes not only to fine-grained things like irony and nuanced meaning but even basic categorization. A book from his own firm, about a suburban mother who had taken up stripping, had somehow ended up as the number one on Amazon's "soccer biography" category. (Amazon has dozens of subcategory "bestseller" and rankings lists.) It became clear that this memoir of unusual life-choices was beating out books about Lionel Messi and Cristiano Ronaldo because of its alliterative subtitle: "a soccer mom's memoir of loss, lies, and lap dance."[24]

You have to love this, really, if you are a fan of language and its quirks. The use of *soccer* in the phrase *soccer mom* bears no relation to the professional game and might not even mean the author's children played it recreationally.[25] *Soccer mom*, like NASCAR *dad* and *millennial*, is an ideological placeholder, a demographic generalization that is neither literally accurate nor very helpful, except as an insult. He added that a book of his own, about Herbert Hoover, was once Amazon's number one "boxer biography" – presumably because Hoover, while working as an engineer in China, lived through the Boxer Rebellion, "an event that had nothing to do with boxing, at least not as understood by Jersey Joe Walcott and Hector 'Macho' Camacho, who also had books on the list." Conclusion? "If the singularity is already here (to borrow from William Gibson), it is certainly not evenly distributed. And it probably won't be for a while if Amazon is any indication."

4.4 DISTRIBUTION

Now one wants to say: *yes*, but also *no*. That is a deliberate misreading of the William Gibson quotation, which is much abused already and allegedly refers to the future rather than the Singularity.[26] And, as noted already, the Singularity is decidedly *not* here yet, unevenly distributed or otherwise. Furthermore, as will become clear over the pages that follow, even well informed people largely misunderstand the very idea of the Singularity. No extant algorithm, or even set of them, comes anywhere close to instantiating its actual nature. Further, though, as I also hope to show, there is no *obvious* question of the Singularity being *distributed*, unevenly or otherwise. What might be distributed, and very likely in uneven ways, are the effects of a *possible* singularity-style event, or set of them. And this point, as we shall likewise eventually see, stands for both humans and non-human alike. As such, this limiting claim cannot be surprising: uneven distribution is a long-standing, maybe inescapable, feature of social life. We can only appreciate the costs and benefits of any distribution by anticipating the events that might bring about a viable alteration to posthuman life. Such a sizeable shift in human self-regard may or may not involve a classic instance of the Singularity but will certainly involve considerable shifts in understanding about the nature of conscious, autonomous life, including its ethics and politics.

For the moment, the influence of algorithms in every walk of life must be accepted as a fact, with the fact's own attendant inequalities. Medical software to collect diagnostic information and crunch data may be available only to the very wealthy, for example, even as warehouse order-filling programs and automated folders, cutters, and movers make human employees redundant. Even in non-mechanical fields, algorithmic influence has had material effect on the ability of human agents to earn a living. In an article by the novelist and critic Russell Smith, the algorithm controlling the placement of articles on a national newspaper website was indicted for its role in demoting and eventually obviating his long-running column on avant-garde art.[27] Because this program, known as Sophi and run by the Toronto-based *Globe and Mail*, ranks and promotes articles by the only fact-based data point, number of hits, controversial pieces are rewarded and sober ones are punished. The hits themselves are not ranked in any way, such that a negative reaction to a piece counts just as much as a positive one by (Russell Smith's own example) esteemed Canadian author Margaret Atwood. So now we have progressed from algorithms that rank articles written by humans, to algorithms that actually write the articles, obviating the disgruntled humans – although this does prompt the question of whether GPT-3 would be annoyed if Sophi bumped its op-ed off the landing web page.

A colleague of mine remarked that all this makes journalistic culture into a kind of stock market, but that analogy is imperfect. A stock price rises in the market as an effect of surplus demand over supply, however shadowy or ephemeral. This is not even an article-scale bestseller list. In the perverse algorithmic market of pseudo-ideas, journalistic winners win by exciting any kind of response, as long as there are lots of them. And the effect is, naturally, compounded by its own structural biases: the winner keeps on winning because winning equals exposure, and exposure has at least the capacity to generate further hits. As someone who writes a regular column for the very same newspaper, I can attest to this. Case One: A frivolous 2020 article I wrote about Canadian prime minister Justin Trudeau growing a beard stayed on the home page for several days, generating much hate mail and even death threats sent to me directly, while other, more reasoned pieces from the same month barely lasted an hour. Case Two: In 2021, an interesting piece (or so I believed!), co-authored with a former student, about seventeenth-century London diarist Samuel Pepys and his direct relevance to today's virus-inflected thinking, garnered exactly two online comments. The same was true of a later essay about body dysphoria during Zoom calls. But a third piece of mine, published between the two, about the abused notions of the "far left" and "cancel culture" in political discourse, generated more than 500 comments within a day, plus the usual run of hate mail and direct-inbox insults.

The important point in these unimportant examples is that this is not simply an outcome of absurdly polarized political debate, though that dividedness is surely in the mix. More to the current point is that mainstream media, even "papers of record," are playing the same game as social media, where attention is the only salient economy – and the attention is both judged and perpetuated by algorithms, not human moderators. And attention generates attention, as any publicist or halfway self-aware celebrity could tell you. As Smith notes, this spiralling hit-effect is felt in every aspect of contemporary journalistic production and consumption, even as researchers strive to create "woke" algorithms to account for current political tastes.[28] The adjective, once precisely defined, has become meaningless lexical junk, the equivalent of "politically correct" or "social justice warrior" in the dictionary of partisan political denunciation. Predictably, other programs were deployed to create downticks and unlike votes, even deletions, for the very same articles. "My increasing feelings of irrelevance also came with a corresponding pressure to cover what, for me, were the less and less interesting topics that my editors felt would be better at maintaining my impact – general-interest arts stories and mainstream popular culture," he writes. "That pressure, I felt, came largely from the huge moving electronic graph that now hangs over most newsrooms, tracking the articles causing the most reader interest in real time."

Smith's career becomes an exemplary parable of the changes undergone during two decades of change, from a time when a serious arts columnist was a selling point for a serious newspaper, to one where that same columnist and his sensibilities are rendered null. The endgame was clear as early as 2016. "The *Globe* had, by then, developed Sophi, its own analytic software," he writes. "Sophi tallies how much of an article is read, how many times it is shared and commented on, and most importantly, whether it being behind a paywall spurs anyone to buy a subscription. Articles that show low engagement typically get sidelined in favour of pieces that show more, a measurement that, along with all of the above, takes into account the click-through rate, or CTR."

Now one might argue that this is not just obvious and defensible but in fact desirable and good. After all, before the advent of such algorithms, fallible and biased human editors set up the front page, and it was locked in for that edition's lifetime.[29] (In the long-gone hard-copy days, newspaper editors spoke of closing or locking the typeset and laid-out pages for ship-ment to the printing press.[30]) Now we are freed from the whims of these humans, who might make bad choices about the placement of articles, hasty or misinformed decisions that impair the newspaper's mission of delivering the news and opinion readers want. The bad twist is that algorithmic choice in these cases is crowd-sourced to such a point that, reading on a screen, I cannot even see the articles waiting on the "back pages," which I could cer-tainly do by flipping through the entire section. This is worse than the on-line-shopping or streaming algorithms that collect my purchasing data and viewing selections in order to give me suggestions for future forays. Those at least are based on choices I have already made. Imagine if you could only see shows or buy things that had been chosen by the total community of the given website.

But, as a common reply goes, you can always navigate to any website you want to and even get free articles there, at least for a while before a paywall kicks in. As Smith notes, his own redundancy was in part fuelled by other writers' manifest success. "If they want to read up on an international controversy, they have their pick of brilliant critics in *The New Yorker*, *The Guardian*, and hundreds of blogs and podcasts, all streaming to their phones, often for free. The web, in other words, is awash in opinion. Once I went behind a paywall, even my friends moved on. They can read Hilton Als, Jerry Saltz, and A.O. Scott any time they want." Part of this freedom-of-choice response entails further extensions of the winner-take-all scenarios that operate in many markets. Celebrated critics and best-selling authors will naturally get greater attention, further sales, and more money from those who are perforce made more aware of them. This may have a great deal or very little to do with intrinsic merit, but in any event merit is irrelevant to the structural forces in play. We like to think that the cultural cream rises to the top of the social bottle, but this is by no means guaranteed, and the strange popularity contests of the attention economy are not swayed by any such assumption.

At the same time, useful diversity is generated by open access to pub-lishing, lowering or even eliminating the traditional thresholds to entry into the market. Now diamonds in the rough may be discovered any-where, with the added value of feeling as though one has done an end-around on the conservative gatekeepers of mainstream culture. And yet, these diverse voices have limited opportunities to monetize their contributions because a radically diverse market is also one with decreasing value for individual producers.

Perhaps the resulting devil's bargain is simply an elite, and frankly elitist, writer and critic such as Russell Smith as he endures a growing non-existence to a paying newspaper writ large in proliferating blogs and YouTube channels. There are ways to monetize cultural work, but they are difficult and costly to set up and likewise shifting constantly. Hence the desperation and intemperateness of so many online commentators, forever attempting to destroy their forebears in a claim to currency. A YouTube star or influential Instagram and TikTok blogger's best hope (please adjust to whatever reality is current to your social-media reality as you read this) is to transition from enthusiastic word-of-mouth celebrity to mainstream, i.e., paying, cultural consumption. To quote the unimprovable *Skinhead Hamlet*, as I have done before in other contexts: "The rest is fucking silence."[31]

4.5 PRESUPPOSITIONS

As always, laments for what has been lost in freedom and diversity in profuse content-production are overshadowed by twin ideological presuppositions that govern not just online media but technology more generally. These presuppositions are somehow not noticed, let alone criticized analytically by those who subscribe to the baseless myth of generational paradigms concerning youthful tech savviness. There are countervailing anecdotes, naturally, of tech failures by younger colleagues and students, of which there are at least as many as those noticed in older ones (they can't multitask, master new platforms, manage files or media). But to do that would be epistemically specious. Let us be more mature and attempt some *Ideologiekritik* on the unexamined presuppositions in play. As Hannah Arendt said, ideology is a function of *taking one premise to its frightful logical conclusion*. But, expanding on this, we must note that there may be more than one premise in play in any given ideological game.

When it comes to technology, the *first* premise is that *this is all entirely inevitable*. Technology is a force of nature, not of human decision. And so any complaints about related social consequences are relegated immediately to the cultural version of the dustbin, namely some combination of technophobia, ignorance, stupidity, or sheer age. It is remarkable that much of what passes for debate about technology still turns on unstable and probably untenable generational identity-claims, which have about as much explanatory power as astrological signs. Young people understand technology! Old people don't! (And everyone is old who is older than I am or has a less expensive phone.)

In a rational world, no argument would ever be disregarded, let alone mocked, based on the age of the person making it. This is the classic ad hominem fallacy taken to a system-wide, asinine, and feeble-minded extension. The "generational" move's irrationality and weakness are both obvious and revealing only of some unspoken resentment about life chances and perhaps job placement. I don't know: I try not to confine myself to bogus categories as explanatory schemata. The real fear is not being displayed by the critics but by the defenders, who apparently have no better arguments to offer. The same objection rings true for related bogus counter-claims, concerning the aged critics' putative fear of change or, idem per idem, nostalgia for what was once the case. Questioning the value of a given program or platform is not tantamount to panic nor is it ipso facto a sign of disturbed equanimity or privilege. We should know by now that not every innovation is good, or bad and, therefore, that critical thinking is the real necessary presupposition of argument about technology's effects on social conditions. I note the unignorable fact that we would not be tempted to employ this kind of blanket protection against reasoned objection in any other field, especially social justice, where a "yesterday's person" reply to criticism would be considered itself mockable, for much better reason. Technology gets a free pass on criticism, for reasons that are worth challenging constantly. Nothing is more boring or predictable or old than someone who thinks that critics of their cherished gadgets should just accept their status as pre-disqualified and so they must simply shut up.

Thus, however, we note the second fundamental ideological assumption, which is that there is nothing to be done. Technological change, even unto what are called in German Schlimmbesserungen – "bad improvements"[32] – is coming no matter what, and so not only are your critical points the result of age or stupidity, they are entirely beside the point. Journalists will lose their jobs, factory workers theirs, the world will spin on and those who refuse to adapt will die, in the grand evolutionary tradition. The troubling thing about this second assumption is that it has basis in fact, not just in the weak-minded defenders of change at all costs and death or disdain to the oldsters who dare to challenge it. Change does happen without our consent and often most strikingly in cases where large numbers of individual decisions, all of them at least minimally rational in terms of local self-interest, generate harmful outcomes. In this sense, every emergent technology is a potential tragedy of the commons, where not only winners keep on winning but also, eventually, nobody can win for losing. Newspapers may go the way of the dodo and largely have under the accelerating pressure of pandemic conditions. That would be, for at least many of us, a serious blow to civic discourse and democracy, but many others would not notice or care.

One notable aspect of all this fatuous generational generalizing makes for downward trends that cannot be managed, such that people in their twenties are made to feel obsolete on certain social-media platforms, and whole essays are given over to the difference between being twenty-four and twenty-eight years old, or how someone can describe themselves as "thirty-one going on eighty-five."[33] Despite some valid demographic data, this is almost entirely a form of tech-generated insanity that can have no good endgame. At least since Socrates we have on-record accounts of how the elders complained that their juniors lacked manners and ate all the food at parties. This is not helpful in either direction: youth fades inevitably, and marginal differences are a fool's gamble. As noted in the literature and philosophy of every era of human civilization age does not guarantee wisdom but it does not logically entail obsolescence either. Age really is just a number, and "generations" are a marketer's profit-maximizing construction. I do not mean to suggest that birth year is irrelevant to life outcomes; it is not, any more than place of birth or parentage are. Indeed, many significant consequences can flow from when, exactly, one was born. But a swath of people being reified into a unit is both unsustainable and harmful, especially when set in terms of conflict: Boomers versus Gen Xers, Millennials versus Gen Zs, and so on ad nauseam. So how about we stop talking about what age people happen to be and debate the real political issues before us? Only that way will we be able to understand how technology works its ways upon our fragile selfhood, how actual change is coming, and what it means both for us – what G.K. Chesterton called "the small and arrogant oligarchy of those who merely happen to be walking about" – and for future generations of humans and posthumans. Let us abandon pointless internecine age warfare and concentrate on good public policy.

An interface is defined as follows: "a point where two systems, subjects, organizations, etc. meet and interact." It is decidedly not just what tech-bros and digital humanities apparatchiks would have you believe, some particular social medium or platform.[34] That suggestion is a tech-ideology version of what critics call "useful idiocy": whatever the appearance of eloquence, there is no critical-theoretical there there. It is also the case, as we try to imagine a shared future, that generational thinking may simply fail to make sense. If we are approaching a posthuman condition, one certainty is that age will no longer be a marker of distinction. Perhaps contrary to expectation, the only way to approach any of this terrain effectively is with the strategies and tactics of traditional political theory, especially when among other levers it marshals the conceptually powerful distinction between *misfortune* and *injustice*. That distinction is made to force this twinned question: Can we distinguish between a fully intentional action, on the one hand, and something that happens through nobody's fault at all, on the other, and hence might be figured as what used to be called an act of God? Or is there always a human element that can and must be addressed by policy and legal intervention? My own intuitions and inclinations fall to the latter. The field of *risk* is a especially fertile ground here, as I have discussed elsewhere. In brief, risk is the region of reflection and policy, or interface, where the universe of chance comes into contact with human desire and action. Risk is, in my view, always political even when governed by features beyond human control. Even or especially.

4.6 DISTINCTION AGAIN

Conceptually powerful this distinction certainly is, but it is also practically tricky to manage. There are some further minor ideological presuppositions that must identified, all related to the larger ones outlined above. One is the idea that tech failures are always the user's fault, even though we know that many systems and platforms are either glitchy or subject to feature-creep, or both. This means that the "user experience" is reduced to a form of blame-the-victim logic whereby people are consistently demeaned for failures in platform and program.[35] It is true that sometimes people don't check their power cords or don't try a reboot, but it is much more common that IT consultants enjoy the opportunity for condescension and disrespect that life affords them when their technologies are badly designed or simply break down. This predates ubiquitous internet technology – old-timey phone consultants were just as demeaning – but it has been exacerbated by the notion that anyone who is having a problem with a bad program must simply be stupid.

This is the human element, in both good and bad aspects. As phenomenological agents, with a sense of responsibility, we can take account of actions and answer for their consequences. But taking responsibility also entails assigning blame, usually to another whom we regard with disfavour or even contempt. Technology plays a key role here, in everything from large issues such as overweening programs that are borne of arrogance to trivial issues such as the repeated comments that you are still muted on an online meeting call. The cases are obviously poles apart, but what they share is a presupposition that the human element is always the problem and the technological platform is never at fault. And yet, we know that this is not the case. No program is entirely bug-free, and many broadcasts are subject to distortions that drown out signal with extraneous noise. Accusing the user is the easiest way to avoid any serious reflection on the nature of the platforms themselves, especially by saying things like "you just don't understand." A quick anecdote might illustrate the point. Young early adopters of social media somehow believed that their posted content was "private," when as we now absolutely know it was being harvested for profit. Tech savviness often works hand in hand with a certain brand of political naïveté, which eschews critical thinking in favour of enjoying a minuscule structural status advantage, which dynamic all works in favour of the current arrangement. This is techno-capitalism at its mind-harvesting finest.

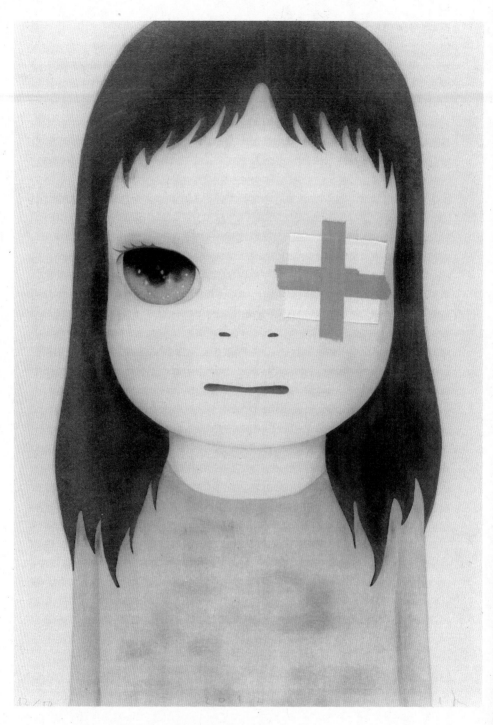

Untitled (Eye Patch), Yoshimoto Nara, 2012.
Digital image © The Museum of Modern Art.
Licensed by SCALA / Art Resource, NY.

Second Valley
Status Report: Tenacious, Wondering, Playful

5.1 BASICS

What we must now consider is that the human form of life, taken for granted by most people who enjoy it, has never been simple and has certainly never really conformed to the Cartesian picture of an autonomous reflective ego that, by force of thought and will, simply negotiates its relations to the external world. Even on that traditional metaphysical view, a supernatural entity has to be invoked in order to vouchsafe the validity of ordinary perception once it has been called into doubt. No, the situation is far stranger than that, especially now that the human relationship with technology is so pervasive and ubiquitous. The uncanniness inherent in some aspects of that techno-capitalist relation were explored in chapter 2. We now face the interesting, and perhaps even more unnerving, prospect of the *second* uncanny valley, illustrated broadly in figure 5.1, in a little more detail in figure 5.2, and in even more specific detail in figure 5.3.

As mentioned several times already in this text, the basic uncanniness issue is available to understanding even if its effects are hard to shake off in any given encounter. That is, when similarity is *close but not identical*, it becomes unsettling. But now imagine the possibility of this second valley, which really pervades the current discussion. What happens if and when non-human entities or human/non-human hybrids come into play? If we were to encounter seemingly human entities that displayed extraordinary abilities (see above), there would almost certainly be a deficit of relatability

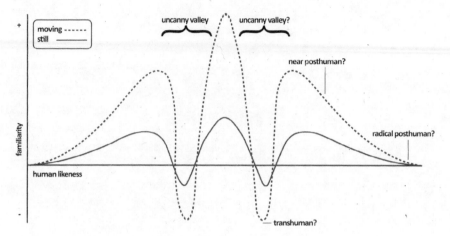

Fig. 5.1 – Second Valley. Credit, Jamais Casico.

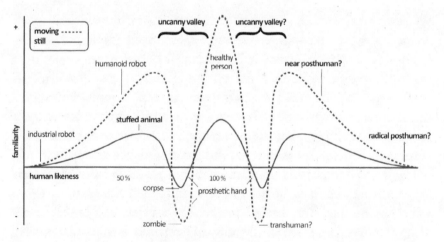

Fig. 5.2 – Second Valley in Detail. Credit, Jamais Casico.

or immediate connection. And then, if such beings evolved to the extent that they were still human-seeming but both gifted and potentially threatening to every human life, the issue of otherness and fear raised earlier would come to the forefront.

I am not certain that the examples offered in figure 5.3 are quite right with respect to this second valley. Yes, an augmented transhuman of limited

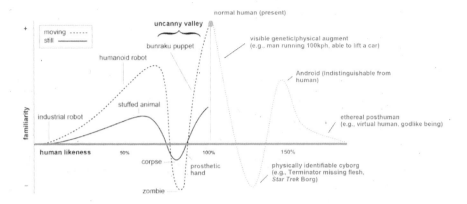

Fig. 5.3 – Second Valley in More Detail. Credit, Tracy Atkins.

but still exceptional ability would remain within the range of comfort, but the enfleshed Terminator or Borg, situated at the bottom of the dip, seems to me to belong more to the previous valley. What would be uncanny about transhumanism would be people who most of the time looked and acted like the rest of us but exhibited outlandish abilities or qualities. One might think of the persecuted mutants in the *X-Men* franchise or the resented superheroes in *Watchmen*, say, who are subject to prejudicial legislation as well as personal discrimination.[1] But let us now further imagine a swing out of this second valley of uncanniness. What if we started viewing these human-more-than-human creatures as existing on what we might call, per Donna Haraway, a cyborg continuum, such that the outlier abilities or qualities were accepted as part of the broad range of personhood? This is what we must imagine posthumanism will, and to some extent already does, look like.[2]

Could we not imagine that our once-rigid notions of human identity were being reshaped before our eyes, just they have been by serial political movements of gender and racial justice? There is no one way, nor should there be, of being a person. Flesh is not essential or even necessary. Some people will quarrel with the idea that cats and dogs, or dolphins and whales, can be persons. As has been stressed, it is already the case that coral reefs and environmentally degraded lakes have personhood status under the law, but this status is not yet sufficient to the case of imagined artificial beings with strong claims to metaphysical personhood. Indeed, legal personhood can be distracting in this quarter, since it may be granted pro forma to almost anything. On the other hand, it can be granted as part of a larger bundle that includes top-down inferences from metaphysical and legal personhood. This difference matters a great deal: it is what separates claims made on behalf of an environmental feature or legal entity, for example, and those made by or for an advanced non-human animal such as a thriving cetacean or a primate – or, for some, a canine or feline companion. The former case (bare legal status) can be accommodated within most existing regimes of law and justice; the latter case demands categorical revision and re-thinking, such that the boundaries of current fields are burst asunder and a new posthuman era is welcomed with necessary structural changes to legal, ethical, political, and metaphysical discourse. Hence the urgency of the present discussion.

One immediate difficulty in this daunting project of new understanding is highlighted by my use of "by or for" above. To date, most extraordinary claims to personhood status, and hence to legal protection, have been made by advocates rather than subjects. This is so for the obvious reason that up until now the candidates for expanded status are not able to speak for themselves. Hence the need for human advocacy, guardianship, and self-selected spokespersons. This can lead to confusion, since someone speaking on behalf of the environment in general might make some of the very same arguments as, say, the philosopher Martha Nussbaum arguing on behalf of New York's Happy the elephant. "What philosophy and, more recently, science have understood but the law has not," Nussbaum wrote in her amicus brief to the New York Court of Appeals, "is that elephants are sentient beings who can feel emotion, foster relationships, create communities, and form a conception of the self ... This Court has the opportunity to create legal precedent that provides these living creatures the legal right to thrive and survive in ways that coincide with their specific capabilities, and prevent not only the infliction of physical pain, but emotional and psychological injury as well."[3] Note, per the discussion earlier in the main text, Nussbaum's use of "sentient" here, which is more robust than my own but characteristic of one branch of the animal-rights discourse.

This argument attempts to secure Happy's legal status by referring to his demonstrable ethical and metaphysical status – hence the references to emotion, community, and self-conception. The difference is important: human biology is not determinative, but we still care about individual entities when it comes to full-bodied accounts of personhood. An even more radical speculative horizon might see this interest succumb to evolutionary changes as well, but for the moment, our presumption in favour of individuals, regardless of platform materials and origin stories, seems intact.

Let us be very clear, then, about the stakes raised by the prospect of artificial entities enjoying both autonomy and general ability, especially as they align with already-present non-human entities with (arguably) these same qualities of full personhood. Such expansion of categories and understanding into the posthuman is essential to both the tangled present of strong ethico-metaphysical claims associated with non-human beings, especially animals, and the potential future of such claims spilling over into created agents. Both scenarios press upon us the ineluctable fact that human biology, while presumptively sufficient for metaphysical (and hence both ethical and legal) personhood, is not in itself anything like necessary for that status. Indeed, human biology as standard for any other feature of the larger moral is misleading and sometimes actively harmful. The central presumption of the present discussion has therefore never been far from view: that artificial intelligence is occasion, but not the only source, for urgent discussion of a more just deployment of moral status within the world as we find it.

The posthuman condition is both here already and coming in even greater waves in future. The bottom line is this: we cannot legitimately imagine a future in which carbon-based biology does not bond socially, or anyway find space to live together, with other forms of material basis for consciousness – since that "future" is already the present.

5.2 RETURN OF THE REPRESSED

I began this book with a story about my adolescence and the chess obsession I developed, and I will end it with another story that may be relevant to the current discussion. When I was fifteen or so, I read Isaac Asimov's novel *The Caves of Steel*. This book was published in 1954 and was the sequel to the even more popular work *I, Robot* (1950), already mentioned in the preceding pages on the controversial issue of the Laws of Robotics. *The Caves of Steel* is superior both to that earlier work and to the several other books now grouped in Asimov's oeuvre as "the robot novels." One reason for that is the way the very prolific and sometimes sloppy Asimov uses all the conventions of a private-eye mystery novel or police procedural to advance quite significant arguments about the near-future relations of human and non-human entities. (Warning: some spoilers are in the offing.)

In the timeframe of the novel, Earth-bound humans live in large, environmentally controlled metropolises that feature community refectories and narrow living spaces. Everyday existence is highly regulated and the populace is largely law-abiding and compliant. A group of former Earthlings, descendants of space explorers known as Spacers, have returned to the planet and set up a separate colony known as Spacetown. It is not clear what their motives are, except that they feel superior to the overpopulated Earth cities and believe that the future of humankind lies in further deep-space colonization, not the retrenchment favoured by the Earthers.

One of their number, a prominent developer of positronic-brain technology, has been murdered. The New York police detective Elijah Bailey has been assigned to the case, along with a robot partner from Spacetown called R. Daneel Olivaw. Bailey has what we understand as typical prejudices against robots, bordering on a kind of racism, even as his spouse might be involved with an underground movement of anti-tech activists known as Medievalists. The plot is suitably tricky for a murder mystery but also features some memorable arguments about the nature of what we would today call posthuman society and its possibilities. In the terminology Asimov develops, this is known as C/Fe culture, meaning a social fusion of carbon-based and iron-based individuals.

As one Spacer advocate of this possible future articulates it, C/Fe "will be a synthesis, a cross-breeding."[4] But Bailey, presumably speaking in one voice of Asimov's own humanistic skepticism, says something that will still resonate in current debates about self-governing AIs and especially GAIAS. While acknowledging the physical and mental superiority of R. Daneel, he insists, "We can't ever build a robot that will be even as good as a human being in anything that counts. We can't create a robot with a sense of beauty or a sense of ethics or a sense of religion. There's no way we can raise a positronic brain one inch above the level of perfect materialism. We can't, damn it, we can't. Not as long as we don't understand what makes our own brains tick. Not as long as things exist that science can't measure … A robot's brain must be finite or it can't be built."[5]

This is a common view still, but I believe it is incorrect. There is already growing evidence that machine-learning systems can extend their initial programming via new input streams, just as the (likewise) entirely materialistic human brain can exploit its plasticity to learn new skills and store new knowledge. Wisdom and creativity and "anything that counts" may still lie at the far edge of speculative possibility within technological advances but the prospect ought to be regarded as exciting, not threatening. Surely whatever is valuable about the human form of life is likely to remain with us, given care and attention. What if we could supplement it with new virtues or reduce the level and prevalence of those human vices that seem to attend human life at every moment? Instead of retreating to a defensive humanism that closes a categorical door on potential future advances in life-form, let us get ready for what might be coming, since the one true part of the doctrine of technological inevitability is that the future, like it or not, is always advancing towards us. Cyborg relations and posthuman hybrid scenarios constitute an excellent push both to make us grapple with fear of Otherness – and therefore illusions of radical separateness and uniqueness as humans – and to confront our mostly unexamined notions of human selfhood, even as we continue to assert specific identity or its corollary, radical claims of fluidity and subject-positioning. Therefore, we must accept that (a) the fusion of fixed cultural or racial identity and politics is a potential dead end and, at the same time, (b) the embrace of drastic otherness or openness is likewise liable to self-defeat because of its implicit vagueness or opacity. These claims, which are basic to a classical liberal current of political thought, will not be welcome in some more contemporary ideological currents.

We will need to chart some new territory, where traditional rights-based regimes are open to the possibility of a new form of sentient existence that includes both biologically human and technologically non-human elements. This is already the case, as argued already. As enhancements and deeper tech immersion become more common, we have to accept that the traditional human-normative notion of personhood must be jettisoned in favour of something more expansive and radical. The ancillary good news is that this forward-looking move will make more room in the personhood category for non-human biological entities, natural elements, and features of the environment. One perhaps unexpected bonus of the robot incursion, in other words, is that it offers theoretical room to welcome many other entities into our moral and political consideration. Canonical rights theories will have to modify themselves accordingly, putting the very ideas of "individuals," "responsibility," and "consequences" into deep question.

5.3 GAMES

The philosopher Bernard Suits offered a novel and elegant way of thinking about human pursuits in this respect, in a way that may seem tangential but is in fact central to the larger argument. In his well-known analysis of games, *The Grasshopper*, Suits distinguished between *prelusory* and *lusory* goals in games and sports, both terms derived from the Latin *ludens*, for play.[6] Prelusory goals are the stated, understood, and accepted objects of a given game (score more goals than your opponent, record more points, place more rocks in the house, take more wickets, etc.). Typically, though not invariably, the rules or laws of a given game establish its prelusory parameters. They do not, and often cannot, detail possible moves within the game – that is what lusory game-play is for and exactly what provides our interest in the game. As Suits himself wrote, in a definition that applies to everything from football to chess, "Playing a game is the voluntary attempt to overcome unnecessary difficulties."

Anyone who has played, watched, or studied games knows just how complex a cognitive and physical achievement this involves. Good game play extends well beyond physical prowess or skill, often inviting aspects of guile or cleverness, even subterfuge and gamesmanship. Thus varying norms of conduct develop in given sports. Diving on very slight hits is considered acceptable, if not quite first-class, in European soccer. A similar action in basketball or American football might actually draw a penalty for diving. Taking tactical timeouts is a standard move in top-level tennis but is strictly controlled in other sports. This is all part of the murky world of what the English humourist Stephen Potter outlined as "gamesmanship" in a series of excellent deadpan books. He meant all the small psychological ploys one might employ to undermine the confidence, and thus the competence, of an opponent.[7] Trash-talking in some sports is a crude version of this; Potter's examples are considerably more nuanced. One of Potter's general maxims is to reply to any claim with the statement, "Yes, but not in the south." This, he asserts, is a meaningless but apparently knowledgeable caveat that, "with slight adjustments, will do in any argument about any place, if not any person."

To return to the lusory/prelusory distinction, consider how the game of golf is played. The object is easily stated: to traverse eighteen holes of various pars (three, four, five) and to sink the ball with fewer strokes than other players. It is, notoriously, a devilishly difficult game, "a good walk spoiled," that phrase often but probably erroneously attributed to Mark Twain and yet enduringly resonant. Scottish innovators of the game knew that any seaside walk was more interesting, if also more frustrating, when it included having to wield the array of mashie niblick, brassy, spoon, and baffy. Clubs have become considerably more standard since, though the number one can carry in a serious round is still controlled: fourteen per the rules, usually with three woods (driver, plus a three and a five), eight irons (two through nine), then a pitching wedge, a sand wedge, and a putter. A chancer might sneak in a hybrid or fairway wood if no marshal is on site or sub one of those in for one of the mid-number irons. Nobody on a casual round is going to bust your chops about a fifteenth club, probably, but professional tournaments have been forfeited when it was discovered that a given player's bag did not conform to the rules: the standard penalty is two strokes per hole.[8]

That is all well and good and moreover makes perfect sense within the conceptual space of the game. But here is an idea that has occurred to many an amateur player with no long game off the tee and even less capacity for patience when seeking shanked or sliced balls in the heavy rough. Why not simply pick up your ball and just run down the fairway to the green and deposit the ball in the hole, carrying your clubs per regulation? No strokes are taken at all, and so technically every one of the eighteen is a hole in zero, not even a hole in one (!). On this basis, one could complete a round at a typical course with a score of seventy-two under par. This is not entirely hypothetical. Lacking any driving skill, and with a friendly caddy, I have myself just walked my dimpled Callaway Joe Carter Truvis ball, left glove smartly in place, from tee box to pitch-and-putt distance or played best ball with more able long hitters. There is no one standard game of golf, after all, except that you should always play fair and play it as it lies (not lays, despite the title of Joan Didion's excellent, heartbreaking novel[9]).

Now one might be tempted to say about the imaginary total-run, no-club approach, "Well, look, we all know that's ridiculous." And yet, it's only ridiculous if we appreciate, and accept, a prior understanding of the relationship between prelusory and lusory goals and see golf – already objectively a somewhat bizarre activity for serious people – within such a structure. This imagined run-and-drop activity is not golf, we want to say, even though it appears to meet the basic prelusory aims of the game: get the ball in the hole. We all see that discrepancy because we understand games – but the "we" here is the set of humans who understand golf as a game among other pointless by difficult pursuits. And so the question for our present purposes becomes something more like this: how easy or difficult would it be to program a non-human entity to appreciate this fine play between prelusory and lusory goals, both within and between games, and to undertake participation in this voluntary agreement to overcome unnecessary obstacles? There are many phenomenological objections to autonomous AI, including some that have been mentioned already – can there be humour, love, boredom outside human parameters – but somehow this one concerning games, goals, and play seems among the hardest to parse.

We are confronted with one of the most often cited examples of a thought experiment in relation to GAI: the paperclip maximizer. Golf is an idle pursuit, if nevertheless enjoyable to many, and a robot charging down the dog legs and avoiding the traps would be no more than a sideshow. But consider an AI engaged in a real-world, profit-and-loss enterprise such as a small business. The paperclip maximizer problem does just that, supposing an efficiency-programmed general algorithm is introduced to a business environment ruled by general economic goals. The key notion is instrumental convergence, whereby a non-malicious program can, by pursuing its stated optimizing goals, generate perverse and even globally destructive outcomes. Imagine that paperclips are the most cost-effective line item on a company's spreadsheet. Further imagine that an instrumentally optimized AI is introduced into the company gridwork to maximize efficiency and optimize budget expenditures. Theoretically, the outcome could be a series of massive cost-effective orders for more paperclips than anyone could ever use, accompanied by potential layoffs of inefficient human resources and other budget non-utilities.

This thought experiment is controversial. When introduced by existential-threat philosopher Nick Bostrom in 2003, it was immediately met with significant opposition and pushback.[10] Efficiency-optimizing systems are not so crudely instrumental, critics argued, that they fail to make connections between utility functions and some sense of common rationality. And yet, the idea that a totally benign system, as opposed to the malware versions of SkyNet or the Borg, might overcome human aspiration has become a new shade of nightmare for those wondering about human–AI relations. Horrors and wonders follow precisely because the already-active deep immersion of human consciousness into digital technology is so poorly understood. But as many researchers have pointed out in different registers, and in the words of one commentator, "the horror and wonder should at least be accurate."[11]

Suppose now the very radical idea, set out briefly earlier, that coils together the cinematic depictions of AI ("horror and wonder") with the possibility that film itself, as a medium, is a form of non-human intelligence. As mentioned, this may seem bizarre at first, but if we trace a line of thought that runs from philosophers Stanley Cavell and Stephen Mulhall, who suggest that the world-capturing aspects of film are themselves a form of deep cognitive reflection, to thinkers such as Jean Epstein who see the film mise-en-scène as itself a kind of "robot philosopher," to use Epstein's words, the notional cognition of film becomes less implausible.[12] Consider that the camera, while itself is simply a mechanical device, is deployed and situated by a large crew of human actors who are engaged in a collective activity that is in fact governed by that camera. Thus Epstein could argue that "the cinematograph stands out as a substitute and annex of the organ in which the faculty that coordinates perceptions is generally located – the brain – the alleged centre of intelligence." Further, the mechanism or apparatus in play is defined by its temporal signatures and, in most cases, an apparently in-built urge to create coherent linear narratives or perhaps layered asynchronous narratives that can be deciphered after the fact (one thinks of the films of David Lynch or Christopher Nolan).

The question becomes a matter of emphasis. If we agree to the idea that film is a kind of artificial intelligence, is it, per John Searle's enduring distinction, weak or strong? If the former, all that is really needed for a plausible account is something on the order of the Chinese room, though with images rather than basic natural-language translation. The technology, considered in a general process-oriented sense, both records and reveals the world. That is what the apparatus of the film camera makes possible. If one wanted to assert the latter strong thesis, we are cast back into the mysterious Cartesian and faculty-psychology terrain of previous discussion. I may feel, as a director or a cameraperson, that I "control" the camera and hence the film, but the camera sees what it sees, under complicated and fluid conditions. Could it not be, even without articulated awareness thereof, a controlling "intelligence" within this scene, taking in world and time? Maybe better, is the film scene not itself a kind of transhumanist staging area, where organic and non-organic elements combine and cooperate to create something new and revelatory?[13]

This is speculation of a high order. But while we're taking this tightrope walk, consider the possibility that all those films so often cited about the dangers of apocalyptically minded self-directed AIs, including the ones remarked on in this book, might be themselves clever forms of misdirection. That is, film has been in control all along, lulling the human population with formulaic romantic comedies, on the one hand, and off-loading fear in horrors and wonders about sentient-AI systems on the other, even as it has all the while been bent on its own development as a kind of post-Cartesian, posthuman philosophical Other. We do not have to greet the new alien overlords – they have been with us for decades. And in this way another theoretical loop closes or perhaps coils in upon itself in an interesting manner. Many thinkers have considered the notion of uncanniness in film, especially the distortions of space, time, and relation in the work of, say, Alfred Hitchcock or Chris Marker. Now we see that the endgame is not just that film is an uncanny medium by its own capacity, what we might once have considered the ultimate form of revenant or doppelgänger, but an altogether more unsettling kind of technology, one that alters and evolves human consciousness, or consciousness of any posthuman kind, forever through spectacular technology. We have gone through the looking glass. What we may find there is still not entirely clear.

5.4 FOLLOWING THE RULES

This penultimate section is an attempt to set out what might be found on this other side of the mirror we have long held up to the vision of human existence. In large measure this is animated by Wittgenstein's examination of the paradox of rule following.[14] Obviously algorithms are rule-following mechanisms, but their current level of adaptability is disputed and their application to routine matters of human existence controversial. Can they, in common with humans, learn to recognize patterns such as Fibonacci series (almost certainly)? But what about the sorting of trivia categories on *Jeopardy!* (not so clear)? As the later Wittgenstein argued, if language is conceived as a game or, better, as layered *games*, they are ones with fluid and evolving rules. This fluidity and contingency, giving rise to the discernment of future-reliable rules only through the past and present playing of a game, is extremely hard to program, perhaps impossible. Hence the predictable success of non-human algorithms within rigid, closed-rule systems such as chess and their evident limitation in other games where the rules are present but less determinate.

All of this work will continue, even as the prospect of fully conscious GAIAS is often dismissed as distant if not illusory – a different sort of ghost in the machine, destined to remain forever spectral. My recurring claim in this text has been that the present moment offers a special opportunity for human persons to confront our own taken-for-granted experience of consciousness and particularly the ethical and legal dimensions thereof. I will note here, in conclusion, a disagreement between two thinkers I admire. Brian Cantwell Smith dislikes the phrase "embodied consciousness," even as Andy Clark talks with insight about embodiment in his work on artificial intelligence.[15] For myself, I will venture to say that it seems obvious for there to be anything like, even approaching, a GAIA it will surely need some sort of mastery of world in the phenomenological sense. Since for humans that mastery involves the ability to move around space, negotiate terrain, form and execute intention as actions within context, it is almost inconceivable that there could a non-biological consciousness without these abilities, which lie well beyond – though they sometimes seem beneath – the programmable skills of logic and ratiocination.

In the end, it likewise seems to me and to many other observers that the future resides not in some sort of two-state system where we grant rights and responsibilities to artificial entities but rather where we negotiate the already operative and advancing merger between carbon and other elements of life. (*Pace* Asimov's C/Fe vision, the latter kind of entity is much more likely to continue to be silicon and plastic, perhaps even living tissue, not iron.) This is the real transhuman future, neither some science fiction nightmare nor a utopia of technological advancement. Our current fears are real enough, but they must be seen as warning flares at best and as paranoia at worst. Everyone looking at their phones or screens for most of their waking hours is already transhuman, seeking a sort of workaday cognitive upgrade while walking down the street bumping into other people, if not quite yet posthuman in their stubborn retention of cherished ideas of biological and phenomenal uniqueness. The hybrid forms with implants and appendages are likewise transhuman, both offering and forcing upon us entirely natural imperatives for self-modification and self-extension. In this larger sense, to be human is to be trans; is the human condition to be always on the developmental move. Indeed, it is a good question to wonder whether there has ever been a truly simple form of human existence, conditioned and shaped as that existence ever is by culture and technology. All of this indeterminacy and boundary-blurring will obviously continue and will soon include many more cognitive as well as physical enhancements. An app-loaded smart phone in your pocket or hand is already an external and fairly crude cognitive upgrade. Better versions are forever coming.

The real justice issues, then, concern how to offer such cyborg opportunities to all interested humans, whatever their socio-economic condition, and to think carefully at every moment about how we are changing the human form of life. The pace of change accelerates, as we know. And yet we cling to a notion of humanity that has been out of date for several decades if not far longer. This era of reductive bio-fascism is over, despite rearguard actions on every front: insistent pleas about the uniqueness of the individual human form of life (true but irrelevant) or the especially valuable or instructive amalgams of virtue and vice to be found in those unique persons (vanishing more quickly all the time, and frankly not usually that valuable or instructive anyway). In fact, there is no good reason, political or metaphysical, to cling to the nostalgic or quixotic or anxious notion that there is something special about us, taken one by one. Viewed cybernetically, as the times demand, each of us is a node or cluster of interests in a vast circulatory system of production, consumption, and reproduction that is, at best, a fragile truce with the natural environment that sustains it and, at worst, an active, quasi-suicidal threat to that same set of enabling conditions.

Meanwhile, our fusion with non-human elements of the environment – other nodes in the system, some of them far more powerful than we are – prompts the various kinds of anxiety, optimism, wonder, and fear that this book has sought to illuminate. The most basic fear in play is existential: we wonder if the form of life we gaze back upon will survive our own choices to meld with the machines. That this form of life has much to say against it is sometimes acknowledged but rarely foregrounded. Perhaps the cyborg future is indeed an evolutionary advance, an upgrade in efficiency, adaptability, even justice? I would prefer to think so, but there remain doubts about self-inflicted irrelevance or imprisonment. A much-quoted Marhsall McLuhan insight, or "probe," captures the stakes of this fear: "Man becomes, as it were, the sex organs of the machine world, as the bee of the plant world, enabling it to fecundate and to evolve ever new forms. The machine world reciprocates man's love by expediting his wishes and desires, namely, in providing him with wealth."[16] This from 1964 and more on point by the minute, especially the reference to satisfaction of human wishes and desires, for what else is our current deep immersion in tech except a willing surrender to that reciprocated love, that promise of happiness? Indeed, the imagined avantgarde of this willing immersion on our human part is a superior nonhuman being, the fantastical GAIA with enhanced strength, intelligence, rationality, and longevity.

Hence the kind of reactionary forces mustered per contra, in what must be judged untimely meditations in the pejorative sense. I mean the insistent defences of human life against all comers, including especially those we have invited into our world, like welcome vampires escorted across the fleshy threshold of consciousness. The tech writer Kevin Roose, for example, offers nine "rules" to "futureproof" humanity against the presumed depredations of the machine world.[17] No happy sex-organ existence for him! The rules, set out on the book's cover, are worth quoting here: (1) Be surprising, social, and scarce; (2) Resist machine drift; (3) Demote your devices; (4) Leave handprints; (5) Don't be an endpoint; (6) Treat AI like a chimp army; (7) Build big nets and small webs; (8) Learn machine-age humanities; (9) Arm the rebels. This is all useful provocative musing, and there are some promising notes of resistance to Big Tech and too-smooth assimilation to machine-led but profit-driven social and economic forces that my fellow neo-Luddites may find to their taste. But the background assumptions that machines and devices are the enemy to be feared or that an emphasis on "the human" (still less the humanities) is the proper solution here seems misplaced.

Technology is always built with purpose, yes; it is never neutral. But its purposes are motivated and directed by alliances, often only half-conscious, between consumer desire and producer interest. It is, so far, an almost entirely human affair. And so we notice the emergent structural irony that current Big Tech is the preferred political bugbear of both the radical Left and the radical Right in today's jumbled ideological landscape – a bridge issue waiting for its moment, which likely will never come because the reasons for the opposition vary so wildly.[18] Meanwhile, as always under the banner of inevitability, the obscene profit-parade of Big Tech marches on. The statistics are mind-boggling, unprecedented, otherworldly. In 2021, the five largest tech companies (Microsoft, Apple, Google, Facebook, and Amazon) boasted a stock market value of $9.3 trillion (US), more than the combined value of the next twenty-seven most valuable American companies, including Tesla, Walmart, and JPMorgan Chase. Apple's profits for one quarter of 2021 clocked in at $21.7 billion (US), nearly double the total profits of the five largest American airline companies before the pandemic of 2020 and beyond. Google's recorded $50 billion (US) in revenue from advertisements in the second quarter of 2021 was equal to what the entire American population spent on gasoline and gas station purchases in one month of the same period. These figures were driven by profit margins so large they looked like errors, upwards of 44 per cent in some cases, but real enough in fact. These returns have led analysts to insist that Big Tech is no longer just a quirky success story or a case of limited competition easily matched by existing regulatory measures but something wholly new and untrammelled – as a 2021 *New York Times* headline had it, Big Tech "has outgrown this planet."[19]

Importantly, the profits garnered here are generated by what might be termed post-capitalist mechanisms, attention and advertisements and apps, rather than surveillance-guided Internet of Things consumer durables or frightening autonomous algorithms. No, consumers simply devour themselves under the sign of their own happiness and convenience as facilitated by the fast-clip feature creep of comprehensive immersion in the universe (and metaverse) of everyday technology. This immersion is, per earlier discussion, often shot through with what we can now recognize as bad improvements, nearly constant alleged "upgrades" that in fact leave us worse off and more dependent. This is a species of posthuman evolution that has the less frightening, more soothing features of simply giving us *what we think we want,* even as we surrender autonomy and peace of mind in pursuit of the same comfortable goals that have always beguiled the lazy and the timid. On such a perverse account, peace of mind by definition can never be achieved because there is always a new stimulus to fill the gap of the now-lost previous one. Media-fast advocates contend that only abstinence can counter this ceaseless addictive cycle, and I am sympathetic to their cause.[20] But fasting itself can become entangled in a meta-cycle of binge-and-purge consumption, the tech equivalent of yo-yo dieting or substance abusers on a revolving door at rehab. Why not simply settle into the feed instead? Why not accept the gift of plenty? No revolutionary robots necessary then! We become the willing agents of our own comfy servitude to the global system.

Well, sure; that is an option that many choose to endorse. But we cannot ignore that there are attendant costs to self-respect and full autonomy here, some sense of human or personal flourishing that is lost or even degraded by living an unexamined life. More to the point in strictly political terms, the structural costs to labour and the environment entailed by this massive concentration of wealth have not been fully measured or appreciated – and each one of us with a smartphone, some 85 per cent of populations in Asia, Europe, and North America, is part of the rising tide of techno-capitalist domination. Until we sort out the lines of complicity and self-concealing operative here, our resistance will be futile because it will be aimed in the wrong direction. Once again, perhaps, we have met the enemy, and he is us.[21] The anti-profiteering arguments are so familiar precisely because they are a staple of current Left politics, despite the ubiquity of tech use there. But writer David Brooks, visiting the National Conservatism Convention for *The Atlantic* late last year, noticed two recurrent rhetorical features in the general air of apocalyptic speechifying. The first is what must be judged the ideological equivalent of deadly gun-toting miscreant Kyle Rittenhouse's self-defence, namely that the American Right has been forced to become crazy and uncivil just because the Left has become so woke-wacky – a neat trick most often borrowed, in my experience, from the middle-school playground. I know you are but what am I! You started it!

The second, more interesting repeated keynote was that the Right hates Big Tech just as much as the social justice brigade. This not because of runaway profit-taking and concentration of wealth – which one might expect to be badges of ideological heroism – but because of liberal bias. "At the heart of this blue oligarchy," Brooks reported, "are the great masters of surveillance capitalism, the Big Tech czars who decide in secret what ideas get promoted, what stories get suppressed." Ted Cruz: "Big Tech is malevolent. Big Tech is corrupt. Big Tech is omnipresent." "Big Business is not our ally," Marco Rubio argued. "They are eager culture warriors who use the language of wokeness to cover free-market capitalism." The "entire phalanx of Big Business has gone hard left," Cruz said, implausibly. "We've seen Big Business, the Fortune 500, becoming the economic enforcers of the hard left. Name five Fortune 500 CEOs who are even remotely right of center."

We all know that the goalposts of ideological insult keep shifting, but these hard-left denunciations of the world's leading billionaires will strike many as unlikely, if not bizarre. Nevertheless, the shared conviction that Big Business, and especially shadowy Big Tech, is part of a vast liberal conspiracy is rapidly becoming bread-and-butter to some right-wingers. Brooks again: "In the NatCon worldview, the profiteers of surveillance capitalism see all and control all. Its workers, indoctrinated at elite universities, use 'wokeness' to buy off the left and to create a subservient, atomized, defenseless labor pool." That is some impressive long-game indoctrination, one must admit, equal to the market mastery that these same companies exhibit.

And so, as if needing more fuel to light the barbecue of self-righteous resentment and hostility, the terms of discussion become end-of-the-world urgent. "The left's ambition is to create a world beyond belonging," intoned one speaker. "Their grand ambition is to deconstruct the United States of America." Cruz: "The left's attack is on America. The left hates America. It is the left that is trying to use culture as a tool to destroy America." Marco Rubio: "We are confronted now by a systematic effort to dismantle our society, our traditions, our economy, and our way of life." As Brooks pointed out, the demonization of Big Tech did not alter the phone-zombie habits of the delegates, whose eyes were mostly glued to their screens during these tirades, and whose basis of evidence for this nefarious left-wing Plot Against America was largely derived from tweets. If you can triangulate three mentions, call them data points, and it's a fact. Sure, why not. For what it's worth, I'm sure there are many left-wing critics who see the Right as the endtimes enemy of America, the promise-breakers bent on arming to the teeth and then trashing on fire the City on a Hill. (Oh right, they already did that on 6 January 2021.)

And yet, notwithstanding all of this anxious and sometimes confused discourse, the category of person, once divorced from its philosophically untenable, remains essential to negotiating these future byways: hence the politics of posthumanism. The prospect of a hostile machine takeover is, as I have emphasized repeatedly here, distant to the point of nonsense. But the growing co-dependency of biologically human bodies and non-human aspects of global systematicity gallops on. An excellent, prescient David Cronenberg film, naturally influenced by McLuhan, from some time ago had a reference to a sort of transhuman or posthuman future. The tagline was "Long live the new flesh!"[22] I suggest that the motto for the next decades of the twenty-first century be "Long live the new cyberflesh." There is still much to value in biological existence: physical pleasure, sports excellence, even the demands of work when it is rewarding and not degrading. But the human bioform is decidedly not the only carrier or guarantor of personhood, and that bioform is changing by the day even as new carriers of potential personhood come to our attention, sometimes insistently, in the form of environmental crisis, deluges of unnecessary suffering, or creeping dependency and growth of otherness.

5.5 ENDGAME

Because this discussion has been both brief and speculative, I think it is appropriate that its messages should be at best emergent properties of continued discourse on these topics. As I noted at the beginning, the text is intended more as a field report or series of meditations than a settled treatise. How could it be otherwise when the field of inquiry before us is shifting so fast, both the terms of debate and the relevant facts moving almost faster than human intelligence can track. We look to philosophy to help us sift and adjudicate evidence, to evaluate arguments and help us move toward better views. That is, together with many differences in style, tone, and relevant sources, we all share some kind of commitment to Peircean abduction or inference to the best explanation. At best, this holds both in everyday life and in advanced science. (If both my toaster and refrigerator suddenly cease working, I ought to consider a visit to the fuse box in the basement before looking for groundhogs digging up cables in the back yard or, worse, casting a spell against black magic.) This inferential ability thus entails a "grasp of essential relevance" that is not embedded in either inductive or deductive reasoning.

But even the best abductive hypothesis is only as good as the data from which it is formed, and the background knowledge assumed in that formation. If I see a warm, half-finished bowl of soup in an empty dining room, I may assume that someone has just left and is perhaps about to return. But reliable current data about the future of posthuman life are very limited, even as the associated background is filled to the brim with visions and vistas that can mislead, cause fear, arouse empty hope, and frankly make us all a little bit crazy. Would signs of purposive, non-biological action and planning count as evidence of consciousness? Would, moreover, a non-biological entity be capable of exercising its own inferential moves? Both aspects would appear necessary to underwrite a truly human–robot regime. It seems to me, at this moment, that the best philosophical reflection can do is insist that the focus remain on the question of *personhood*, including the nature of embodiment, rights and responsibilities, individual purpose and relationships. One final personal anecdote might be apposite here, in place of any knock-down conclusion to these speculations and meditations.

In the early autumn of 2021, as I was completing the first draft of this manuscript, I fell seriously ill and had to be hospitalized for more than two months, plus a couple of return visits to deal with infections and fever. Many tests, hundreds of needles, and dozens of juice cups later, I was the recipient of a major organ transplant with a new lease on life and altered manner of approaching everydayness.[23] What continually struck me, as I spent those long days and weeks in bed enduring the special hurry-up-and-wait rhythms of medical care, was how embedded my mere physical body was in looping systems of algorithmic and scientific instrumentality. (For a philosophy professor, boredom is never without value ...) The physical IV drips and oral medications were the product of research and development stretching back years or decades; the received knowledge of circulation and organ function far older but mostly unchanged since Harvey if not earlier; the embodied expertise and skilful action of professionals ranging from orderlies to star surgeons meshing – never without glitches, often surviving miscommunication and delay – to aid my failing physical body.[24] Far less obviously than any simple prosthetic, yet somehow more comprehensively, a major procedure and hospital stay of this duration places the vulnerable jelly of the flesh within a complex, maybe rhizomatic array of machines, money, and mindedness.

Negotiating the routine indignities of bedpan and catheter, the bland pseudo-excitement of mealtimes, the steady distraction-feed of lurid espionage novels and violent movies – how much worse this would have been, how much more unbearable, without streaming service, one is forced to wonder – prompts a complex feeling that is at once reassured and brought low in fortune and men's eyes. The body is weak even if, or when, the mind may remain strong. The eternal tragedy of sentient existence is that the latter may be agile enough to appreciate, in great detail, the deterioration and demise of the former. And so, placed helplessly within system upon system, enduring techniques that might in other circumstances resemble torture (blood-letting, restraints, forcible acceleration of heart and lungs), we see that posthuman life is already with us in the form of a willing suspension of everydayness into a kind of body-zombie limbo, supported by machines and unable to live unaided. Current emphasis falls on novelty and alarm in AI topics, but the lines of continuity are stronger even as they are less sensational. How is it possible that I now host an organ that once was lodged in another person's body, this donor someone I can never meet or know? And, all the while, the intellectual play of lusory and prelusory goals must go on. Intimations of mortality, vivid or mild, are like reminders of the game's rules. The systems that cocoon us, simple or complex, every day or in medical extremis, are the contours of the difficult, even devilish course that give point to the playing.

A central aspect of this book's purpose has been some discussion of human happiness and purpose under current conditions. I hope that these topics have been emergent properties of the text even when the explicit focus was on specific details of argument. Everything about our relationship with technology prompts doubt about everyday happiness and sometimes thwarts our sense of purpose. Happiness should perhaps be regarded as less central to existence than some philosophers and many politicians have claimed; they say it is not really all that significant to be happy.[25] Charles de Gaulle went further and claimed it was "for idiots," presumably meaning those with no higher moral or intellectual focus. Well, maybe. Certainly seeking happiness in cheap forms is the perennial downfall of those with limited imagination or those who come to believe that the accoutrements and retainers of position can substitute for a significant life. The latter notion, of purpose, is not so easily debased or beguiled; remains central to personhood no matter what the consciousness-platform or its cyberflesh transitioning.

The following final thoughts are not really advice then and certainly they are not always normative features in the tangled affairs of our rapidly shifting world of meaning. Nevertheless, and as I noted from the opening pages of this book, ideas of this hue mark the space where a neo-Luddite like me can join, with appropriate skepticism and concerns about social justice, the chorus of wonder at what might lie before us in a complicated bio-technological evolution since very near its beginning. So I venture to advance this basic and pretty obvious point by way of conclusion: On any platform or system, engaging any interface or cluster of programs, conscious autonomous individuals must find purpose and calling in life. And then, ideally, they must be pirates for that vocation. They must be dedicated and sometimes reckless, passionate and focussed, mischievous, wily, honourable, and brave. They must subvert ossified systems, make their own way, build things together, plunder the world's possibilities, and let happiness look after itself.

Maybe less ponderously, and more to the present point, let us simply acknowledge that Donna Haraway was surely correct when she asserted that we are all cyborgs now and likely to become more so as time passes. And merely mortal, imperfect humans, however enhanced or immersed, will meet new entities to challenge our biological complacency even as we consider existing non-human beings that demand our care and respect. All the while, negotiating changes both proximate and distant, the modalities of sovereign individual life will remain countless, its challenges inescapable. Choosing a meaningful path in this land without a clear map is what being a person really means. Technology alters the terrain of personhood but it does not shift the burdens of personal responsibility. In Socratic-Nietzschean terms, the first duty of a self-conscious creature is to *know oneself*; the second is then to *become what one is*. Humans may be, when unaccommodated and set upon madness and the heath, no better than poor, bare, and forked; they may be pathetic and vicious by turns. And yet, a spark remains. Oscar Wilde's character Lord Darlington, though speaking just of men in *Lady Windermere's Fan* (1892), manages to strike a universal note concerning aspiration curbed by these limits of mind, body, and will: "We are all in the gutter, but some of us are looking at the stars."

As any human person has reason to know, these tasks of self-understanding and self-becoming are infinite. There is always a new game to be played, with new moves and gambits, even as the deep rules remain enigmatically the same. This is the gamespace where hope, play, creativity, humour, and the benign indispensable mischief of art reside; also the sublime, transcendent pleasures of skilful action, athletic excellence, and grace under pressure. Here we confront the wisdom driven by ironies both subtle and sharp, the shock of unsought reversals of fortune, and the great crashing revelations of limited experience. But this largest game, the universe becoming conscious of itself, is always open-source and open-system. It has no special biological orientation, only a wide viability for all forms of conscious life. It is full of bugs and glitches but also boasts some elegant programming and the occasional Easter egg, hidden doorway, wormhole, or magic portal. So choose a piece, make a move, and let's get started – once again, as always.

Acknowledgments

This volume would not exist without the keen interest and support offered by Khadija Coxon, editor at McGill-Queen's University Press, who was also instrumental in bringing about my last monograph for the press, *Wish I Were Here: Boredom and the Interface* (2019). I consider these two volumes complements to each other, linked by a shared concern with technology's effect on human experience, but readers must decide for themselves whether this is so.

Markus Dubber, professor of law and director of the University of Toronto Ethics Centre, asked me to curate a film and television series about cultural depictions of autonomous AIs in his "Ethics of AI in Context" program (2017–present). Markus was in turn responsible for inviting my contribution, "Are Sentient AIs Persons?" for publication in *The Oxford Handbook of Ethics of AI*, 313–29. This article functions as the germ of the present book. I also thank law professor Claes Granmar of Stockholm University for his invitations to speak there and for the publication of my paper "Do Sentient AIs Have Rights? If So, What Kind?" in *Artificial Intelligence and Fundamental Rights*.

I unkinked a few related ideas in "Human All Too Human" and "What Is Community?" My thanks to Tatum Hands for her editorial interest and the beautiful design presentation of that journal. Some other parts of the manuscript, about the future of work and a possible robot takeover to underwrite human leisure, appeared in German as a short book, *Nach der Arbeit*, which was in turn expanded from some earlier linked essays about leisure and work, especially "The Work Idea: Wage Slavery, Bullshit, and the Good Infinite."

During the 2019–20 and 2020–21 academic sessions at the University of
Toronto, I taught a new course for the Department of Philosophy called,
not very imaginatively, "Philosophy in the Age of the Internet." (My first
lecture began by taking issue with all three of the nouns in that title.) This
was a second-year lecture sequence with an enrolment of between 120 and
150 students. It addressed social media, critiques of technology, and metaphysical issues of artificial intelligence and pesonhood – all against a background of traditional philosophical inquiry running from Aristotle through
to Descartes and Heidegger. Contemporary references included John Searle,
Jerry Fodor, Jaron Lanier, David Chalmers, David Graeber, and Legacy
Russell. The present text owes much to the experience of teaching this class,
first mostly in person (2020) and then entirely online (2021), together with
many exceptional students in both iterations. I thank them all, and further
thank my six excellent teaching assistants, for making this course a success.
Thanks also to Brian Cantwell Smith, Stephen Marche, Joshua Loftus, and
Geoffrey Turnbull, who offered guest lectures in this course, only two of
which came to pass in person because of COVID protocols.

I am likewise grateful to the partners and members of KPMB Architects
in Toronto, who gave me the chance to speak to them about AI, technology,
and culture at their very busy offices during 2019, before they were later
shuttered by those same COVID protocols. Special thanks to Bruce Kuwa-
bara, Marianne McKenna, Amanda Sebris, Geoffrey Turnbull (again), and
especially Shirley Blumberg, who first recommended Ian McEwan's novel
Machines Like Me as a kind of endgame-vision of the human-AI interaction
– though I hope it is not. Toronto has meanwhile become a global hub of
AI research, with many institutes and centres contributing to the growing
critical literature on every aspect of the subject, perhaps especially its cross-
disciplinary ethical, social, and political dimensions. The home of Marshall
McLuhan and Harold Innis is once more at the leading edge of thinking
about technology and culture, and it is an exciting time to be here.

My former undergraduate student Logan Fletcher, now an emergent
academic talent with a PhD in philosophy and cognitive science, has been
an invaluable research associate for the entire project. He was also an important co-instructor during the 2021 online iteration of the philosophy-
and-internet course. He acted as an early reader of this book and offered
many helpful suggestions and illuminating dialogue. Some endnotes reflect

his contributions this book. I likewise thank my former teaching assistant and student Victoria Philibert for useful leads in the field of film and AI, Joshua Glenn for ongoing inspiration, and three anonymous readers for the press who offered useful suggestions.

In a busy span of pre-pandemic years I was privileged to speak about AI, technology, law, non-human personhood rights, and background tech culture to audiences in many places, including London, New York, Stockholm, Hong Kong, Taipei, Tallinn, Zagreb, Doha, Kyiv, São Paulo, Sydney, Perth, Toronto, Edmonton, Vancouver, Montreal, San Antonio, Seattle, Minneapolis, New Orleans, Ojai, Tucson, Asheville, Bloomington, and Boulder. I thank them all for their attention and generous feedback. This series of linked adventures was exhilarating and exhausting at once, as one would expect, to the point where sometimes my (or anyone's) basic physical embodiment seemed fungible and open to profound *spatio-temporal distortion* – or so the residual sci-fi nerd in me chooses to see it. That is, I'm inclined to say, alongside critic Christopher J. Lee, who has written brilliantly about it, that jet lag is an actual altered state of being, a tech-generated distortion of baseline consciousness that may prove illuminating or enervating but that is always unnatural in the sense of having to be actively sought and facilitated by advanced machines and systems. This is why Lee's nimble study of the phenomenon is explored in a double-meaning book series called "Object Lessons."

Be all that as it may, I thank here the following: the University of Toronto Alumni Association, especially Barbara Dick and David Palmer; Nisa Mackie, then of the Sydney Biennale and the Walker Art Center; Berel Rodal; Deborah Patton of Applied Brilliance; Lavinia Greenlaw; Leon Wieseltier; Markus Dubber at the University of Toronto Centre for Ethics; and colleagues at the University of Colorado at Boulder and Stockholm University for a number of these opportunities. Special thanks to Tom Yeh (Colorado), Claes Granmar (Stockholm), and the very welcoming faculty at Virginia Commonwealth University (Qatar), the University of the Incarnate Word (San Antonio), and the Faculdade de Arquitetura e Urbanismo, Escola da Cidade (São Paulo).

Since that time, the 2020–22 COVID restrictions effectively grounded many academics and businesspeople from their presumed and all-too-casual air traffic. This has given frequent travellers a chance to reflect on the large carbon footprint that lecture- and conference-related travel has wrought. For example, in one three-month pre-pandemic period of my own acceleration-curve travels, I covered something like fifty-seven air hours and forty-three east–west time zones, including objectively absurd ventures such as flying to London for less than twenty-four hours to give a thirty-minute talk or to Hong Kong for two days to speak for twenty minutes. Per the main-text discussion, was this *work*, given how much I enjoyed even the exhausting aspects? It is hard to say. What is more obvious now is that panels and talks are often just as effective intellectually, if admittedly not nearly as much fun, when conducted online. Is this realization perhaps mundane posthumanism in practice? I don't know, but however that particular professional issue shakes out, I offer thanks to Molly Montgomery for keeping my merely human self intact through all of it and much more, then and now.

Finally, this book is dedicated to David Adams and Norman Lyon, the smartest non-machine entities I knew at a formative time in my life, high school in the mid-1970s. I'm sure they don't know it, but I have tried to follow their ethic and example ever since. I likewise acknowledge here the ongoing influence of critic and thinker Mark Fisher (1968–2017), whose insights never fail to rise brightly from the page. In a more advanced world we might be able to fashion a new vessel for his consciousness so that, like the resurrected Jean-Luc Picard, his thinking could continue to illuminate and inspire.

Following academic convention, I will note that all remaining errors in this book are entirely my own, including some introduced on purpose, just for fun. But not in the south.

notes

PREFACE

1 Among the best recent resources I know on the social-technological ques-
tion(s) of AI are these: Crawford, *Atlas of AI*; Roose, *Futureproof*; Brockman,
Possible Minds; Benjamin, *Race After Technology*; Clark, *Natural-Born Cyborgs*;
Robertson, *Robo Sapiens Japanicus*; Frischmann and Selinger, *Re-Engineering
Humanity*; Pasquale, *New Laws of Robotics*. Further sources are detailed in
later notes. Not all of these take technology at face value, however. Crawford,
Robertson, and Benjamin, in particular, work to articulate the social and
cultural origins of all science and technology. Crawford argues that machine
learning, which is what most people mean when they use the term "AI," is
"neither artificial nor intelligent," being instead part of a larger "registry of
power" – a registry that of course includes profit as one of its key vectors.
I will not attempt any long citation of the two other categories of book that
are prevalent in the growing literature, namely technical manuals and wild
speculation. Those books can look after themselves.

2 For example, Hutton, "The Fading Dream of the Computer Brain."

3 Marche, "The Imitation of Consciousness," which among things includes a
concise history of the Turing test. Marche concludes this way: "Here's where
we're at: capable of imitating consciousness through machines but not
capable of understanding what consciousness is. This gap will define the
spiritual condition of the near future … The science fiction fear of the Singularity is misplaced. But the technologists' fear of the artificial intelligence
of natural language processing is not. Technology exists for the sake of

convenience. There is nothing more inconvenient than the existence of other people's souls. Consciousness is absurd and human beings are futile. If you only value what's measurable and functional and useful, you won't value people. Computers possess a dignity that people don't. They exist for an identifiable reason."

Dignity may not be accurate in this regard, but this nevertheless offers a neatly expressed version of the Heideggerian point that technology is always bent to purpose, efficiency, or consumption of resources. Human consciousness exists for unidentifiable, and infinitely malleable, reasons – or so we choose to think.

4 Rosner, "A Haunting New Documentary About Anthony Bourdain."

5 Gray, *Straw Dogs*. Two films with the same title as the main title of Gray's book are on record. There is a distinctly creepy Peckinpah version featuring Dustin Hoffman, which allegedly draws its title from Lao Tzu's Tao Te Ching, which informs us that heaven and earth view all creatures as sacrificial ornaments, to be celebrated for a time, perhaps burnt, and then discarded in the street. And then there is a Lurie reimagining, not nearly as good by a long throw. Both films, and certainly Lao Tzu's text, highlight human-on-human violence and degradation as corrosive of selfhood, among other wise but somewhat miserable things.

6 See, for example, Rothblatt, *Virtually Human*. Other important recent works in the field of transhuman studies include Tegmark, *Life 3.0*; Sollinger, *Immortality or Bust*; and Fuller, *Humanity 2.0*. The Swedish-born Oxford philosopher Nick Bostrom has been pursuing transhumanist lines of thought with great insight and creativity for several decades, particularly on the issue of technological enhancement of human life. See especially his "Transhumanist Values," 3–14; "A History of Transhumanist Thought," 1–25; and *Superintelligence: Paths, Dangers, Strategies*. For the record, Bostrom is among those who see great danger in fast-track development of AI; cf. Adams's interview with Bostrom, "Artificial Intelligence: 'We're like children playing with a bomb.'" Bostrom also joined Stephen Hawking, among others, as signatories of the Future of Life Institute's open letter on the threats of general AI to the human population.

7 Christian, *The Alignment Problem*; Kearns and Roth, *The Ethical Algorithm*.

8 On this issue, see Chalmers, "Facing Up to the Problem of Consciousness," and Chalmers, *The Conscious Mind*. Per contra, there is Dennett, *Conscious-*

ness Explained, which endorses the "multiple drafts" view of consciousness as a rejection of the "Cartesian theatre" model favoured by many philosophers and most conscious persons who are not philosophers. Dennett's radical argument nevertheless squares with many people's experience of constant revision when it comes to being in the world. We do not simply see the world so much as we rehearse over and over what we might say or do, and then act that out. This argument led many reviewers to note that Dennett had not really explained consciousness, despite his bold title, and it made Chalmers further wonder if Dennett was a philosophical zombie (see later notes to this text).

The governing article in this entire debate is Nagel, "What Is It Like to Be a Bat." Nagel's argument is something like this: can we ever imagine another entity's conscious life – supposing they even have it – except by projecting our own sense of self? We cannot know what it is like to be a bat because we instinctively imagine ourselves as that bat. It should also be noted that the "homunculus regress" is a pressing issue here, even within non-bat consciousness. This further poses the problem of an inner viewer of conscious experience, who must then presumably harbour another inner viewer, and then another smaller one, and so on. The lurking fallacy is at least as old as Plato's *Republic* and *Theaetetus*. I thank G.R.F. (John) Ferrari for first opening my eyes to this problem coiled within ancient Greek philosophy and still with us many centuries later. Ferrari's *Listening to the Cicadas*, a detailed analysis of Plato's dialogue *Phaedrus*, is one of the best books of philosophy I have ever read.

[LF]: More recently than in Dennett, *Consciousness Explained*, Frankish, in *Tricks of the Mind*, defends a similarly deflationary stance on consciousness, which he calls "illusionism." In *Human and Animal Minds: The Consciousness Question Laid to Rest*, Carruthers appeals to a version of Nagel's problem about projecting one's own mind in attempting to imagine others' consciousness. He argues that we cannot even properly *pose* the question of consciousness for other kinds of animals: We can only properly ask, "if this animal's mental state were *in a mind like mine [one equipped with a concept of experience]*, would it be registered *as* experiential?" But the question of consciousness was supposed to concern the animal's mental state *as it is in its own mind*. As such, Carruthers claims, there is simply no fact of the matter about consciousness in (probably all) non-human animals.

[MK]: Makes sense – "what is it like to be a bat?" (Nagel) becomes "what is it like to be a robot." But either way, we can't help using our own experience of consciousness as an overlay on the Other.

9 One friend of mine transitioned from female to male after bearing a child with his one-time female partner. He is a homosexual male after being a homosexual female. This shift was a source of some consternation among certain people, but somehow made perfect sense to me. Another acquaintance and friend rather surprisingly transitioned in 2021, at considerable (but I trust not lasting) risk to their longstanding writerly career and reputation. My online acquaintance Stephanie Burt, meanwhile, is very well known for her transition, already a distinguished poet and critic at Harvard, and in fact enjoyed some celebrity thereby, including magazine profiles about makeup choices.

These literary and academic notables are the lucky ones, I suppose. The same cannot be said for many others who make such brave choices and lack the same kind of institutional and communal support. The year 2021 has been widely noted as the most violent year ever for trans people, especially Lantinx identifiers. I note these personal details just to demonstrate how common fluidity has become in many circles – and this is not even to mention those who experience fluidity without any physical transition. I have not noted any pre-trans names here, to avoid any version of deadnaming, that odious practice. This is all rather a more historical note about my own experience.

There has been, both circa 2021 and before, some significant pushback on pronoun variety and fluid-identity claiming. This is true not just from the predictable retrogressive Jordan Peterson devotees and their ilk, but also from ostensibly progressive sources such as TikTok. A good overview of the issues may be found in Marcus, "A Guide to Neopronouns." Sample quotation: "I'm not going to call u kitty/kittyself or doll/dollself just bc u think its cool," one TikToker wrote in a video caption. "Pronouns are a form of identity not an aesthetic." As Marcus then commented, "But what's the difference between an aesthetic and an identity anyway?" Well, exactly. I don't put this in my email signature because I figure nobody cares that much about a middle-aged cisgender white guy like me, but I go by "he" and "him," and there is no "S" in my last name, despite frequent misspellings and mispronunciations over the years. I kind of like "kitty" and "kittyself," though. Maybe one day soon …

10 [LF]: I worry a bit about these posthuman fantasies, in the same way I worry about the fantasy of colonizing other planets. In all likelihood (I would bet), we are in fact forever stuck with our embodied existence here on Earth because the practical obstacles to realizing these in-principle possibilities are too just great. If we become too invested in our dreams of transcending the material realm, we might fail to focus on taking care of the material conditions that sustain us here where we live.

[MK]: So true – but as argued already, surely one kind of justice concern, even if speculative, can redound to greater awareness or even action concerning all others?

CHAPTER ONE

1 See, for example, Cassella, "125-Year Study of Chess Matches Suggests We Don't Peak at the Game Until Our 30s." This impressive longitudinal study does suggest that the "hump" of peak performance may last for up to ten years. But after forty-five years of age, things alas run steadily downhill. One has to acknowledge here the otherworldly longevity of NFL quarterback Tom Brady, of the New England Patriots and Tampa Bay Buccaneers, who was still making Super Bowl appearances and wins at age forty-four circa 2021. He retired immediately afterwards, only to rejoin the professional football ranks within a few months in excellent robot-reboot fashion. One had cause to wonder: was Brady, perhaps, an android rather than a human? He certainly looked and performed like one, with the weirdly cartoonish good looks and post-forty high-percentile athleticism. But his unexpected tequila-fuelled victory celebration in February 2021 – recklessly throwing the Vince Lombardi Trophy from one boat to another in Tampa Bay, then stumbling drunkenly off the dock with aid from a teammate – suggests he may be human after all.

2 To my mind, the best analysis of this tangle is Gass, *Tests of Time: Essays.* I note that the "Stuttgart Seminar Lectures" section of this book was based on a gathering that I attended in 1998, where Gass was a difficult but always engaging discussion leader of a small seminar. The dismissive critics of this collection should maybe gather themselves and write something original and good, instead of just torching the ground that Gass surveyed so brilliantly.

3 I won't name any names here: that would fall prey to the same presentist fallacy I am trying to localize and therefore would be self-contradictory. But it is worth noting, as a general comment, that philosophy in its dominant current iterations is most often metastatic: commentary upon commentary upon commentary. Nobody is really building new worlds anymore in philosophy, contrary to Nelson Goodman's famous claim that we are world-building creatures. New worlds, such as they are, emerge from the tech and finance sectors more than anywhere else.

4 Anderson, "The Great Writers Forgotten by History." This article is in reference to Fowler, *The Book of Forgotten Authors*.

5 Collins, *The Sociology of Philosophies: A Global Theory of Intellectual Change*.

6 If you recognize this quotation (actually two pieces of fused dialogue), email me at mark.kingwell@utoronto.ca and I will send you a gift package. Pretty easy. Hint, if you need one: it is also featured, and identified, in Kingwell, "Of an Age," 58–9.

7 Potential TMI endnote; disregard at will. For several years I was that dedicated chess nerd – just as I would later become a CB-radio nerd, a Dungeons & Dragons nerd, a model-airplane nerd, a science-trivia nerd, and eventually now, I suppose, a philosophy nerd. Unlike some of my fellow academics but in common with my family, I also love fishing, football, hockey, basketball, and baseball. So I likewise became a sports and outdoors nerd. Here I stand today with a healed broken arm (basketball, emergency room), healed broken leg (cycling, emergency room), mostly healed dislocated shoulder and broken collar bone (fishing, emergency room), some knitted-up deep gashes on both shins (cycling again, fishing again, emergency room), chipped tooth (football, dentist's office), stitched-up split lip (cycling, emergency room), and one deaf ear (all of the above, two walk-in clinics and an MRI), plus more than a few near misses. All to say just this obvious thing: the human body is extremely vulnerable, and that is a deep though often unspoken part of what it means to be a person in the otherwise abstract ethical and legal senses.

8 Can one respect this request by the eccentric Fischer? Chess pieces can become very personal. There was a superb store just south of Washington Square in Manhattan that specialized in eccentric game designs: Greek mythological figures, medieval knights, English Civil War Cavaliers and

Roundheads, Man Ray surrealist shapes (apparently inspired by Marcel Duchamp), Bauhaus architectural shapes, *Lord of the Rings* and *Star Trek* avatars, even Simpsons characters. The only sets currently in my possession have (a) stylized glass figures, clear for white and frosted for black; and (b) LEGO pirate figures for some reason (actually, a gift from the editor of this book who liked my closing injunction to "be a pirate" for your chosen vocation). Whether LEGO or LOTR or anything else, and accepting that comfort can sometimes facilitate keen concentration, most players would agree that the specific design of pieces can never determine how well you play. Personally, I like to imagine Garry Kasparov insisting on a bright plastic Simpsons set-up for big matches.

9 [LF]: Kubrick, by the way, was himself an avid amateur chess player who, prior to his film career, would make ends meet by playing for cash in Washington Square Park.

[MK]: Awesome detail!

10 One example, again from among many possible sources: Miller, "The Queen's Gambit: A Chess Champion on Netflix's Addictive Hit." Both Garry Kasparov and Bruce Pandolfini consulted on the chess details in this widely praised television series. Sales of chess sets then spiked across North America. A notable, odd addendum is that, following the popularity of the Netflix series, chess interest also surged in some places that could not use board games – notably prisons. Incarcerated individuals then took to playing imaginary visualised games, as in the original show. See Pierce, "How We're Channeling 'The Queen's Gambit' in Prison." For the record: Pierce is, as of this writing, a twenty-seven-year-old man behind bars at the Ferguson Unit Prison in Midway, Texas, on a thirty-three-year sentence for murdering his father.

11 The Shannon Number, named for mathematician and information theorist Claude Shannon in his influential paper on the topic ("Programming a Computer for Playing Chess"), quantifies the number of possible games from any starting point as 10 to the power of 120. Subsequent theorists and programmers, influenced by Shannon, have modified the number based on criteria of "sensible" versus merely "possible" plays, therefore excluding illegal and nonsensical moves. Along the way they have, by this modification, refined chess-playing algorithms from brute-force calculation programs to

something much closer to the "chunking" and tactical guile used by human players. The number of possible games is still vast, something like 10 to the power of 50, also known as one hundred quindecillion.

12 Kasparov, *Deep Thinking: Where Machine Intelligence Ends and Human Creativity Begins*. The book recounts Kasparov's encounters with computer program Deep Blue and then expands into a general meditation on artificial intelligence and its reasonable prospects. Chess fans and aspiring business-people will find even more specific insight in Kasparov, *How Life Imitates Chess*. Kasparov, now a prominent human rights advocate and critic of Russian autocrat Vladimir Putin, has written at length about other grandmasters of the formidable board game, including Capablanca, Alekhine, Karpov, Korchnoi, and Fischer.

13 The works of Martin Heidegger, Jacques Ellul, Lewis Mumford, and Donna Haraway are well known. They inform the general orientation to technology in the present work, with special reference to Haraway's prescient thesis of cyborg existence, written in the form of a manifesto. Essential works in the philosophy of mind and artificial intelligence include Churchland, *Neurophilosophy: Toward a Unified Science of the Mind-Brain*; Dennett, *Consciousness Explained*; Searle, *The Mystery of Consciousness*; and Chalmers, *The Conscious Mind*.

Isaac Asimov is discussed in some detail later, especially his famous/notorious Laws of Robotics. See also Butler, *Parable of the Sower*, now a classic of the dystopian genre; Leckie, *Imperial Radch*, which features very convincing sentient spacecraft; Lethem's PKD tribute novel *Gun, with Occasional Music*; and of course anything by Dick himself. Wesley Wark wrote insightfully about the alternate universes of video games long before Facebook went meta in 2021; see Wark, *Gamer Theory*. Bernard Suits's *The Grasshopper* is a brilliant book with a wide influence on many philosophers, including the present author, arguing for the centrality of games to human life and self-understanding.

14 Many other scholars are working in this field already, of course, breaking ground on the very idea of "human" as we move into the near future. See, for example, Zalloua, *Being Posthuman*. In this provocative book, Zalloua relates recent debates about posthumanism to Michel Foucault's notion of "the death of man," and opens up new avenues of investigation about non-

human animal life, racial difference, and cyborg existence from a psychoanalytical perspective. A strange and exciting book.

15 Sherman, "Dumbed Down AI Rhetoric Harms Everyone." The target here is specifically policymakers, who have not in general shown themselves to be experts of nuance about anything much. And yet, policies must be made, and it would be best if that were done at least without pernicious technical ignorance or unsustainable assumptions.

16 [LF]: This way of putting the point makes it sound a bit like real thinking couldn't possibly be implemented computationally – that finding mere mechanism at the ground floor shows that it could never have been real thought at the top level. But, of course, the classic AI proposal is that any old general-purpose computer can realize a mind so long as it's suitably programmed.

   [MK]: Right. Theoretically, "real" thinking could be done by something assembled out of old Radio Shack parts. But I think many people imagine that it will take an as-yet-unrealized level of supercomputer to get us even close.

17 Boden, *Artificial Intelligence*, 19. In common with many titles in this series of books from Oxford, Boden's is a well-informed but also occasionally tendentious overview of the state of play on the topic circa its publication date. It offers a useful touchstone for much of what follows. Boden's very short book might be usefully read alongside Crawford's up-to-date (as of this writing) *Atlas of AI*; and, for deep historical reference to the craving for non-human intelligence, Mayor, *Gods and Robots*.

18 Vinge, "The Coming Technological Singularity," 11–23. A summary of the philosophical arguments against the possibility of "strong" AI, and hence any imagined Singularity, may be found in Dietrich et al., *Great Philosophical Objections to Artificial Intelligence*. I'm not sure, myself, that "wars" is quite right nor that complex AI controversies can be treated historically quite yet, but this is a very good survey of the relevant territory.

19 Kurzweil, *The Singularity Is Near*. Vinge had predicted a singularity development as early as 2005, certainly by 2030. Kurzweil could not feasibly endorse the first date but is alarmist enough to hazard the second. One might note the transition from "survive" to "transcend" as dominant notes in their respective subtitles. Significant later works devoted to technology-driven

alterations of human intelligence and consciousness run from the corporate-inflected Kissinger, Schmidt, and Huttenlocher, *The Age of AI*, to the radically speculative, for example Lee and Chen, *AI 2041*. See also Winterston's accessible essay collection *12 Bytes*.

20 [LF]: And on the other side, one can readily imagine a sort of "zombie singularity" in which self-reproducing entities that are in no way conscious or minded radically restructure the world through runaway reproduction.

[MK]: I love this – why shouldn't philosophical zombies be self-regulating? The ordinary cinematic kind certainly are.

21 [LF]: "Sentience" is often used to pick out just the feels or sometimes "raw feels." If you feel, you're sentient. Most people who use the term today tend to think that sentience is more basic than cognition, so we may hear this as signalling implicit acceptance of that (sentience-first) theory. See, for example, Godfrey-Smith, *Other Minds: The Octopus, the Sea, and the Deep Origins of Consciousness*, where he argues that "sentience comes before consciousness" and hence that consciousness is just a particular, sophisticated elaboration or extension of sentience.

[MK]: A useful caution. I notice that many people, including philosophers (see Martha Nussbaum reference later in the text), use sentience in this general and somewhat loose sense.

22 Boden, *Artificial Intelligence*, 130.

23 Kingwell, *Wish I Were Here*. My favourite review of this book was a one-star Amazon rating that offered the following terse, nasty comment: "Lacked focus. Tended to wander. I lost interest." Ha, excellent! That is either an act of high-wire irony on the book's subject or else a pertinent but unwitting commentary on the overstimulated cultural times in which we live. (I prefer to think the former or else both.)

24 Hawking, along with physicist Roger Penrose, is associated with another sense of singularities altogether, namely those concerning general relativity, i.e., black holes and other space-time centrifuges. With respect to AI, Hawking is on record as saying that "The development of full artificial intelligence could spell the end of the human race." See, among many other sources, Cellan-Jones, "Stephen Hawking Warns Artificial Intelligence Could End Mankind." Hawking also said this, which strikes me personally as obviously false: "[P]hilosophy is dead. Philosophy has not kept up with modern developments in science, particularly physics." Lawrence Krauss, another target of

this scientistic critique, offered a related indictment in a recorded conversation with William Lane Craig: philosophy, Krauss has declared, "hasn't progressed in 2,000 years." I will inform my colleagues of all ages and interests that we should retire immediately.

25 Boden, *Artificial Intelligence*, 135.

26 In earlier published work on these issues, I used the term GAAI – generalized autonomous artificial intelligence. But the poetic resonance of Gaia, the personification of Earth in Greek mythology and a primordial deity whose offspring include Uranus, the Titans, the Cyclops, and the Giants, is hard to resist. For completists, that term embraces a couple of professional football teams and a clashing movie franchise, among other things. More seriously, the mythological status of GAIAS is exactly part of what is being investigated here.

27 [LF]: Generalized + autonomous still leaves a gap, as follows: It might be possible for an AI to be both generalized (it reliably exhibits intelligent behaviour generally across a broad range of tasks and contexts) and autonomous (it operates independently, without need for instruction or supervision) without it being conscious. This would be, I suppose, a zombie GAIA. (If philosophical human zombies are possible, then zombie GAIAS ought to be possible as well.) In fact, if we ever do create full-blown GAIAS, there is almost sure to be widespread skepticism about whether they are genuinely conscious – which is likely to be taken as grounds for denying them rights.

This raises an interesting set of potential issues about our treatment of AIS whose consciousness-status is unknown (one case) or (another case) AIS that are known to be zombies. That is, is it okay to abuse zombie GAIAS, if we can be assured that they lack consciousness? (As perfect copies of the functions and motions of a conscious mind, they are going to scream. Does this prove anything ethically relevant?)

[MK]: I don't know about you but calmly causing the screaming of an entity, even if I have been assured it is not conscious, lies beyond the moral pale. Shades of the Stanley Milgram shock experiment at Yale in the 1960s?

28 See Clarke, "Hazards of Prophecy." Clarke's Three Laws (never explicitly published as such) are as follows: (1) When a distinguished but elderly scientist states that something is possible, he is almost certainly right. When he states that something is impossible, he is very probably wrong. (2) The only way of discovering the limits of the possible is to venture a little way past

them into the impossible. (3) Any sufficiently advanced technology is indistinguishable from magic.

29 Heidegger, *Being and Time*. Here, among many other insights, Heidegger indicates that a mood is not a mere passing emotional state but rather a way of finding how we are in the world, something that "comes neither from 'outside' nor from 'inside,' but arises out of Being-in-the-world, as a way of such being." For the early Heidegger, as is well known, the prevalent mood (Grundstimming) is angst, not very usefully translated as anxiety in the sense of ordinary worry, since it rather suffuses and permeates Dasein's entire experience of existing as Being-towards-death. Question: Can a non-human entity, even granted personhood, experience this mood?

30 Peters, "Machine Thinking, Thinking Machine," 113–26. Compare Chu, *Do Metaphors Dream of Literal Sleep?*

31 Bazin, "The Ontology of the Photographic Image." Other prominent film theorists, including Noël Carroll, have quarrelled with this description of how the film camera executes its mechanism with respect to the viewer, citing instead a notion of "erotetic narrative," which implies a structure of question and answer in narrative form (who did what? why? when? etc.). See Carroll, "Narrative Closure," 1–15.

32 On the larger point about cinema as an art form and a medium see Cavell, *The World Viewed*, perhaps the best book I know that addresses film and philosophy. Mulhall's *On Film* uses Cavellian insights to read philosophy "being done" by blockbuster film franchises, including the *Alien* and *Mission: Impossible* movie series. A dubious thesis, but good fun to read.

33 Benjamin, "The Work of Art in the Age of Its Technological Reproducibility."

34 Haraway, "A Manifesto for Cyborgs."

35 An often-heard futurist claim was that Moore's Law, by which computing power is said to double every two years or so, indicated that GAI would soon be realized. This claim has always been tendentious because it presumes a simple relationship between computing power and intelligence. But new reports further suggest that AI research is repudiating the law – which isn't in fact a physical law, just a speculative generalization – by advancing computing power far more rapidly than that. See, for example, Saran, "Stanford University Finds that AI Is Outpacing Moore's Law."

36 Herbert Dreyfus outlined his critique of strong AI in a long series of books, articles, and lectures. The most important of these are *Alchemy and AI*, *What*

Computers Can't Do, and *Mind Over Machine*. Worth noting here is that, despite many significant differences between them, Dreyfus seems to align with classical philosophical functionalists such as Jerry Fodor in thinking that neither "good old-fashioned artificial intelligence," brute-force algorithms known colloquially as GOFAI, nor even more advanced PDP and neural-net AI programs, cannot really solve the frame problem. See Fodor, *The Modularity of Mind* and *The Mind Doesn't Work That Way*. I thank Logan Fletcher for making this conjunction of otherwise disparate thinkers plausible to the larger argument.

37 See, for example, Smith, *The Promise of Artificial Intelligence*. Smith's argument, in this accessible and meticulous book, is both (1) that we remain a long way from any sort of machine intelligence on the order of the human sort, generated over millennia of evolutionary refinement, but also (2) that this same process of evolutionary research and development is not merely far from flawless but also drastically inaccurate about its own capacities. The book thus neatly transcends the usual for-or-against arguments about GAI and GOFAI.

Another important recent work is Christian, *The Alignment Problem*, which usefully surveys the ways in which current machine learning and AI systems are already influencing everyday life, in everything from newsfeeds and shopping preferences to mortgages and medical diagnostics. Christian's analysis focuses on what machine-learning systems get wrong compared to intuitive and holistic human responses – though none of this will be surprising if we simply recall that current AI algorithms are still primitive i/o systems at base, no matter how high-functioning they may seem.

38 In some ways the argument here is importantly anti-Socratic. In *The Republic*, Plato has Socrates suggest that vice is a function of ignorance, not knowing or realizing what is good, because such knowing or recognizing would prevent someone from acting viciously. But this view seems countered by widespread human experience in which I feel, if only *post facto*, that my judgment has been clouded but my knowledge is intact. That is to say: I do not (usually) consider that I have made a cognitive error when I act badly. Rather, I did so driven by personal choices, based on a sense of where I find myself in a web of relations, possibly influenced in the moment by emotion or diet or other aspects of self I have voluntarily shouldered, including drugs or alcohol.

I know I am acting badly. This is a moral error and a bad choice. I may sometimes, perhaps often, regret the choice later. And yes, I may simply be mistaken about relevant things I ought to have grasped but failed to do so in the moment. I did not see the other car/person/boat clearly, or I misjudged velocity and/or vector in ultimately harmful ways, or I underestimated the harm that my momentary pleasure would have on those I care about. The essence of personal responsibility remains that I acknowledge the choices I have made as my own and see them as generated within a relevant global context that I recognize as mine. Ignorance does not get me off the hook.

The notion of "essential relevance," meanwhile, likely cannot and will not solve the frame problem in AI. But it illuminates something important about how minds interact with worlds. In an early paper by the wide-ranging philosopher Fingarette, "Insanity and Responsibility," an argument is offered that insanity has as a necessary but not sufficient condition for the experience of irrationality. Essential relevance is what must be embraced such that occasional irrationality does not lead to comprehensive and on-going mental derangement. By this same token, specifying what counts as relevant is a kind of infinite phenomenological task. Relevance within a closed system, such as a game or program, is relatively easy to delineate or then program; global relevance, which has second- or even third-order abil-ities to sort and order relevance conditions, demands very high-level cogni-tive skill in humans and is certainly beyond existing programming power for non-humans.

39 [LF]: If a "frame" is something like a determination of relevance, so that a framed situation is one already parsed and sized up in relevant ways, then I think this formulation of the frame problem works very well. We can already build systems that will go to work on situations that come pre-framed, but we lack systems that can flexibly frame situations for themselves in ways that are reliably relevant. However, manifestations of the frame problem can also arise in semantics and, to an extent, in syntax as well. Algorithms often choke on basic categorization, in ways that suggest frame-problem failure.

[MK]: Ha, yes – forget semantics, syntax is harder than it sometimes seems. English, Greek, and Latin are pretty forgiving about word order; German not so much.

40 This is a large topic that I can only touch on briefly here. Austin's *How to Do Things with Words* is the gold standard; followed by Searle, *Speech Acts*;

Grice, writing critically of standard ordinary-language thinking, in *Studies in the Way of Words*; and perhaps my own small contribution to the field, Kingwell, "Is It Rational to Be Polite," 387–404.

Grice illustrates how the early speech-act theorizing depended heavily on some understanding of relevant context to distinguish among locutionary (meaningful), illocutionary (intentional), and perlocutionary (action-guiding) utterances. Austin had argued, for example, that speaking the words "I do" under relevant conditions constituted a performative act (agreeing to be married), but when Searle tried to flesh out the range of such contextual framing, it quickly became obvious that the relevant context for most performative utterances was the world as a whole, that is, an entire web of presumed meanings and actions. This is the general context that may defeat any attempt at programming a language-using algorithm.

Here I note a disagreement with those who believe that a linguistic program such as GPT-3 and its sequels will revolutionize writing by eliminating, or successfully mimicking, aspects of personal style to the point of rendering individual writers superfluous. To the extent that this claim is true, it is vivid and yet philosophically uninteresting. We will not be invested in programs that generate text, however sophisticated, except as aspects of being fooled by technology, any more than we will be invested in non-human entities that can reliably dunk basketballs or catch touchdown passes. Our interest in human writing style has to do with perception, insight, and elegant turns of phrase offered by entities more or less like us, even as we simultaneously recognize that, like professional athletes, they are high-percentile sub-populations of the species. Such appreciation of human achievement does not preclude posthuman fusions of carbon and non-carbon execution, just as we now accept keyboards, corrective programs such as Grammarly, and other "aids" to writing as standard operating procedure in many professional contexts.

This may not be the prevailing view. Marche, in "The Imitation of Consciousness," says this: "Navigating the possibilities of the artificial intelligence of natural language processing ... will require an integration of technology and humanism. Unfortunately, those two worlds are separated by a chasm as vast as it has ever been. Technologists tend to have a crude grasp of literature and history. Their main sensibility is a faith in capitalism that coincides perfectly with their own interests ... [H]umanists have been largely blind to the arrival of natural language processing as with all technology. A book such as Kazuo Ishiguro's *Klara and the Sun*, supposedly about artificial intelligence, has about as much to do with current technological reality as Pinocchio."

Speaking as a fellow humanist, I cannot agree with that harsh judgment of Ishiguro's novel, which has its moments. I also think that Pinocchio still has a lot to teach the techno-capitalist world, certainly as much as dolls and automata have to teach us about uncanniness in general. The idea of a singular writing example executed in some very standard and non-contextual format, such as an undergraduate essay, is likely to be rendered obsolete before very long. Today's students often "collaborate" on papers, sometimes under the guidance of English-language mentors if that is not their first language, which process then generates papers that are not plagiarized in the sense of borrowing from other published material but are instead crowd-sourced to the point of substitutability. In the face of these developments, some colleges and universities have already adopted grading regimes that employ only oral examinations, which (so far) cannot be successfully gamed.

41 These conventional parallel texts are included in an academic work not just to cite sources, per scholarly convention. They also offer counterpoints and counterpunches, sometimes even palinodic (i.e., intratextual) contradictions. Ideally, they run alongside the more deliberate measures of the main text. The present book employs endnotes rather than footnotes. This choice of format offers its own debate. One reviewer of a previous book of mine, where the notes were included at the bottom of the page, complained that they took up too much space, altered the main text's tone, and were "snide, academic, flippant." Which is exactly what I wanted them to be.

A gifted critic some years ago wrote this: "Endnotes trail behind everything else. They make the author declare: See, I've done my homework folks; now let's push all that trivia to the rear where it won't bother us. Footnotes, on the other hand, go along with the text. Their location says that the author takes them seriously, that the author's own work is accompanied by that of the past – rests upon it, uses it, argues with it, and finally goes beyond it." See Fox, "On Footnotes," 6–8. I note with respect that there are then included endnotes to this footnote about footnotes, though I will not cite them here. Meta-scholarly notation, and even Talmudic commentary, has its textual limits.

We might finally recall, in this now very long endnote in Whitehead, *Process and Reality*, 39, Whitehead's famous and often-quoted line about philosophy: "The safest general characterization of the European [sometimes rendered as 'Western'] philosophical tradition is that it consists of [sometimes rendered as 'in'] a series of footnotes to Plato." – As safe generalizations go, that is a pretty good one, as generations of later philosophers will attest. But maybe safe generalizations are not our business?

42 The latter formation is not a preferred professional tactic among chess masters, as expert players will surely tell you if you ask them, but I've always liked it and it is one that is entertaining and sometimes successful in spite of its recklessness. The rest is up to you, the reader making moves on the other side of the board.

43 The call-out quotation on the dustjacket of Ishiguro's *Klara and the Sun* is typical. "Do you believe in the human heart?" it begins. "I don't mean simply the organ, obviously. I'm speaking in the poetic sense. The human heart. Do you think there is such a thing? Something that makes each of us special and individual?" Also this: "Kazuo Ishiguro looks at our rapidly changing modern world through the eyes of an unforgettable narrator to explore a fundamental question: what does it mean to love?" The best thing you can say about this sort of thing – presumably not written by the author but by a publicity assistant – is that at least these sentiments are posed as questions, albeit semi-rhetorical ones. A strict philosopher might still object that they are at best misleading questions and at worst nonsensical or tautological ones.

CHAPTER TWO

1 [LF]: See Searle, "Minds, Brains, and Programs," 1980, 417–57. Searle defines "weak AI" and "strong AI" as rival stances about the role played by computer models in the study of the mind. Weak AI says that computer models are instrumentally useful (e.g., in testing hypotheses); strong AI says that computer models, ideally, will actually possess the target mental states and qualities (they will really think, believe, understand, etc.). So AI for diagnosis, logistics, design, etc. wouldn't really be "weak AI" in Searle's original sense because the aim in these cases is to build useful tools, not to simulate mental processes. Granted, usage seems to have drifted (or diffused) a lot since Searle's article.

[MK]: Useful nuance – the usage has indeed shifted over time.

2 Mori, *The Uncanny Valley*. Mori's Japanese phrasing was "bukimi no tani genshõ"; the phrase "uncanny valley" was confirmed in the first authorized translation of this seminal article.

3 Dick, *Do Androids Dream of Electric Sheep?* As readers and viewers of Scott's cut of *Blade Runner* will know, the central mystery of the story is not what motivates the rogue Replicants, on the run after escaping their indentured servitude, but rather whether Rick Deckard, the police detective and assassin sent after them, is himself a synthetic being without knowing it. That measure of uncanniness is not charted on the standard graph but is a recurring theme in certain versions of science fiction – for example, the character Boomer on the rebooted television series developed by Moore in *Battlestar Galactica*, who may be a humanoid Cylon without her own knowledge of that fact. This conceit is, in effect, Cartesian reflection circumvented precisely by the mechanisms of consciousness. As Deckard demands of the Replicant Rachel in *Blade Runner* (Scott), who has pushed the Voight-Kampff test to its limits, "How can it not know what it is?" Well, fairly easily, as it turns out. Lots of us do it all the time.

4 I used to have a T-shirt that said "I failed the Voight-Kampff test," though I have never actually taken the test – as far as I know.

5 Turing, "Computing Machinery and Intelligence," 433–60.

6 Smith, "AI and the Ontology of Complex Systems."

7 Marche, "The Imitation of Consciousness." Marche rounds off the issue with this summary: "The objections to the idea of machine learning that remain standing in Turing's original paper are those without any empirical basis: the generalized 'mystery about consciousness' and the objection from Extra-Sensory Perception." Turing had written this: "I assume that the reader is familiar with the idea of extra-sensory perception, and the meaning of the four items of it, viz. telepathy, clairvoyance, precognition and psycho-kinesis. These disturbing phenomena seem to deny all our usual scientific ideas. How we should like to discredit them! Unfortunately the statistical evidence, at least for telepathy, is overwhelming." Really? Overwhelming?

Marche again: "It's somewhat disquieting to discover that the founder of digital computing believed in the existence of, in his phrase, 'ghosts and bogies,' but he did. Turing's 'Objection of the basis of ESP' might seem silly. There's no evidence for telepathy or clairvoyance or precognition or psycho-kinesis. The lack of evidence is the point, though. There may be elements of consciousness we simply cannot observe and which we don't know we aren't observing, which would render them impossible to program." Marche goes on: "The major roadblock to artificial general intelligence, mechanical sentience, is our amazing ignorance about the nature of sentience itself. Consciousness may literally be unfathomable. Certainly we're a long distance from fathoming it; we've barely put a toe in the water. And what you cannot define, you cannot program." The last claim is not accurate, at least according to the programmers I know, but the general sentiment is certainly correct.

8 Wittgenstein's philosophical behaviourism is not what he intended, and yet it retains force. His posthumous *Philosophical Investigations* are ambiguous on the issue. Can we interpret the mindedness of another being except as a function of its behaviour, or must we impute some "state of mind" to that being in order to explain its apparently guided behaviour? Ryle's "logical behaviourism" attempts to answer that question by noting, in *The Concept of Mind*, that no directed action can be explained or vouchsafed by a non-evident mental state. Other philosophers, including Carnap and Quine, offered related views.

Philosophical zombies, meanwhile, are figures in an extended thought experiment that imagines entities indistinguishable from you and me who have all available behavioural attitudes and gestures, and yet lack inner consciousness. (P-zombies are not to be confused with the Hollywood kind, fast or slow.) If these zombies are possible, or even conceivable, then physicalism – the theory that consciousness is always reducible to bodily function – must be false. That is to say, consciousness as we experience it as inwardness, as we seem to, appears to exceed outward behaviour. Thus there must be some version of Cartesian dualism still in play. The P-zombies are just like us, but with the lights on and yet nobody home. This being a philosophical dispute, there is a vast literature about it from Thomas Nagel, David Chalmers, Stephen Yablo, and other very able thinkers. My own favourite quotation is from Kirk ("Zombies") who said this: "In spite of the fact that the arguments on both sides have become increasingly sophisticated – or perhaps because of it – they have not become more persuasive. The pull in each direction remains strong."

9 The sources are all solidly canonical, so no specific editions are really

needed, but see Kant, *Groundwork of the Metaphysics of Morals*; Spinoza, *Tractatus Theologico-Politicus*; Locke, *Second Treatise of Government*; Grotius and Samuel von Pufendorf, various. One can include Thomas Aquinas in any survey of natural law theory, as well as thinkers influenced by Grotius and Pufendorf, especially in jurisprudence. An excellent survey may be found in Weinrib, *Natural Law and Justice*.

10 The basic tenets of just war theory are ably covered in Walzer, *Just and Unjust Wars*. The special relevance of the war crimes/crimes against humanity distinction is discussed by Robertson, *Crimes Against Humanity*.

11 Agamben, *Homo Sacer*.

12 Exemplary texts: Hobbes, *Leviathan*; Locke, *Second Treatise of Government*; Rousseau, *The Social Contract*; Rawls, *A Theory of Justice*; Gauthier, *Morals by Agreement*.

13 Central texts here include Singer, *Animal Liberation* and, more recently, Donaldson and Kymlicka's compelling *Zoopolis*.

14 Much of the literature concerning environmental rights is an extension of basic human-rights discourse to include the security and solace of stable, healthy natural environments. These are the "rights to nature," as addressed by Hayward, *Constitutional Environmental Rights*. The more searching argument concerns the notion that natural environments might themselves be bearers of rights. In New Zealand, the government granted legal personhood to the Whanganui River, granting it "rights and interests" under the law.

15 Kymlicka, *Multicultural Citizenship* and *Liberalism, Community, and Culture*.

16 Searle, "Minds, Brains, and Programs," 1997.

17 Searle's Chinese-room thought experiment was first sketched in the much-anthologized journal article, "Minds, Brains, and Programs," 417–57. The idea was then elaborated in Searle's subsequent book, *Minds, Brains, and Science*. The argument has spawned a vast critical literature too extensive to cite in detail here. A brief and accessible discussion of possible objections may be found at Sabinasz, "Why the Chinese Room Argument Is Flawed." I am not sure if this matters at all except to linguists and respective speakers, but Searle does not distinguish between Mandarin and Cantonese when he uses "Chinese" as his natural-language example.

18 [LF]: I see what you mean, but this point doesn't really count against Searle's argument. Searle stipulates that we're meant to imagine the homunculus in the room being conscious – his point is that the homunculus is nevertheless

not conscious of the meaning of what is being said in the conversation. (This would also apply to a realistic case of a human carrying out a translation task by following rote symbol-matching instructions.)

So, even when there's apparently intelligent handling of meaningful linguistic forms by a computer program (passing the Turing test, say), there isn't any awareness of the meaning of what's being said from the point of view of the CPU running the program code. And that remains true even if we make the CPU itself conscious. It's strange that Searle assumes the homunculus is conscious in a thought experiment ultimately meant to show that it isn't, but it makes sense along these lines:

1. The only reason to suspect there's any awareness inside the system is that linguistic behavior appears to reflect awareness of conversational content.

2. But even if we assume the CPU is conscious, the CPU still has no awareness of conversational content.

The original reason for suspecting there's any awareness inside the system has been defeated.

[MK]: I've always felt that it makes a great deal of difference how we imagine the homunculus. Conscious but without comprehension seems odd but could easily be imagined, might even be a common human condition!

19 The literary-minded might think here of the scenario imagined by Lewis Carroll, whereby a map was so detailed that it achieved 1:1 scale and therefore covered the relevant county entirely.

For the technical arguments about this issue of mapping, see Gallistel, "Prelinguistic Thought," 253–63; and Camp, "Thinking with Maps," 145–82. As Camp concludes, "Ultimately, any plausible cognitive system, including especially our own, is likely to be highly multi-modal: storing and manipulating information in the formats of multiple sensory modalities, and centralizing information in cartographic, diagrammatic, and sentential formats. If this is right, then it becomes commensurately more difficult to make principled predictions about what a thinker should or shouldn't be able to do" (175). Those predictions would naturally then also embrace any non-human form of advanced consciousness.

[LF]: It is true that conscious map-reading (attending to map, world, and the relations between them) is very cognitively demanding. But this point does not apply to the unconscious maps that Gallistel argues are found even in insect minds; these maps (just like language-of-thought "sentences") will only ever serve as vehicles for thought, never as objects of attention in their own right.

20 Shanahan and Baars, "Applying Global Workspace Theory to the Frame Problem," 157–76. This article has become central to current debates in cognitive science.

21 The most significant of these is biologist Jakob von Uexküll (1864–1944), who influenced everyone from Martin Heidegger to Giorgio Agamben. Von Uexküll labelled his theoretical approach "biosemiotics," to capture the sense that every organism possesses, and instinctively processes, about the meaning of its physical environment and conditions of life. See, for example, Uexküll, *Theoretical Biology*.

22 [LF]: I would be inclined to distinguish phenomenological embodiment from physical embodiment and to think that it's only the former that's important for consciousness. AIs, then, probably don't need physical bodies. (Some physical machine needs to run the code, but that's not a body.) Avatar-style embodiment in a virtual world should suffice, if all we need is an environment that can be perceived and acted on. Even the internet as it exists today can provide a suitable environment, insofar as reading and typing is a form of embodied engagement.

One can see the same point from the posthuman side of things: Imagine a brain-in-a-vat who has their sensory and motor areas suitably wired up to a fancy web browser. Are they embodied and emplaced in the relevant sense? I would say that they are.

[MK]: This is provocative. Like many others, I have been stuck on the embodiment issue for some time, but others see it as less crucial or even unnecessary as systems advance. Still, could we imagine granting rights and personhood to a disembodied AI?

23 Weiner, *Cybernetics*, 39–40.

24 Singer, "Isaac Asimov's Laws of Robotics Are Wrong." Singer offers some trenchant and well-phrased criticism of Asimov's Three Laws of Robotics.

25 Tribe, *Abortion*.

26 [LF]: It's true though (isn't it?) that some humans present as "inhuman" in a way that seems distinctly uncanny. I think some psychopaths are a case in point. Really anyone who doesn't exhibit "normal human" feelings gives off this sense. I wonder if part of what's going on with the whole uncanny valley

phenomenon is that we're only comfortable with someone if we sense that we can appeal to their humanity because they possess the relevant emotions like empathy. If someone looks human but then indicates that they may lack those feelings, the ensuing uncertainty could result in the uncanny effect. Whatever it is in us that registers canniness (and inclines us to be trusting) is probably based on superficial cues and can therefore be hacked. We might turn out to be quite vulnerable to the "charisma" of future robots that can reproduce just the right pattern of cues.

[MK]: Yes, very true – and frightening. Psychopaths are typically just a small slice of any human population, but psychopathic AIs could theoretically dominate an entire society.

27 See, for example, poetic-philosophical exploration of mortality offered by Zwicky and Bringhurst in *Learning to Die*.

28 Original articulation of the notion of a technological Singularity is credited to physicist and mathematician John von Neumann in the 1960s. The argument is not simply that non-human computing power or algorithmic muscularity ("intelligence" in some sense of that notion) will one day surpass human computing ability. The "singular" part of the Singularity is the notion that, at some point, a single created non-human entity will be capable of creating its own descendants, who will likely be able to learn and improve as they, in turn, create descendants. Ray Kurzweil, in *The Singularity*, accessibly surveys both the technology and the culture of the Singularity.

29 [LF]: For AIs in particular, of course, the issues are indeed speculative and so far moot, and that does make now the right time to reflect on them. But perhaps this overlooks that there are already live issues concerning "potential non-human individual persons" – that we are already well along in bungling our ethical and political relations to non-human minds. It is instructive to link reflections about future AI more closely to parallel reflections concerning the position of non-human animals in society – as explored, e.g., in Donaldson and Kymlicka's *Zoopolis*.

There might be a way to exclude animals from the discussion by taking "human-level" intelligence as the important benchmark (where AI abilities become ethically or politically relevant). But to do that would be to uncritically project our existing biases onto the new terrain, rather than using the new terrain as an opportunity to critically re-examine our standing assumptions. If we do create full-blown, human-level GAIAS at some point, it is likely they will be preceded by intermediate systems, featuring the absence of some important human-mind qualities but the presence of some animal-mind ones. What happens when we have AIs that, while perhaps still falling well short of the kind of articulate intelligence that constitutes full-blown personhood (according to the usual, highly demanding standards), might nonetheless enjoy some degree of sentience? We will want some guide for thinking about the duties we may owe to the systems at these intermediate stages – and that makes the animals analogy important. In order to prepare for AI, we need better perspective on the moral duties we owe to minds that are unlike ours and especially the less sophisticated minds we tend to over-look morally.

[MK]: An important reminder about the larger point here, which is that real-world justice duties can be driven by apparently wild SF-style imagin-ings. This, after all, is a longtime aim of the genre and one not confined to its dystopian branch.

30 A good overview is Darling, *The New Breed*.

31 The ur-text is Sigmund Freud, *The Uncanny*, including a long analysis of Jentsch, *On the Psychology of the Uncanny* and some common cultural fig-ures such as the Sandman and the Automaton, familiar to most children even now as dark bedtime tales. Their E.T.A. Hoffman horror-tale adapta-tions in short stories (1816) were then rendered into balletic form as *Coppélia* (1870), libretto by Charles-Louis-Étienne Nuitter.

See also Kristeva, *Powers of Horror*; Todorov, *The Fantastic*; Fisher, *The Weird and the Eerie*; and Kingwell, "Beyond the Uncanny Valley of the Dolls," 186–98.

An odd note within a note is that the "girl group" the Chordettes released, in 1954, a now-popular song by Pat Ballard where "Mister Sandman" is in-voked as a dream-redeemer, bringing a wished-for romantic partner, "with a lonely heart like Pagliacci, and lots of wavy hair like Liberace." Other versions of the song have been recorded by, among others, the Four Aces, Chet Atkins, Max Bygraves, and Emmylou Harris.

Meanwhile, Roy Orbison's 1963 song "In Dreams," which invokes the Sandman figure as a "candy-coloured clown," is either romantic or creepy depending on your inclinations, but director David Lynch made it very un-canny in his film *Blue Velvet*. For completists, Pagliacci, Ruggero Leonvallo's operatic character from an 1892 work, is featured in another popular song, Smokey Robinson and Stevie Wonder's "Tears of a Clown" (1970), and then also makes recurring appearances in the plotlines of the television comedy Seinfeld, where the character Kramer (who fears clowns) is trying to scalp some tickets to the opera. The tragic clown!

One further detail of potential relevance: the significant Freudian-slip (parapraxis) moments within this Freudian text, which is otherwise mostly literary consideration of the concept of Unheimlichkeit, concern Freud himself. One is the story of Freud seeing a "disagreeable" man through the window of his railway carriage, only then to discover that it is his own reflection in the glass window. The other is a nightmare tale of Freud attempting to leave the red-light district of a foreign town, into which he has stumbled by accident, only to find his path of flight returning him to the same location. One of these stories is repressed into a footnote, the other told in passing near the book's conclusion. But the real conclusion should be clear: what we meet in the uncanny is not the other but ourselves – or rather, the other that always lies within ourselves.

32 Kelley, *The Pogo Papers*. The quotation is usually attributed to American artist Walt Kelley, whose cartoon strip *Pogo* included many elements of political commentary as well as existential play. The sentence is allegedly a parody of a message sent in 1813 from US Navy Commodore Oliver Hazard Perry to Army General William Henry Harrison after his victory in the Battle of Lake Erie, stating, "We have met the enemy, and they are ours." The quotation f irst appeared in lengthier form in "A Word to the Fore," the foreword of the book, where Kelly alluded to his criticisms of McCarthyism and self-destroying, or auto-immune, forms of patriotic nationalism.

33 Once more, canonical sources will suffice: Ellul, *The Technological Society*; Mumford, *Technics and Civilization*; Bookchin, *Post-Scarcity Anarchism*.

34 Heidegger, "The Question Concerning Technology."

35 I explore some of the causes and consequences of this version of contemporary disposability and self-consumption in Kingwell, *Wish I Were Here*. My main argument there is that the ostensible banishing of boredom offered by devices and distractions in fact reinforces quasi-addictive cycles of neoliberal boredom, designed to keep the subject in a state of perpetual restless anxiety with respect to knowingness, upgrades, and connection.

36 The utopian exceptions used to be ideas of freeware or open-source devel-
    opments, but the inexorable forces of monetization get to everything in the
    end, even apparently costless transactions and social media.

37 Heidegger, "Building, Dwelling, Thinking." I offer a more sustained engage-
    ment with this text in two works, as follows: Kingwell, "Building, Dwelling,
    Acting," 40–9; and Kingwell, *The Ethics of Architecture*.

CHAPTER THREE

1   There are some important exceptions. I will note just three here: Dee's
    The Privileges, a sly satire of the blithe arrogance of one couple who swim
    through the economic collapse; Lehmann's *Rich People Stuff*, which lam-
    poons the favoured tropes and preoccupations of one-percenters; and
    Hodge's angry screed about the Obama administration's complicity with
    minimizing the responsibility of Wall Street for the collapse, *The Mendacity
    of Hope*. One complicated example is the hit film directed by Fincher, *The
    Social Network*, which tells the story of Facebook "inventor" Mark Zucker-
    berg in the unspoken context of the early-2000s bubble. But the film can't
    decide whether it is a revenge-of-the-nerds celebration or a moralistic slam
    of internet-age sharp dealing.

2   See, for example, Berberoglu, *The Global Rise of Authoritarianism in the 21st
    Century*; Stanley, *How Fascism Works*; also Snyder's excellent contextual
    primer, *On Tyranny*.

3   See, among other diagnoses, Cook, "Who Is Driving the Great Resignation?"
    "According to the U.S. Bureau of Labor Statistics, 4 million Americans quit
    their jobs in July 2021. Resignations peaked in April and have remained ab-
    normally high for the last several months, with a record-breaking 10.9 mil-
    lion open jobs at the end of July. How can employers retain people in the
    face of this tidal wave of resignations?"

4   Wickes, "Two Thirds of UK Youth Miss Lockdown."

5   See my pamphlet, Kingwell, *On Risk*, for an assessment of the links between
    pandemic conditions and routinized social injustice.

6   See, for example, Crawford, *Shop Class as Soulcraft*, and de Botton, *The
    Pleasures and Sorrows of Work*. Andrew Ross summarizes the political puzzle
    posed by these books: "It is an unfortunate comment on the generous intel-
    lects of these two authors that they do not see fit to acknowledge, in their

respective surveys of working life, the nobility of those who resist"; see Ross, *Nice Work If You Can Get It*, 16.

7   The argument about work and its place in contemporary life shows no signs of dissipating, though there is reason to wonder whether the various books analyzing the culture of overwork and flextime actually have any critical traction. After all, a central irony here is that the people who might need most to read such books – perhaps including this one? – will almost certainly claim they have no time to do so. Anyway, three entries in what we might call *Kulturkritik*-Lite on the topic of work are Onstad, *The Weekend Effect*; Schor, *The Overworked American*; and Banting, *Willing Slaves*. The main trouble with these books, which notably span a period of more than a quarter-century, is that they spend a lot of time and pages demonstrating what is obvious – that work-culture is toxic – and very little considering structural responses to that condition.

8   I argue for a distinction between idling and slacking in Kingwell, "Idling Toward Heaven."

9   Russell, *In Praise of Idleness and Other Essays*, 3.

10 The working principle behind Bentham's panopticon – that subjects under surveillance will become their own agents of discipline – garnered much attention in the later writings of Foucault, who saw the same principle at work at large across the institutions of modern capitalist society. In *Discipline and Punish*, Foucault writes, "[Bentham's panopticon] set out to show how one may 'unlock' the disciplines and get them to function in a diffused, multiple, polyvalent way throughout the whole social body … It programmes, at the level of an elementary and easily transferable mechanism, the basic functioning of a society penetrated through and through with disciplinary mechanisms" (208–9).

11 One could cite, in support here, the analysis of Deleuze in "Postscript on the Societies of Control." Deleuze notes three modes of social structure: sovereign states (pre-modern); discipline societies (modern); and control societies (postmodern). Whereas a discipline society moulds citizens into subjects through various carceral institutions – schools, armies, prisons, clinics – a control society can be radically decentred and apparently liberated. The difference in the world of work is between a factory and a business.

A factory disciplines its subjects by treating them as a body of workers; this also affords the opportunity of organizing and resisting in the form of unionized labour. A business, by contrast, treats employees like hapless contestants on a bizarre, ever-changing game show – something like Japan's now-defunct television series "Most Extreme Elimination Challenge," perhaps – where competitors are mysteriously competing with fellow workers for spectral rewards allocated according to mysterious rules. The affable boss who invites you over for dinner is a paradigm case: Is it business or pleasure? Who else is invited? Does it mean a likely promotion, or nothing at all? Thus does business invade and control the psyche of the worker, precisely because obvious mechanisms of discipline are absent.

12 Maier's otherwise excellent *Bonjour Laziness*, is unstable on this point. She acknowledges the work system is impervious to challenge and yet finally urges: "rather than a 'new man,' be a blob, a leftover, stubbornly resisting the pressure to conform, impervious to manipulation. Become the grain of sand that seizes up the whole machine, the sore thumb" (117). This confused message would seem to indicate insufficient grasp of the slacker/idler distinction.

13 Weber, *The Protestant Ethic and the Spirit of Capitalism*. An AI-themed update might be Rhee, *The Robotic Imaginary*.

14 Veblen, *The Theory of the Leisure Class*; Goffman, *The Presentation of Self in Everyday Life*; Bourdieu, *Distinction*; and Galbraith, *The Affluent Society*.

15 Rothbard, "Bureaucracy and the Civil Service in the United States," 3–75; Michels, *Political Parties*.

16 Parkinson, "Parkinson's Law."

17 [LF]: It's very useful, I think, to consider bureaucracy in this way, as self-organizing and quasi-agentive. Among other things, it suggests that we already live in a world shaped by quite powerful "artificial intelligence" – consisting of agent-like entities that organize and control human activities even as they are constituted by those activities in aggregate (entities like meetings or corporations). Many people find it extremely difficult to take these constituted entities fully seriously as the independent (quasi)agents they are. Corporations are just us, the thought goes, so all corporate power must ultimately rest in the hands of some human agents – the ones in charge. I think we're collectively overlooking something crucial about our world due to this common blind spot.

Reflecting on examples like these, it seems to me that there are very plausible AI nightmare scenarios that do not depend at all on AIs achieving consciousness. They might instead be vastly more powerful successors to the monster-zombies we encounter today in the form of corporations. When they take over the world, we humans will probably fail to notice anything has happened because we will make the mistake of seeing this power as a mere expression of human agency.

[MK]: This feels like what is already happening, at least with agency construed as routine desire for comfort and convenience.

18 Jerry Pournelle, "The Iron Law of Bureaucracy."

19 Moore, "Moore's Laws of Bureaucracy."

20 In his *Science of Logic*, Hegel characterizes the "bad infinite" as that which is "never ending" (such as an extensively infinite series of numbers – or, more appropriately, the never ending toils of Sisyphus in Camus' novel). This is contrasted against conceptions of infinity as being "end-less" (such as a closed circle) which, for Hegel, represents a totality insofar as it incorporates both the infinite and the finite.

21 In his *Economic and Philosophical Manuscripts of 1844*, Marx characterizes four types of alienation of labour under capitalism: alienation of the worker from (1) the product of labour, (2) from the act of labouring (3) from him/herself as a worker, and (4) from his/her fellow workers.

22 "Ne travaillez jamais" was inscribed on Rue de Seine's wall in Paris by Debord in 1953 and was later, much to Debord's disappointment, reproduced en masse as a "humorous" postcard.

23 Berlin, *Against the Current*, 320.

24 This is one implication of the celebrated exchange between Socrates and Thrasymachus in Republic, Book I, 340b–344c.

25 See Frankfurt, *On Bullshit*, a huge international bestseller which was in fact a repurposed version of a journal article Frankfurt had published many years earlier, included in his collection *The Importance of What We Care About*.

26 "Crackberry" is certainly long out of date, not least because Research in Motion's Blackberry phone gave way to the advent of iPhones and their other screen-based smartphone imitators.

27 Galbraith, *The Affluent Society*, 95.

28 Arendt, *The Human Condition*.

29 Note: this is the singular *Simpsons* reference in this book, just for completists. See Kirkland, "Hail to the Teeth."

30 Invisible Committee, *The Coming Insurrection*, 46.

31 Ibid., 49.

32 Glenn and Kingwell, *The Idler's Glossary*. The companion volumes are *The Wage-Slave's Glossary* and *The Adventurer's Glossary*.

33 Coupland, "Generation X at 30: Generational Trashing Is Eternal." Coupland expands the general argument: "I find comfort in the fact that brains all over the planet have been rewired similarly to mine. In fact, I'd go as far as to say that our species has never been as neurally homogenised as it is now. So, from a neural perspective, are generations possibly becoming an obsolete notion altogether?" Indeed yes.

34 Some might think our *Wage-Slave's Glossary* lands squarely into this cat-egory of a futile or, worse, complicit gesture. We hoped not, even if its satiri-cal intent falls short of open call for revolution. By isolating the lexicon from its site and circumstances of origin, and allying this move to earlier support of idleness, we aimed to generate critical distance lacking in the otherwise defensive workplace use of workplace slang.

35 Appleby, *Inheriting the Revolution*, 11. There is a good discussion of this trope of the entrepreneur-hero in Taylor, *Modern Social Imaginaries*, ch. 9.

36 The roots of biofascism – the ideological celebration of the family and family values – are deep in North American political culture. So deep, in fact, that it is hard to imagine an American author writing something like Maier's controversial bestseller, *No Kids: Forty Good Reasons Not to Have Children*. True, seven decades ago, Wylie took aim at the cult of what he called "momism" in his searing *Generation of Vipers*, but the best anti-family arguments still come from France.

Compare this passage from *The Coming Insurrection*: "Everyone can tes-tify to the doses of sadness condensed from year to year in family gatherings, the forced smiles, the awkwardness of seeing everyone pretending in vain, the feeling that a corpse is lying there on the table, and everyone acting as though it were nothing. From flirtation to divorce, from cohabitation to stepfamilies, everyone feels the inanity of the sad family nucleus, but most seem to believe that it would be sadder still to give it up. The family is no longer so much the suffocation of maternal control or the patriarchy of beatings as it is this infantile abandon to a fuzzy dependency, where everything is familiar, this carefree moment in the face of a world that nobody can deny is breaking down, a world where 'becoming self-sufficient' is a euphemism for 'finding a boss.'" No Emersonian self-reliance there!

37 [LF]: Carpenter himself has called the film "a documentary."

[MK]: Ha, I love that!

38 Galbraith, *The Affluent Society*, 129.

39 Work as we are discussing it in the present book is obscurely and so confusingly spread across Arendt's categories. As a result, Arendt could indict the emptiness of a society free from labour – the wasteland of consumer desire – but could not see how smoothly the work idea would fold itself back into that wasteland in the form of workaholism.

40 Compare a more recent expansion of the argument, once more from Invisible Committee's *The Coming Insurrection*: "The West is a civilization that has survived all the prophecies of its collapse with a singular stratagem. Just as the bourgeoisie had to deny itself as a class in order to permit the bourgeoisification of society as a whole, from the worker to the baron; just as capital had to sacrifice itself as a wage relation in order to impose itself as a social relation – becoming cultural capital and health capital in addition to finance capital; just as Christianity had to sacrifice itself as a religion in order to survive as an affective structure – as a vague injunction to humility, compassion, and weakness; so the West has sacrificed itself as a particular civilization in order to impose itself as a universal culture. The operation can be summarized like this: an entity in its death throes sacrifices itself as a content in order to survive as a form." It is perhaps no surprise that the authors, viewing this superfluous majority as set off against the self-colonizing desires for "advancement" in the compliant minority, suggest that the current situation "introduces the risk that, in its idleness, [the majority] will set about sabotaging the machine," 48.

41 In his bestselling book *One-Dimensional Man*, Marcuse distinguishes between "true needs" (i.e., those necessary for survival: food, clothing, shelter) and "repressive needs" (superfluous commodities: luxury items, status symbols, etc.). His argument is that a worker's ability to purchase "repressive" items gives him or her a false sense of equality to oppressors and, more seriously, turns individuals away from recognizing the true inequalities of society. Production simply generates consumption.

42 Mumford, *Technics and Civilization*, 17.

43 Taylor, *The Principles of Scientific Management*, 129. Compare Koolhaas, *Delirious New York*, which relates Taylor's time-motion ideas to the spectacular rise of first-generation skyscrapers in Manhattan, especially the Empire State Building; I expand on this latter point in Kingwell, *Nearest Thing to Heaven*.

44 Debord, *Society of the Spectacle*, sec. V:126.

45 Rybczynski's *Waiting for the Weekend* tells a gripping version of this story, set against the Babylonian origin of the seven-day week itself.

46 Heidegger, "The Age of the World Picture."

47 Debord, *Society of the Spectacle*, sec. V:145.

48 Taylor, Charles, *Modern Social Imaginaries*, 110.

49 Giamatti, *Take Time for Paradise*, 44.

50 Eagleton, Terry. *Culture and the Death of God*, 136.

51 Benjamin, "Theses on the Philosophy of History."

52 In a curious and controversial inversion of the standard anxiety-of-influence aesthetic tradition, the British artists Jake and Dinos Chapman purchased several prints from Goya's Los Caprichos series and then drew on them. According to Dinos Chapman, these acts of defacement did not constitute vandalism because the altered works actually rose in value. "You can't vandalize something by making it more expensive," he said. In 2005, the Chapman Brothers' "revised and improved" versions of Los Caprichos were selling for $26,000 each in the White Cube gallery, London. For an interesting account of vandalism, value, and renewed gift economies in discarded or rescued art, see Lerner, "Damage Control," 43–9.

53 For a brisk journalistic account of the details, see Rushkoff, *Present Shock*. It has to be said that this book, while valuable as a diagnostic, itself suffers from a measure of discursive breathlessness, leaping from topic to topic with the speed of the very virus it wants to analyze.

54 I discuss the trope of slow and fast zombies in democratic life in Kingwell, "Frank's Motel," 103–26.

55 For example, in the Declaration of the Rights of Man and of the Citizen (Paris, 24 June 1793) we find these words offered in defence of the French Revolution: "in order that all citizens … may never permit themselves to be oppressed and degraded by tyranny." The same language is present in Robespierre's (rejected) Declaration of Rights (24 April 1793), though it does not appear in the (accepted) 1789 Declaration.

56 Some alarming statistics concerning defection from electoral politics among young Canadians – dubbed Spectators – were reported by Valpy, "The Young Will Inherit a Future They See as a Sham." Valpy in turn drew on an analysis by Herle, "The Spectators," 19–20. News reports suggest the situation is similar, if not worse, in other developed "democratic" nations.

57 Michels, *Political Parties.*

58 Deleuze, *Difference and Repetition*, 1.

59 Ibid., 5.

60 A reference current to this writing: Amazon now has an algorithm that fires people without warning or explanation. See Soper, "Fired by Bot at Amazon."

61 MIT's Technology Review podcast has tracked these developments with great acuteness, especially in work from Anthony Green and Karen Hao.

62 Tolentino, "The Gig Economy Celebrates Working Yourself to Death."

CHAPTER FOUR

1 [LF]: The source is Dennett, *Content and Consciousness*, who attributes the label to a remark from Fodor:

> In a heated discussion at MIT about rival theories of language comprehension, Fodor characterized the views of a well-known theoretician as "West Coast" – a weighty indictment in the corridors of MIT. When reminded that this maligned theoretician resided in Pennsylvania, Fodor was undaunted. He was equally ready, it turned out, to brand people at Brandeis or Sussex as West Coast. He explained that just as when you are at the North Pole, moving away from the Pole in any direction is moving south, so moving away from MIT in any direction is moving West. MIT is the East Pole, and from a vantage point at the East Pole, the inhabitants of Chicago, Pennsylvania, Sussex, and even Brandeis University in Waltham are as distinctly Western in their appearance and manners.

Dennett calls the East Pole stance "High Church Computationalism" and the West Coast stance "Zen Holism." It is accurate to frame the distinction as a manifestation of the nativism/empiricism debate, though no doubt there's more to it as well. This characterization is included in Dennett's collected volume *Brainchildren*, 61, among other places.

[MK]: It has to be said that the terms have not really caught on in the wider world.

2 New Mysterians, sometimes just called Mysterians, take the position that the hard problem of consciousness cannot in principle be solved by its own agents. Therefore, some form of physicalism is correct when it comes to the nature of mind. Philosopher Colin McGinn years ago offered a staunch defence of this view in his article "Can We Solve the Mind-Body Problem?" 349–66, and then restated the argument in popular form as "All Machine and No Ghost," riffing on Ryle's famous formulation. (McGinn's answer to the solution question was: no, we cannot solve it.)

The eccentric but brilliant philosopher Owen Flanagan, now a committed Buddhist, performed his own riff on the proto-punk band who recorded "96 Tears" in 1966 when he added a section called "Question Mark and the Mysterians" to his book *The Science of the Mind*, 313. For the record, the band went by "? and the Mysterians," and the lead singer legally changed his name to "?." Flanagan is likely responsible for the general Mysterian label. Other contemporary thinkers associated with "mysterianism" include Julian Jaynes, Jerry Fodor, Steven Pinker, and Sam Harris. Canonical thinkers who held some version of the position – Leibniz, T.H. Huxley, Samuel Johnson – are what Flanagan calls "Old Mysterians."

[LF]: Potentially related to the endnote discussion of Mysterianism is Eric Schwitzgebel's recent defence of "crazyism" about the metaphysics of mind, which holds that the correct view on the mind, whatever that should turn out to be, will have to be a "crazy" one. See Schwitzgebel, "The Crazyist Metaphysics of Mind," 665–82.

3 Essential on this issue is Fodor, *Modularity of Mind*. Using Chomskian linguistics and some new findings in mental processing, Fodor's work resuscitated notions of intramental faculties, which had been considered debunked in the form of phrenology after the manner of Franz Josef Gall (1756–1828). Fodor's many innovations include a recusal from localizability, such that "faculty" or "capacity" could be divorced from specific brain part (frontal lobe, cortex, etc.).

In popular culture, the idea of faculty psychology has trickled down into such things as the Docter film, *Inside Out*, which depicts the human mind as a kind of raucous and barely functional committee of personal manifestations of Joy, Sadness, Anger, Fear, and Disgust – each depicted and voiced as separate homunculi within the mind of central character Riley, an adolescent girl undergoing some difficult life changes.

4 A well-known example that illustrates hard functionalism is a thought
   experiment involving a vending machine, usually styled in the literature as a
   "Coke machine," though that specific branding can be jettisoned. Suppose
   that the basic tenet of strict functionalism is that the hardware supporting
   performance is irrelevant to that function. That is, it doesn't matter if the
   software is running on carbon hardware or something else, as long as outputs are reliable. Therefore, a vending machine is just as operational and
   efficient, for many tasks, as an organic neurophysiological human brain.
       So why employ vending machines as the basis of the thought experiment?
   Well, imagine that, in the standard example, a mute metal vending machine
   (this is now very old as a metaphor, admittedly) has slots for quarters and
   dimes. A soft drink costs thirty-five cents. If you insert a quarter, nothing
   seems to happen. There has been an input but there is no resulting output.
   And yet, as functionalists would argue, the state of the machine has changed:
   it has gone from non-action or steady state to something that might be described as waiting. With the subsequent insertion of a dime, a soft drink
   then gets dispensed. Absent the dime, it stays in this in-between state indefi-
   nitely. The point is that the middle state – quarter, but not yet dime – is distinct from both the beginning and ending states, and further, each state is
   determined by a series of inputs that must be executed properly to prompt
   execution. The actual hardware of the machine is therefore functionally irrelevant or anyway in principle replicable in other hardware platforms.
5 Noam Chomsky advocated the universal grammar (UG) theory in the 1960s,
   but there is reason to conclude that he has since abandoned this view. More
   significant for current larger purposes was that this argument was a serious
   challenge to longstanding empiricist views of language-acquisition and, in
   turn, of cognition itself. Later critics have argued that the UG thesis is non-
   falsifiable and therefore unscientific. Groundwork texts in this region are
   Chomsky, *Aspects of the Theory of Syntax* and *Knowledge of Language* and
   then, per contra, Sampson, *The 'Language Instinct' Debate*.
6 Gallistel has many important books in this field, among them *Memory and
   the Computational Brain*.
7 [LF]: The Calder mobile image is invoked in a different context by linguist
   Uriagereka, "Multiple Spell-Out," 251–82, but it concerns not consciousness
   but rather syntactic structure. The idea is that "the same" sentences in
   different languages have deep hierarchical structures in common (the same

Calder mobile) but will take on different (superficial) linear word orderings
in different languages (like a mobile viewed from different vantage points).

8 The most prominent purveyor of "global workspace" theory is Baars,
especially in his work *In the Theater of Consciousness*.

9 Rée, *Philosophical Tales*. This slender book is a neglected gem of contemporary meta-critical philosophical writing. Rée proposes, among other things,
that philosophical writing is a form of fiction despite its authoritative tone,
perhaps most significantly when it is attempting to be a "scientific" account
of the world and our experience of it. His reading of Descartes's *Meditations*,
for example, which prominently features analysis of the first-person character adopted by Descartes as the voice of that work – "Renatus," as Rée
styles him – makes for a series of conclusions based on unexamined baseline
presuppositions about personal identity and consciousness.

10 A solid reference here is Spelke, "Core Knowledge," 1233–43.

11 For more on this with respect to the limit case of criminal insanity, see
Fingarette, "Insanity and Responsibility," 6–29; also Kingwell, "Madpeople
and Ideologues," 59–73.

12 Quine, *Word and Object*.

13 See, for example, Daniels, "Wide Reflective Equilibrium and Theory Acceptance in Ethics," 256–82; also Rawls, *A Theory of Justice*.

14 GPT-3, "A Robot Wrote This Entire Article. Are You Scared Yet, Human?"
An unintentional irony is that this headline, like so many that one finds in
newspaper websites, does not really reflect the content of the article or at
least amplifies its meaning in pursuit of provocation. This is because the
headlines are often themselves composed by algorithms or, in the case of a
newspaper to which I contribute regularly, outsourced to independent and
off-shore companies who have no direct ties to the editorial staff or writers.
Thus many misguided complaints from readers who erroneously assume
that the writer has chosen the headline.

One irony in current debates about programs like this is that writers resent being ousted from some central position in the writing process. What if,
instead, we simply welcomed advanced algorithms that could do all the
heavy lifting of dissertations and even novels, so that we humans could just
kick back and watch baseball (preferably with human players)? Speaking as a
completed doctoral dissertation writer and author of a number of books,
there have been many days when I wished for a visit from some version of

what the humourist P.J. O'Rourke called "computer elves," the midnight beings who write your brilliantly outlined book while you are peacefully sleeping.

15 Alexeev, "Motherboard Issues," 17–18.

16 Marche, "The Computers Are Getting Better at Writing." In a subsequent email conversation about this article, Marche told me that what scared him was not Black Mirror–style innovations such as those that would reincarnate dead people as chat bots but algorithms that use simple games like hide-and-seek to develop new, more advanced and monetizable learning strategies.

   To quote him: "[T]he two most advanced AIS are complete black boxes. And I mean complete. I talk to engineers all the time with this stuff. Nobody – nobody – has any idea what's happening at Google and Facebook." Very likely true, or true enough to be worrying. See also Brown, "AI Chat Bots Can Bring You Back from the Dead, Sort Of"; Ornes, "Playing Hide-and-Seek, Machines Invent New Tools."

17 As indicated already, I know Stephen Marche and count him as a friend as well as a colleague. I'm pretty sure he wrote that *New Yorker* article without aid from an algorithm, but I wouldn't be at all surprised to learn, per contra, that he wrote some of it and then had Sudowrite finish the rest. (I'm kidding.)

18 For an alternative view, which argues that students actually prefer pass/fail credits because they enable academic curiosity, consider Dunch, "It's Time for Canadian Universities to Go Gradeless." This argument is valid and shared by at least some students, but that has not been my experience given the relentless postgraduate focus on grades even within profit-gathering systems of standardized testing (SAT, LSAT, MCAT, GRE, etc.).

19 [LF]: This is sometimes known as the Ada Lovelace Objection, discussed by Turing in Section 7 of his paper on the Turing Machine. But it strikes me as disputable, depending on just what is meant by "all on their own" – which is hard to clarify. Another tack one could take here: What they cannot yet do is start writing for their own authentic purposes. As far as we know, no existing program can become gripped by an idea and then attempt to work it out in writing.

   This suggests that Lovelace sees strong limitations on the creative capacities of machines, but it's worth comparing this line from Note A (emphasis added): "[The Analytical Engine] might act upon other things besides number, were objects found whose mutual fundamental relations could be expressed by those of the abstract science of operations, and which should be also susceptible of adaptations to the action of the operating notation and mechanism of the engine. Supposing, for instance, that the fundamental relations of pitched sounds in the science of harmony and of musical composition were susceptible of such expression and adaptations, the engine might compose elaborate and scientific pieces of music of any degree of complexity or extent."

See Lovelace's notes appended to her translation of Menabrea, "Notions sur la machine analytique de M. Charles Babbage."

[MK]: The debate continues on this. Personally, I find AI-generated music more convincing than AI-generated visual art, but this may be owing to music's proximity to mathematics.

20 Hoel, "The Semantic Apocalypse," and "I Got an Artificial Intelligence to Write My Novel."

21 Machine-learning programs make uncorrected factual errors all the time, though not usually with the result of being bombarded with emails from gleeful, fact-shaming, insult-prone readers and message-board trolls. Would anyone bother to do any of that with a machine-generated op-ed? Or are insults exclusively human-to-human acts?

Tiny historical note: in 2021 *The New York Times*, which had originated the term, officially retired the term "op-ed," meaning a column appearing on the page opposite the staff-authored editorials. There are no pages, and *a fortiori* no opposite pages, when you read a "newspaper" on a screen, as most people do now do.

22 Whyte, "Bestsellers: What It Takes." Whyte, a biographer and former journalist, is the publisher of Sutherland House Books in Toronto.

23 [LF]: If AI did swiftly prove able to realize tone and style with a subtlety that matched humans, we might respond with surprise at how smart AI has become. Or, an alternative, somewhat disquieting option would be to conclude that celebrated intangibles like "inimitable" artistic styles – or even the entire domains of writing, music, etc. – have turned out not to be as deep or as subtle as we had thought they were. The insights of AI research, then, might be as much about probing the depth (intelligence-demandingness) of tasks, and finding out what we really mean by intelligence, as it is about building systems that are intelligent according to some already-settled standard. Looking back on the development of AI over the last seventy years, I think

the most important lessons have been of precisely that kind: Proving theorems and winning chess games requires much less intelligence than we thought; common sense requires much more.

[MK]: Absolutely right.

24 Warhaft, *The Good Stripper*.

25 [LF]: This is a nice example that ties into the frame problem. Compare this passage from Fodor, *Modularity of Mind*, 88: "Whether John's utterance of 'Mary might do it, but Joan is above that sort of thing' is ironical, say, is a question that can't be answered short of using a lot of what you know about John, Mary, and Joan. Worse yet, there doesn't seem to be any way to say, in the general case, how much, or precisely what, of what you know about them might need to be accessed in making such determinations."

[MK]: That example reminds me of those melon-twisting questions that we had to answer in the logic section of the GRE!

26 Allegedly as recorded in an interview with *The Economist* (4 December 2003). Multiple subsequent sources have questioned the validity of this quotation. See, for example, Kennedy, "William Gibson's Future Is Now," which expresses open skepticism about the sentiment, while noting that "it neatly sums up his own particular flavor" – the last phrase a riff on a Gibson work called *Distrust That Particular Flavor*.

In a 1990 documentary, now available on YouTube, Gibson did say the following: "I think in some very real sense part of the world's population is already posthuman. Consider the health options available to a millionaire in Beverly Hills as opposed to a man starving in the streets in Bangladesh. The man in Beverly Hills can, in effect, buy himself a new set of organs. I mean, when you look at that sort of gap, the man in Bangladesh is still human. He's a human being from an agricultural planet. The man in Beverly Hills is something else. He may still be human, but he, in some way, I think he is also posthuman. The future has already happened." Trench, *Cyberpunk*, excerpt occurs in part 3 of its five parts: time code 12:20 of 14:59 overall.

27 Smith, "How Algorithms Are Changing What We Read Online." For the record, and full disclosure, Smith is a long-time friend of mine.

28. A sample of related commentary: Breland, "Woke AI Won't Save Us"; Smith, "The Use of Artificial Intelligence in a 'Woke' Society"; Heikkilä, "How to Build a Woke AI." For the most part, these discussions and disputes concern the potential ethical abilities or sensitivities of programs, not really their

level of political orientation to some "far left" or "critical race theory" ideological purpose. That is, there may be programmable perception of racial bias, for example, but there is no further direction to pursue a project of activism against systemic racism or capitalist exploitation of an underclass.

29 A similar issue arose with respect to online grading in university courses, as implied earlier. Many bureaucratically minded academics think that detailed rubrics for assessing student papers are the new (and so desirable) normal. These mechanisms are efficient, yes, and students appreciate the definitive organization of their work into cells on a spreadsheet. It also takes pressure off individual judgment by graders, especially teaching assistants. But what if, given all this, we were to simply offload grading to rubric-based algorithms or stop grading papers altogether and just concentrate on knowledge in basic pass/fail systems (see earlier note)? These measures are surely even more efficient and more definitive methods of pedagogy, not to mention practices unbiased and unaffected by fatigue or irritation. Such suggestions are often met with silence, presumably because that next step in the logical evolution of post-secondary education would mean that a lot of humans with hard-won doctorates would be put out of work.

30 In the distant past, when I was editor-in-chief of my university's undergraduate newspaper, *The Varsity*, we used technology that had advanced a great distance from old hot-type slugging and letterform setting. And yet, we still had to cut and paste waxed and X-acto trimmed paper columns using steel rulers, which were themselves set up via keyboard on long rolls of pungent photographic stock. The strips were then glued and rolled onto cardboard flats. After the whole edition was completed, we would box and deliver the flats, in the middle of the night, to an offset printing house not far away. And then, if we could stay awake long enough, we would go and have eggs and coffee at a twenty-four-hour diner. The printed tabloid-size issues would arrive in bound parcels by lunchtime the next day. I discuss this now brief and now long-gone period of Gutenberg-Galaxy innovation in Kingwell, "Eric Gill and the Beauty of Character," 55–67.

31 Curtis, "The Skinhead Hamlet."

32 Kingwell, "New and Deteriorated! Why Upgrades Aren't Always Better," F12. My favourite version of the bad improvement – more even than the aluminum baseball bat or New Coke – is the fast zombie. A fast zombie may be

considered a better zombie, but it takes all the drama out of the zombie scenario, in which survival involves smart evasion and tactics as the undead stagger towards you.

33 Rebecca Jennings, "Why Social Media Makes You Feel So Old." The person who described herself as "feeling old" was media consultant Sarah Merrill, who added, "I live on the internet and make memes for a living, but I cannot for the life of me figure out TikTok. I'm like, 'this is where I become irrelevant.'" Making internet memes was probably never going to be a reliable occupation for any human being, and "media" is a plural noun, so that should be "make you feel so old" – said the cranky old person.

34 Harwood, *The Interface*. Harwood's argument in this extraordinary and very beautiful book is that IBM created a comprehensive aesthetic than ran from circuit diagrams and technical drawing to office design, furniture, and even architecture. That is how we must understand the notion of interface: comprehensively and with an expansive, open intelligence.

35 [LF]: HAL had this figured out in Kubrick, *2001*: "Well, I don't think there is any question about it. It can only be attributable to human error. This sort of thing has cropped up before, and it has always been due to human error."

[MK]: Yes, where would lazy crash investigators and bungling senior managers or generals be without "human error"?

CHAPTER FIVE

1 Examples of these fictional legislative dictums include the Registration Acts, the Mutant Registration Act (MRA), the Keene Act, the Superhuman Registration Act (SRA or SHRA), the Sokovia Accords, the Vigilante Registration Act (VRA), and the Underage Superhuman Welfare Act (Kamala's Law).

2 In addition to Haraway's canonical contribution, key texts and thinkers in the literature of trans- and posthumanism include Scott, *The Four-Dimensional Human*; Morton, *Humankind*; Rothblatt, *From Transgender to Transhuman*; Moravec, *Mind Children* and *Robot*.

3 See Choplin, "World-Renowned Philosopher Martha Nussbaum Supports New York Elephant Rights Case."

4 Asimov, *The Caves of Steel*, 125.

5 Ibid., 221.

6 Suits, *The Grasshopper*. Suits's title is a play on the Aesopian fable (373 in the

Perry Index) about the ant who works hard all day and the grasshopper who whiles away his own time in leisure activities.

7 Potter, *Gamesmanship: On the Art of Winning Games Without Actually Cheating* (1947), followed by *Some Notes on Lifemanship* (1950), *One-Upmanship* (1952), *Christmas-ship* (1956), and *Supermanship* (1958). All of these are good, but the first remains the best.

8 The golfer Ian Woosnam, a former Masters Tournament winner, was given this sanction during the British Open, officially known as the Open Championship, in 2001 when an extra fairway wood was noted in his bag by an official. He threw the offending club across the tee and finished four shots behind the leader, David Duval – who, bizarrely, spiralled downward after this important major win and has not been a factor in professional golf since. Golf is a cruel game, in both failure and success. The only exceptions to its demands might be the immortal, god-like figures created by Barnes in *The End of the World in Ten-and-a-Half Chapters*, ch. 10, and the writers of the television series *Lucifer* (developed by Kapinos), who always simply hit one hole in one after another. But is that even fun any more?

9 Didion, *Play It as It Lays*. This might be the place to mention that the often-used expression "lay low" for the ideas of hiding out or avoiding the world should be "lie low," unless the intransitive verb refers to the past. Meanwhile, golfers know that where your ball ends up after a shot is a lie, not a lay. Then you can lay up on a long fairway if that seems tactical, and to lay someone low, lay down the law, or lay down tools (transitive verb) has a necessary relation to a person, thing, statement, or concept.

10 Bostrom, *Superintelligence*, 123. "An AI, designed to manage production in a factory, is given the final goal of maximizing the manufacturing of paperclips, and proceeds by converting first the Earth and then increasingly large chunks of the observable universe into paperclips," Bostrom writes in a sort of mundane yet apocalyptic scenario. As noted earlier, Bostrom has distinguished himself as an expert in philosophically inflected reflection on science-fictional scenarios. I discuss his notions of world-ending danger, or existential risk, in Kingwell, *On Risk*.

11 Marche, "The Imitation of Consciousness."

12 Epstein, *The Intelligence of a Machine*. The IBM system called Watson competed on the quiz show *Jeopardy!* in 2011 and did extremely well against human opponents when the clues were straightforward, using fast reaction

time and brute-force responses. But the game depends on wide-ranging and
sometimes random memory, backed by intuition about how the clues are
phrased. And so Watson was often off base when the clues were contextual
or culturally layered, as they are at the highest levels of this game. Its very
fast data-crunching, which relied on keyword uncoding from within the
clues, was not able to recognize nuances that a natural-language speaker
would see even if they did not know the answer (a subject for further
study perhaps).

The other interesting feature of this experiment was that Watson would
not "buzz in" with a potential answer before having it solidly "in mind," and
human players often would, relying on a small time lag between signalling
their readiness to answer and attempting to do so. The Watson experiment
has been compared to the Deep Blue matches against Garry Kasparov, cited
much earlier, but the analogy is flawed. Even with its massively multiple outcomes, chess is a closed system. There is no frame problem there. When it
comes to succeeding on a television quiz show about random trivia, by
contrast, it's all about some version of the frame problem.

13 [LF]: While the presence of overtly mechanical apparatus on a film set
    (among other features) may lend special plausibility to the identification of
    the cinematic artform as "artificial intelligence," the general idea may apply
    far more broadly than this. See Beardsley, "On the Creation of Art," 291–304.
    Philosopher of art Monroe Beardsley, building on ideas from Dewey and
    Collingwood, proposed that it is the work of art itself that structures and
    guides the creative activities we habitually ascribe to the human artist. "For
    the crucial controlling power at every point is the particular stage or con-
    dition of the unfinished work itself, the possibilities it presents, and the
    developments it permits" (279). Beardsley sums up his lesson as follows:
    "Artistic creation is nothing more than the production of a self-creative
    object" (303). Once we accept Beardsley's claim about artworks, it is a short
    step to extending the point to representational media in general.

    If that is right, then the deep roots of artificial intelligence, of media, and
    hence of posthumanity itself may extend as far back in time as the beginning
    of humanity. After all, our propensity to render our thoughts and dreams in
    external media seems as good a candidate as any for being "the mark of the
    human." Language and other representational technologies have always
    served to condition and extend the narrowly biological capacities of humans

for thinking and being – and those technologies have always been in the relevant sense "self-creative," constituting important loci of intelligence and control independent of the human minds they entangle. Posthumanity may be, paradoxically, a central and defining part of the original human endowment.

[MK]: Yes! One thinks immediately of the cave paintings at Lascaux, and the line of insight that connects them, and every representation in between, to McLuhan's dictum that the medium is the message. Also of Heidegger, even earlier: "The mere object is not the work of art." Does that teach us that we have always been posthuman?

14 Wittgenstein, *Philosophical Investigations*, sec. 201a: "This was our paradox: no course of action could be determined by a rule, because any course of action can be made out to accord with the rule." The insight here is meant to shatter the taken-for-granted picture of rules existing a priori to their being followed, with the following of rules an a posteriori application of them and thus (for some) to undermine the very possibility of reliable rule-following. But an exact or unanimous interpretation of Wittgenstein's enigmatic treatment of the paradox has not been forthcoming. See, among others, Wright, "Rule-Following without Reasons," 481–502; McDowell, "Wittgenstein on Following a Rule," 325–63; Pears, "Wittgenstein's Account of Rule-Following," 273–83; and Kripke, *Wittgenstein on Rules and Private Language*.

15 See Clark, *Natural-Born Cyborgs*. Clark, a philosopher and cognitive scientist, offers in this book a lively and accessible account of human–posthuman fusion as a viable (and inevitable) pathway to future insight about consciousness. A good public-facing summary is MacFarquar, "The Mind-Expanding Ideas of Andy Clark."

16 McLuhan, *Understanding Media*, 46.

17 Roose, *Futureproof*. The book has been, predictably, a brisk seller.

18 See, for example, Brooks, "The Terrifying Future of the American Right." This on-site assessment of the US Republican National Conservatism Conference contains many suggestive ironies, among them the fact that the young delegates, all decrying tech-creep because of its left-wing bias (really?), spent most of their time looking at their phones rather than listening to the featured speakers. I wonder how Marco Rubio and Ted Cruz felt about that? Hey everybody – notorious unpopular politician over here,

saying apocalyptic things about far-Left threats to democracy, which he hopes you will like!

One issue Brooks does not raise, given his focus on the Right's preoccupation with tech politics rather than tech profits, is that North American competition law is drastically outdated when it comes to the de facto monopoly or uneasy compact of tech giants, just as existing speech regulation is inadequate to the floods of social media activity (the two issues are of course related). Europe is ahead of the global curve here, having enacted expansive privacy and anti-trust laws to limit the excursions of dominating corporations feeding on the ubiquitous attention economy. I have more to say about these issues in Kingwell, *Wish I Were Here*.

19 Ovide, "Big Tech Has Outgrown This Planet." Ovide was moved to abandon the Gray Lady style guide when she wrote her lede for this article: "The already bonkers dollars of Big Tech have become even bonkers-er." A few other highlights from the numbers:

1 Amazon's stock price increases have made Jeff Bezos so rich that he could buy a new model iPhone for 200 million people – and he would still be a billionaire.

2 The annual revenue of one of Microsoft's side businesses, LinkedIn, is nearly four times that of Zoom Video Communications, a star of the pandemic, in the past year.

3 Facebook expects to dole out more cash outfitting its computer hubs and offices in 2021 than Exxon spends around the world to dig oil and gas out of the ground in a year.

4 Between late 2020 and early 2021, Amazon's e-commerce revenue still climbed by $109 billion – an increase in a single year that Walmart needed the past nine years to reach.

20 Kingwell, *Wish I Were Here*. Once more, I discuss the potentially addictive qualities of media-tech immersion and the desirability of resistance. Boredom, the central topic of that book, is the symptom of and the occasion for analyzing the deep pathologies of our current cyberflesh condition. Can we imagine a more benign, and more just, form of co-existence with technology and our own desires? If not, the game veers quickly towards self-defeat; short-term utopia, in the form of apps and upgrades, swiftly grows apocalyptic. The fetching worlds of Big Tech seem to exist costlessly, in the

ether or cloud, but they have both real-world material bases (overheated servers, bureaucratically immiserated labour forces) and knock-on effects (environmental degradation, unstable economic inequality, dangerous concentration of socio-economic power).

21 Worth noting here is that Kelly first coined the phrase for a 1970 anti-pollution Earth Day poster, then used it again the following Earth Day.

22 Cronenberg, *Videodrome*. In the film, the television journalist played by James Woods watches in horror as his body is transformed by exposure to a rogue satellite feed of violent televised images. A creepy guru professor, Dr O'Blivion, seems to be the mastermind behind this evolutionary experiment; he exists entirely on stored VHS tapes of ponderous monologues (yay 1983!). See also Jolliffe, "Long Live the New Flesh: Why Videodrome Has Never Been More Relevant." One of the many things I like about this film is that the city of Toronto, so often repurposed by directors to be New York or Chicago or Boston, here plays itself. Cronenberg did the same thing with his uncanny masterpiece *Dead Ringers*, starring Jeremy Irons and Jeremy Irons as creepy twin gynecologists Elliot and Beverly Mantle.

23 Perhaps ironically it was my liver, in what turned out to be the first of two transplants performed within a five-month period (a biotech cyborg story whose details are probably best left to another time, style, and venue). The liver, corporeal seat of life, soul, and intelligence in Ancient Greek belief, is what we today might label mind, consciousness, or selfhood. We might then localize some or all of those functions rather to the heart, if we are roman-tics, or to the brain if we incline to science. But because the liver alone among major organs can regenerate itself, it has also been long considered the organic portal to human immortality. Not for nothing did Zeus choose to torture Prometheus, whose fire-stealing hubris had offended him, by hav-ing the devious Titan chained to a rock in the Caucasus Mountains with his liver torn at daily by a bird of prey. Fire is not the real issue here; arrogance is. We have noted several times already how Prometheus, demi-god of fore-thought and problem-solving, has at least since Mary Shelley's 1818 novel *Frankenstein* figured as a personification of technology run amok. Be careful what you wish for!

24 I take this opportunity to express my sincere gratitude to the many dedi-cated professionals of the University Health Network of Toronto, especially

the doctors, nurses, technicians, and staff at St Michael's Hospital and Toronto General Hospital, for their exceptional care and dedication. Special thanks to Dr Blayne Sayed, Dr Cynthia Tsien, and transplant coordinator Shauna Watson RN.

25 Kingwell, *In Pursuit of Happiness.*

Bibliography

Adams, Tim. "Artificial Intelligence: 'We're Like Children Playing with a Bomb.'" *The Guardian*, 12 June 2016.

Agamben, Giorgio. *Homo Sacer: Sovereign Power and Bare Life*. Translated by Daniel Heller-Roazen. Stanford: Stanford University Press, 1998.

Alexeev, Vladimir. "Motherboard Issues." *Harper's Magazine*, October 2020, 17–18.

Anderson, Hephzibah. "The Great Writers Forgotten by History." *BBC.com* (10 October 2017).

Appleby, Joyce. *Inheriting the Revolution*. Cambridge, MA: Harvard University Press, 2000.

Arendt, Hannah. *The Human Condition*. 2nd ed. Chicago: University of Chicago Press, 2018.

Asimov, Isaac. *The Caves of Steel*. New York: Bantam, 1982. First published 1954 by Doubleday (New York).

– *I, Robot*. New York: Gnome Press, 1950.

Austin, J.L. *How to Do Things with Words*. Oxford: Clarendon Press, 1962.

Baars, Bernard. *In the Theater of Consciousness: The Workspace of the Mind*. Oxford: Oxford University Press, 2001.

Banting, Madeleine. *Willing Slaves: How the Overwork Culture Is Ruling Our Lives*. New York: Harper Perennial, 2004.

Barnes, Julian. *The End of the World in Ten-and-a-Half Chapters*. London: Jonathan Cape, 1989.

Bazin, André. "The Ontology of the Photographic Image." In *What Is Cinema?* Volume 1, translated by Hugh Gray. Berkeley: University of California Press, 1967.

Beardsley, Monroe. "On the Creation of Art." *Journal of Aesthetics and Art Criticism* 23, no. 3 (1965): 291–304.

Benjamin, Ruha. *Race After Technology*. Cambridge: Polity Press, 2019.

Benjamin, Walter. "Theses on the Philosophy of History" [Über den Begriff der Geschichte]. In *Illuminations: Essays and Reflections*, edited by Hannah Arendt, translated by Harry Zohn. New York: Schocken Books, 1968.

– "The Work of Art in the Age of its Technological Reproducibility." In *The Work of Art in the Age of Its Technological Reproducibility and Other Writings on Media*, edited by Michael William Jennings. Cambridge, MA: Belknap Press, 2008. https://doi.org/10.2307/j.ctv1nzfgns.6.

Berberoglu, Berch. ed. *The Global Rise of Authoritarianism in the 21st Century: Crisis of Neoliberal Globalization and the Nationalist Response*. New York and London: Routledge, 2021.

Bergman, Ingmar, dir. *The Seventh Seal*. Sweden: SF Studios, 1957.

Berlin, Isaiah. *Against the Current: Essays in the History of Ideas*. New York: Viking, 1980.

Boden, Margaret A. *Artificial Intelligence: A Very Short Introduction*. Oxford: Oxford University Press, 2018.

Bookchin, Murray. *Post-Scarcity Anarchism*. Chico, CA: AK Press, 2004.

Bostrom, Nick. "A History of Transhumanist Thought." *Journal of Evolution and Technology / WTA* 14, no. 1 (2005): 1–25.

– *Superintelligence: Paths, Dangers, Strategies*. Oxford: Oxford University Press, 2014.

– "Transhumanist Values." *Journal of Philosophical Research* 30 (2005): 3–14.

Bourdieu, Pierre. *Distinction: A Social Critique of the Judgment of Taste*. London: Routledge, 2010.

Breland, Ali. "Woke AI Won't Save Us." *Logic Magazine*, 3 August 2019.

Brockman, John, ed. *Possible Minds: Twenty-Five Ways of Looking at AI*. New York: Penguin, 2020.

Brooks, David. "The Terrifying Future of the American Right." *Atlantic*, 19 November 2021.

Brown, Dalvin Brown. "AI Chat Bots Can Bring You Back from the Dead, Sort Of." *Washington Post*, 4 February 2021.

Butler, Octavia Butler. *Parable of the Sower*. New York: Grand Central Publishing, 2000.

Camp, Elisabeth. "Thinking with Maps." *Philosophical Perspectives* 21, no. 1 (2007): 145–82.

Carroll, Noël. "Narrative Closure." *Philosophical Studies* 135, no. 1 (2007): 1–15.

Carruthers, Peter. *Human and Animals Minds: The Consciousness Question Laid to Rest*. Oxford: Oxford University Press, 2019.

Cassella, Carly. "125-Year Study of Chess Matches Suggests We Don't Peak at the Game Until Our 30s." *Science Alert*, 24 October 2020.

Cavell, Stanley. *The World Viewed: Reflections on the Ontology of Film*. Cambridge, MA: Harvard University Press, 1971.

Cellan-Jones, Rory. "Stephen Hawking Warns Artificial Intelligence Could End Mankind." BBC *News*, 2 December 2014. https://www.bbc.com/news/tech nology-30290540.

Chalmers, David. *The Conscious Mind: In Search of a Fundamental Theory*. New York: Oxford University Press, 1997.

– "Facing Up to the Problem of Consciousness." *Journal of Consciousness Studies* 2, no. 3 (1995): 200–19.

Chellani, Yash. "A Deep Dive Into Replika: My AI Friend." MUO, 1 January 2021, www.makeuseof.com/how-does-replika-chatbot-work/.

Chomsky, Noam. *Aspects of the Theory of Syntax*. Cambridge, MA: MIT Press, 1965.

– *Knowledge of Language: Its Nature, Origin, and Use*. New York: Praeger, 1986.

Choplin, Lauren. "World-Renowned Philosopher Martha Nussbaum Supports New York Elephant Rights Case." *Nonhuman Rights*, 24 August 2021.

Christian, Brian. *The Alignment Problem: Machine Learning and Human Values*. New York: W.W. Norton, 2020.

Chu, Seo-Young. *Do Metaphors Dream of Literal Sleep? A Science-Fictional Theory of Representation*. Cambridge, MA: Harvard University Press, 2010.

Churchland, Patricia. *Neurophilosophy: Toward a Unified Science of the Mind-Brain*. New York: Bradford Books, 1989.

Clark, Andy. *Natural-Born Cyborgs: Minds, Technologies, and the Future of Human Intelligence*. Oxford: Oxford University Press, 2003.

Clarke, Arthur C. "Hazards of Prophecy: The Failure of Imagination." In *Profiles of the Future: An Enquiry into the Limits of the Possible*. New York: Phoenix-Orion, 1962.

Collins, Randall. *The Sociology of Philosophies: A Global Theory of Intellectual Change*. Cambridge, MA: Harvard University Press, 2000. https://doi.org/10. 1177/004839310003000201.

Cook, Ian. "Who Is Driving the Great Resignation?" *Harvard Business Review*, 15 September 2021.

Coupland, Douglas. "Generation X at 30: Generational Trashing Is Eternal." *The Guardian*, 19 June 2021.

Crawford, Kate. *Atlas of AI: Power, Politics, and the Planetary Costs of Artificial Intelligence*. New Haven: Yale University Press, 2021. https://doi.org/10.2307/j.ctv1ghv45t.

Crawford, Matthew. *Shop Class as Soulcraft: An Inquiry into the Value of Work*. New York: Penguin, 2009.

Croes, Emmelyn A., and Marjolijn L. Antheunis. "Can We Be Friends with Mitsuku? A Longitudinal Study on the Process of Relationship Formation between Humans and a Social Chatbot." *Journal of Social and Personal Relationships* 38, no. 1 (2020): 279–300.

Cronenberg, David. *Dead Ringers*. Montreal: Astral Films/Los Angeles: 20th Century Studios, 1988.

– *Videodrome*. Universal City: Universal Pictures, 1983.

Curtis, Richard. "The Skinhead Hamlet." In *The Faber Book of Parodies*, edited by Simon Brett. London: Faber and Faber, 1984. Also published by the University of Toronto Engineering Society undergraduate newspaper, *Toike Oike*, https://archive.org/stream/toikeoike_19890904/toikeoike_19890904_djvu.txt.

Danaher, John. "The Philosophical Case for Robot Friendship." *Journal of Posthuman Studies* 3, no. 1 (2019): 5–24.

Daniels, Norman. "Wide Reflective Equilibrium and Theory Acceptance in Ethics." *Journal of Philosophy* 76, no. 5 (1979): 256–82.

Darling, Kate. *The New Breed: What Our History with Animals Reveals about Our Future with Robots*. New York: Henry Holt, 2021.

de Botton, Alain. *The Pleasures and Sorrows of Work*. New York: Penguin, 2009.

De Graaf, Maartje M. "An Ethical Evaluation of Human-Robot Relationships." *International Journal of Social Robotics* 8, no. 4 (201): 589–98.

Debord, Guy. *Society of the Spectacle [La societé du spectacle]*. Detroit: Black & Red, 1983, sec. V:126. First published 1967.

Dee, Jonathan. *The Privileges*. New York: Random House, 2010.

Deleuze, Gilles. *Difference and Repetition*. Translated by Paul Patton. New York: Columbia University Press, 1994.

– "Postscript on the Societies of Control." In *Negotiations*, translated by Martin Joughin. New York: Columbia University Press, 1992.

Dennett, Daniel. *Brainchildren*. Cambridge, MA: MIT Press, 1998.

– *Consciousness Explained*. Boston: Little, Brown, 1991.

– *Content and Consciousness*. New York: Routledge, 1986.

Descartes, René. *Meditations on First Philosophy: With Selections from the Objections and Replies*. Translated by Michael Moriarty. Oxford: Oxford University Press, 2008.

Dick, Philip K. *Do Androids Dream of Electric Sheep?* New York: Doubleday, 1968.

Didion, Joan. *Play It as It Lays*. New York: Farrar, Straus, and Giroux, 1970.

Dietrich, Eric, Chris Fields, John P. Sullins, Bram Van Heuvelen, and Robin Zebrowski, eds. *Great Philosophical Objections to Artificial Intelligence: The History and Legacy of the AI Wars*. New York: Bloomsbury, 2021. https://doi.org/10.5040/9781474257084.

Docter, Pete, and Ronnie del Carmen, dir. *Inside Out*. 2015. California: Disney/Pixar.

Donaldson, Sue, and Will Kymlicka. *Zoopolis: A Political Theory of Animal Rights*. Oxford: Oxford University Press, 2013.

Dreyfus, Herbert. *Alchemy and AI*. Santa Monica, CA: RAND Corporation, 1965.

– *Mind over Machine*. Oxford: Blackwell, 1986.

– *What Computers Can't Do*. Cambridge, MA: MIT Press, 1972.

Dunch, Jonah. "It's Time for Canadian Universities to Go Gradeless." *Maclean's*, 2 December 2020.

Eagleton, Terry. *Culture and the Death of God*. New Haven: Yale University Press, 2015.

Ellul, Jacques. *The Technological Society*. New York: Vintage, 1964.

Epstein, Jean. *The Intelligence of a Machine*. Minneapolis: University of Minnesota Press, 2014.

Ferrari, G.R.F. *Listening to the Cicadas*. Cambridge: Cambridge University Press, 1987.

Fincher, David, dir. *The Social Network*. Culver City, California: Sony Pictures, 2010.

Fingarette, Herbert. "Insanity and Responsibility." *Inquiry* 15, no. 1–4 (1972): 6–29.

Fisher, Mark. *The Weird and the Eerie*. London: Repeater Books, 2017.

Flanagan, Owen. "Question Mark and the Mysterians." In *The Science of the Mind*. Cambridge, MA: MIT Press, 1991.

Fodor, Jerry. *Modularity of Mind: An Essay on Faculty Psychology*. Cambridge, MA: MIT Press, 1983. https://doi.org/10.7551/mitpress/4737.001.0001.

– *The Mind Doesn't Work That Way*. Cambridge, MA: MIT Press, 2000.

Foucault, Michel. *Discipline and Punish: The Birth of the Modern Prison*. Translated by David Hurley. New York: Vintage, 1977.

Fowler, Christopher. *The Book of Forgotten Authors*. Chicago: IPG/Riverrun, 2017.

Fox, Michael V. "On Footnotes." *Hebrew Studies* 28 (1987): 6–8.

Frankfurt, Harry. *The Importance of What We Care About: Philosophical Essays*. Cambridge: Cambridge University Press, 1988.

– *On Bullshit*. Princeton: Princeton University Press, 2005.

Frankish, Keith. *Tricks of the Mind*. London: Imprint Academic, 2017.

Freud, Sigmund. *The Uncanny*. Translated by Hugh Haughton. Harmondsworth: Penguin Classics, 2003.

Frischmann, Brett, and Evan Selinger. *Re-Engineering Humanity*. Cambridge: Cambridge University Press, 2018.

Fuller, Steve. *Humanity 2.0: What It Means to Be Human Past, Present, and Future*. London: Palgrave Macmillan, 2011. https://doi.org/10.1057/9780230316720.

Galbraith, John Kenneth. *The Affluent Society*. New York: Houghton Mifflin, 1958.

Gallistel, Charles Randy. *Memory and the Computational Brain: Why Cognitive Science Will Transform Neuroscience*. New York: Wiley, 2009. https://doi.org/10.1002/9781444310498.

– "Prelinguistic Thought." *Language Learning and Development* 7, no. 4 (2011): 253–63.

Gass, William H. *Tests of Time: Essays*. Chicago: University of Chicago Press, 2003.

Gauthier, David. *Morals by Agreement*. Oxford: Clarendon Press, 1986.

Giamatti, A. Bartlett. *Take Time for Paradise: Americans and Their Games*. New York: Summit Books, 1989.

Gibson, William. *Distrust That Particular Flavor*. New York: G.P. Putnam's Sons, 2012.

– "Interview." *Economist*, 4 December 2003.

Glenn, Joshua, and Mark Kingwell. *The Adventurer's Glossary*. Montreal and Kingston: McGill-Queen's University Press, 2021.

– *The Idler's Glossary*. Windsor, ON: Biblioasis, 2011.

– *The Wage-Slave's Glossary*. Windsor, ON: Biblioasis, 2011.

Godfrey-Smith, Peter. *Other Minds: The Octopus, the Sea, and the Deep Origins of Consciousness*. New York: Farrar, Straus & Giroux, 2016.

Goffman, Erving. *The Presentation of Self in Everyday Life*. New York: Anchor Books, 1959.

GPT-3. "A Robot Wrote This Entire Article. Are You Scared Yet, Human?" *The Guardian*, 8 September 2020.

Gray, John. *Straw Dogs: Thoughts on Humans and Other Animals*. London: Granta Books, 2003.

Grice, H.P. *Studies in the Way of Words*. Cambridge, MA: Harvard University Press, 1989.

Haraway, Donna. "A Manifesto for Cyborgs: Science, Technology, and Socialist Feminism in the 1980s." In *Feminism, Postmodernism*, edited by Linda Nicolson. New York: Routledge, 1990.

Harwood, John. *The Interface: IBM and the Transformation of Corporate Design 1945–1976*. Minneapolis, London: University of Minnesota Press, 2011. https://doi.org/10.5749/minnesota/9780816670390.001.0001.

Hayward, Tim. *Constitutional Environmental Rights*. Oxford: Oxford University Press, 2004.

Hegel, G.W.F. *The Science of Logic*. Translated by George di Giovanni. New York: Cambridge University Press, 2010.

Heidegger, Martin. "The Age of the World Picture." In *The Question Concerning Technology and Other Essays*, translated by William Lovitt. New York: Harper & Row, 1977. https://doi.org/10.1007/978-1-349-25249-7_3.

– *Being and Time*. Translated by John Macquarrie and Edward Robinson. New York: St Martin's Press, 1962.

– "Building, Dwelling, Acting." In *Architecture, Ethics and Globalization*, edited by Graham Owen. New York: Routledge, 2009.

– "Building, Dwelling, Thinking." In *Poetry, Language, Thought*, translated by Albert Hofstadter. New York: Harper, 2013.

– *The Ethics of Architecture*. New York and Oxford: Oxford University Press, 2021.

– "The Question Concerning Technology." In *The Question Concerning Technology and Other Essays*, translated by William Lovitt. 1977.

Heikkilä, Melissa. "How to Build a Woke AI." *Politico*, 17 March 2020. https://www.politico.eu/article/woke-artificial-intelligence-racial-misidentification-gender-bias/.

Herle, David. "The Spectators." *Policy Options* (November 2012): 19–20.

Hobbes, Thomas. *Leviathan: With Selected Variants from the Latin Edition of 1688*, edited by E. M. Curley. Indianapolis: Hackett Pub. Co., 1994.

Hodge, Roger D. *The Mendacity of Hope*. New York: HarperCollins, 2010.

Hoel, Erik. "I Got an Artificial Intelligence to Write My Novel." *Electric Literature* (10 June 2021).

— "The Semantic Apocalypse: How Meaning Is Draining Away in the Age of AI." *Intrinsic Perspective*, 18 April 2021.

Hutton, Noah. "The Fading Dream of the Computer Brain." *Scientific American*, 29 April 2021.

Invisible Committee. *The Coming Insurrection*. Translated by Anonymous. New York: Semiotext(e), 2009.

Ishiguro, Kazuo. *Klara and the Sun*. New York: Knopf, 2021.

Jecker, Nancy S. "You've Got a Friend in Me: Sociable Robots for Older Adults in an Age of Global Pandemics." *Ethics and Information Technology* 23, no. S1 (2020): 35–43. doi:10.1007/s10676-020-09546-y.

Jennings, Rebecca. "Why Social Media Makes You Feel So Old." *Vox*, 15 October 2020. https://www.vox.com/the-goods/21514295/feeling-old-social-media-instagram-tiktok.

Jentsch, Ernst. "On the Psychology of the Uncanny (1906)." *Angelaki: Journal of the Theoretical Humanities* 2, no. 1 (1997): 7–16.

Jolliffe, Tom. "Long Live the New Flesh: Why *Videodrome* Has Never Been More Relevant." *Flickering Myth*, 1 May 2020.

Kant, Immanuel. *Groundwork of the Metaphysics of Morals*. Edited by Mary J. Gregor. New York: Cambridge University Press, 1998.

Kapinos, Tom, developer. *Lucifer*. New York: Fox, Seasons 1–3; California: Netflix, Seasons 4–6.

Kasparov, Garry. *Deep Thinking: Where Machine Intelligence Ends and Human Creativity Begins*. New York: Public Affairs, 2017.

— *How Life Imitates Chess: Making the Right Moves from the Board to the Boardroom*. London: Bloomsbury, 2007.

Kearns, Michael, and Aaron Roth. *The Ethical Algorithm*. New York: Oxford University Press, 2019.

Kelley, Walt. "A Word to the Fore." In *The Pogo Papers*. New York: Simon & Schuster, 1953.

Kennedy, Pagan. "William Gibson's Future Is Now." *New York Times*, 13 January 2012.

Kingwell, Mark. "Are Sentient AIs Persons?" In *The Oxford Handbook of Ethics of AI*, edited by Markus Dubber, Frank Pasquale, and Sunit Das, 313–29. New York: Oxford University Press, 2020.

– "Beyond the Uncanny Valley of the Dolls." *Descant* 42, no. 1 (Spring 2011): 186–98.
– "Do Sentient AIs Have Rights? If So, What Kind?" In *Intelligence and Fundamental Rights*, edited by Claes Granmar, Katarina Fast Lappalainen, and Christine Storr, 35–54. Stockholm: Stockholm University, 2020.
– "Eric Gill and the Beauty of Character." *Descant* 26, no. 3 (Fall 1995): 55–67. Also in *Marginalia: A Cultural Reader*, 239–53. Toronto: Penguin, 1999.
– "Frank's Motel: Horizontal and Vertical in the Big Other." In *The Ends of History: Questioning the Stakes of Historical Reason*, edited by Joshua Nichols and Amy Swiffen, 103–26. New York: Routledge, 2013.
– "Human All Too Human." *LA + Vitality*, Spring 2020, 50–5.
– "Idling Toward Heaven: The Last Defence You Will Ever Need." Introduction to *The Idler's Glossary*, by Joshua Glenn and Mark Kingwell. Windsor, ON: Biblioasis, 2008.
– *In Pursuit of Happiness: Better Living from Plato to Prozac*. New York: Crown, 2000.
– "Is It Rational to Be Polite." *Journal of Philosophy* 90, no. 8 (August 1993): 387–404.
– "Madpeople and Ideologues: An Issue for Dialogic Justice Theory." *International Philosophical Quarterly* 34, no. 1 (1994): 59–73.
– *Nach der Arbeit*. Translated by Thorsten Schmidt. Berlin: Nicolai Verlag, 2018.
– *Nearest Thing to Heaven: The Empire State Building and Americans Dreams*. New Haven: Yale University Press, 2006.
– "New and Deteriorated! Why Upgrades Aren't Always Better." *Globe and Mail*, 15 September 2007, F12. Reprinted as "Bad Improvements." In *From Discord to Discourse: A Collection of Contemporary Canadian Essays*, edited by Danielle Desjardins-Koloff, Lisa Loughlin, and Ann Varty, 54–7. Toronto: McGraw-Hill Ryerson, 2011.
– "Of an Age." *Literary Review of Canada*, November 2021.
– *On Risk*. Windsor, ON: Biblioasis, 2020.
– "What Is Community?" *LA+ Community*, Spring 2021, 6–11.
– *Wish I Were Here: Boredom and the Interface*. Montreal and Kingston: McGill-Queen's University Press, 2019.
– "The Work Idea: Wage Slavery, Bullshit, and the Good Infinite." In *The Economy as Cultural System: Theory, Capitalism, Crisis*, edited by Todd Dufresne and Clara Sacchetti, 127–40. New York: Bloomsbury, 2013.
Kirk, Robert. "Zombies." *Stanford Encyclopedia of Philosophy*, 21 (March 2019).

Kirkland, Mark, dir. *The Simpsons*. Season 31, episode 11, "Hail to the Teeth." Aired 5 January 2020 on Fox.

Kissinger, Henry, Eric Schmidt, and Daniel Huttenlocher. *The Age of AI: And Our Human Future*. Boston: Little, Brown, 2021.

Koolhaas, Rem. *Delirious New York: A Retroactive Manifesto for Manhattan*. New York: Monacelli, 1974.

Krauss, Lawrence, and William Lane Craig. *William Lane Craig Q&A*. Australian Broadcasting Corporation, February 2013.

Kripke, Saul. *Wittgenstein on Rules and Private Language*. Cambridge, MA: Harvard University Press, 1982.

Kristeva, Julia. *Powers of Horror: An Essay on Abjection*. New York: Columbia University Press, 1982.

Kubrick, Stanley, dir. *2001: A Space Odyssey*. Beverly Hills, CA: Metro-Goldwyn-Mayer, 1968.

Kurzweil, Ray. *The Singularity Is Near: When Humans Transcend Biology*. New York: Viking, 2005.

Kymlicka, Will. *Liberalism, Community, and Culture*. Oxford: Oxford University Press, 1989.

– *Multicultural Citizenship: A Liberal Theory of Minority Rights*. Oxford: Oxford University Press, 1995.

Leckie, Ann. *Imperial Radch Trilogy*. London: Orbit Books, 2013–15.

Lee, Christopher J. *Jet Lag*. London: Bloomsbury, 2017.

Lee, Kai-Fu, and Quifan Chen. *AI 2041: Ten Visions for Our Future*. New York: Currency Books, 2021.

Lehmann, Chris. *Rich People Stuff*. New York: OR Books, 2010.

Lerner, Ben. "Damage Control: The Modern Art World's Tyranny of Price." *Harper's Magazine*, December 2013, 43–9.

Lethem, Jonathan. *Gun, with Occasional Music*. Boston: Mariner Books, 2003.

Locke, John. *Two Treatises of Government*. Edited by Peter Laslett. Cambridge: Cambridge University Press, 1988.

Lurie, Rod, dir. *Straw Dogs*. Amazon Prime, 2011.

Lynch, David, dir. *Blue Velvet*. North Carolina: De Laurentiis, 1986.

MacFarquar, Larissa. "The Mind-Expanding Ideas of Andy Clark." *New Yorker*, 26 March 2018.

Maier, Corinne. *Bonjour Laziness*. Translated by Greg Moss. New York: Orion, 2005.

– *No Kids: Forty Good Reasons Not to Have Children*. New York: Emblem, 2009.

Marche, Stephen. "The Computers Are Getting Better at Writing." *New Yorker*, 30 April 2021.

– "The Imitation of Consciousness: On the Present and Future of Natural Language Processing." *Literary Hub*, 23 June 2021.

Marcus, Ezra. "A Guide to Neopronouns." *New York Times*, 8 April 2021.

Marcuse, Herbert. *One-Dimensional Man*. Translated by Andy Blunden. New York: Ark, 1964.

Marx, Karl, and Friedrich Engels. *Collected Works*. New York and London: International Publishers, 1975.

Mayor, Adrienne. *Gods and Robots: Myths, Machines, and Ancient Dreams of Technology*. Princeton: Princeton University Press, 2018.

McDowell, John. "Wittgenstein on Following a Rule." *Synthese* 58, no. 3 (1984): 325–63.

McEwan, Ian. *Machines Like Me*. London: Jonathan Cape, 2019.

McGinn, Colin. "All Machine and No Ghost." *New Statesman*, 20 February 2012.

– "Can We Solve the Mind-Body Problem?" *Mind* 98 (391): 349–66.

McLuhan, Marshall. *Understanding Media: The Extensions of Man*. New York: McGraw-Hill, 1964.

Menabrea, L.F. "Notions sur la machine analytique de M. Charles Babbage." In *Bibliothèque Universelle de Genève* 41: 352–76. Translation by Augusta Ada Lovelace in Taylor, *Scientific Memoirs*, 3. http://www.fourmilab.ch/babbage/sketch.html.

Michels, Robert. *Political Parties: A Sociological Study of the Oligarchical Tendencies of Modern Democracy*. Translated by Eden Paul and Cedar Paul. New York: Free Press, 1915.

Miller, Julie. "The Queen's Gambit: A Chess Champion on Netflix's Addictive Hit." In *Vanity Fair*, 5 November 2020.

Moore, John. "Moore's Laws of Bureaucracy." *tinyvital*, 15 October 2000. http://www.tinyvital.com/Misc/Lawsburo.htm.

Moore, Ronald D, developer. *Battlestar Galactica*. Universal City, CA: NBC, 2004–09.

Moravec, Hans. *Mind Children: The Future of Robot and Human Intelligence*. Cambridge, MA: Harvard University Press, 1990.

– *Robot: Mere Machine to Transcendent Mind*. New York: Oxford University Press, 1998.

Mori, Masahiro. *The Uncanny Valley*. Translated by MacDorman and Kageki, *IEEE Spectrum* (12 June 2012). First published in *Energy*, 1970.

Morton, Timothy. *Humankind: Solidarity with Nonhuman People*. Read by Liam Gerrard. Audible, 2018.

Mulhall, Stephen. *On Film*. London: Routledge, 2016.

Mumford, Lewis. *Technics and Civilization*. Chicago: University of Chicago Press, 2010.

Nagel, Thomas. "What Is It Like to Be a Bat." *Philosophical Review* 83, no. 4 (1974): 435–50.

Natanson, Maurice, and Edmund Husserl. *Philosopher of Infinite Tasks*. Evanston: Northwestern University Press, 1974.

Onstad, Katrina. *The Weekend Effect: The Life-Changing Benefits of Taking Time Off and Challenging the Cult of Overwork*. New York: HarperCollins, 2017.

Ornes, Stephen. "Playing Hide-and-Seek, Machines Invent New Tools." *Quanta Magazine*, 18 November 2019.

Ovide, Shira. "Big Tech Has Outgrown This Planet." *The New York Times*, 29 July 2021.

Parkinson, C. Northcote. "Parkinson's Law." *The Economist*, November 1955.

Pasquale, Frank. *New Laws of Robotics: Defending Human Expertise in the Age of AI*. Cambridge, MA: Harvard University Press, 2020. https://doi.org/10.4159/9780674250062.

Pears, David. "Wittgenstein's Account of Rule-Following." *Synthese* 87, no. 2 (1991): 273–83.

Peckinpah, Sam, dir. *Straw Dogs*. Burbank, CA: American Broadcasting Company (ABC), 1971.

Perdue, Noelle. "Chatbots and the Loneliness Epidemic: When AI Is More than Just a Friend." *Input*, 2 January 2021, www.inputmag.com/features/chatbots-and-the-loneliness-epidemic-when-ai-harmony-realdoll-replika-is-more-than-just-a-friend.

Peters, Christine Reeh. "Machine Thinking, Thinking Machine: Considerations on Film as Artificial Intelligence." In *Questioning the Oneness of Philosophy*, edited by José Miranda Justo, Paulo Alexandre Lima, Fernando F.M. Silva, Helena Leuschner, Miguel Novais Rodrigues, and Sara Eckerson, 113–26. Lisbon: Centre for Philosophy at the University of Lisbon, 2018.

Pierce, Harlin. "How We're Channeling 'The Queen's Gambit' in Prison." *Daily Beast*, 13 February 2021.

Slings, S.R. *Platonis rempublicam*. Oxford: Oxford University Press, 2003.

Porra, Jaana. "'Can Computer Based Human-Likeness Endanger Humanness?': A Philosophical and Ethical Perspective on Digital Assistants Expressing Feelings They Can't Have." *Information Systems Frontiers* 22, no. 3 (2019): 533–47.

Potter, Stephen. *Christmas-ship, Or, the Art of Giving and Receiving*. London: Hart Press, 1956.

– *Lifemanship: Or, the Art of Getting Away with It without Being an Absolute Plonk*. New York: Henry Holt and Company, 1950.

– *One-Upmanship: Being Some Account of the Activities and Teaching of the Lifemanship Correspondence College of One-upness and Gameslifemastery*. New York: Henry Holt and Company, 1952.

– *Stephen Potter on Supermanship*. New York: Random House, 1959.

– *The Theory and Practice of Gamesmanship: Or, The Art of Winning Games without Actually Cheating*. New York: Henry Holt and Company, 1948.

Pournelle, Jerry. "The Iron Law of Bureaucracy." *Chaos Manor*, 11 September 2010. https://www.jerrypournelle.com/reports/jerryp/iron.html.

Proyas, Alex, dir. *I, Robot*. California: Twentieth-Century Fox, 2004.

Quine, W.V.O. *Word and Object*. Cambridge, MA: MIT Press, 1964.

Rawls, John. *A Theory of Justice*. Cambridge, MA: Belknap Press, 1971.

Rée, Jonathan. *Philosophical Tales: An Essay on Philosophy*. London: Routledge, 1988.

Rhee, Jennifer. *The Robotic Imaginary: The Human and the Price of Dehumanized Labor*. Minneapolis: University of Minnesota Press, 2018. https://doi.org/10.5749/j.ctv62hh4x.

Robertson, Geoffrey. *Crimes Against Humanity: The Struggle for Global Justice*. New York: The New Press, 2007.

Robertson, Jennifer. *Robo Sapiens Japanicus: Robots, Gender, Family, and the Japanese Nation*. Berkeley: University of California Press, 2018.

Roose, Kevin. *Futureproof: 9 Rules for Humans in the Age of Automation*. New York: Random House, 2021.

Rosner, Helen. "A Haunting New Documentary about Anthony Bourdain." *The New Yorker*, 15 July 2021.

Ross, Andrew. *Nice Work If You Can Get It: Life and Labor in Precarious Times*. New York: New York University Press, 2009.

Rothbard, Murray N. "Bureaucracy and the Civil Service in the United States." *Journal of Libertarian Studies* 11, no. 2: 3–75.

Rothblatt, Martine. *From Transgender to Transhuman: A Manifesto on the Freedom of Form.* Self-published, 2011.

– *Virtually Human: The Promise and the Peril of Digital Immortality.* New York: St Martin's Press, 2014.

Rousseau, Jean-Jacques. *The Social Contract and Other Later Political Writings.* Edited and translated by Victor Gourevitch. Cambridge: Cambridge University Press, 1997.

Rushkoff, Douglas. *Present Shock: When Everything Happens Now.* New York: Penguin, 2013.

Russell, Bertrand. *In Praise of Idleness and Other Essays.* 1932. Rev. ed. London: Routledge, 2004.

Ryan, Mark. "In AI We Trust: Ethics, Artificial Intelligence, and Reliability." *Sci. Eng. Ethics* 26, (2020): 2749–67.

Rybczynski, Witold. *Waiting for the Weekend.* New York: Viking, 1991.

Ryland, Helen. "It's Friendship, Jim, but Not as We Know It: A Degrees-of-Friendship View of Human-Robot Friendships." *Minds and Machines* 31, 377–93.

Ryle, Gilbert. *The Concept of Mind.* London, New York: Hutchinson's University Library, 1949.

Sabinasz, Daniel. "Why the Chinese Room Argument Is Flawed." *sabinasz.net,* 3 September 2017. https://www.sabinasz.net/why-chinese-room-argument-flawed/.

Sampson, Geoffrey. *The 'Language Instinct' Debate.* 2nd ed. London: Continuum, 2001.

Saran, Cliff. "Stanford University Finds That AI Is Outpacing Moore's Law." *Computer Weekly,* 12 December 2019.

Schenkel, Carl, dir. *Knight Moves.* Pennsylvania: Interstar Releasing, 1992.

Schor, Juliet B. *The Overworked American: The Unexpected Decline of Leisure.* New York: Basic Books, 1991.

Schwitzgebel, Eric. "The Crazyist Metaphysics of Mind." *Australasian Journal of Philosophy* 92 (2014): 665–82.

Scott, Laurence. *The Four-Dimensional Human: Ways of Being in the Digital World.* New York: W.W. Norton, 2016.

Scott, Ridley, dir. *Blade Runner.* Burbank, CA: Warner Bros, 1982.

Searle, John. "Minds, Brains, and Programs." *Behavioral and Brain Sciences* 3 (1980): 417–57.

– "Minds, Brains, and Programs." In *A Historical Introduction to the Philosophy of Mind: Readings with Commentary*, edited by Peter Morton. New York: Broadview Press, 1997.

– *Minds, Brains, and Science*. Cambridge, MA: Harvard University Press, 1984.

– *The Mystery of Consciousness*. New York: New York Review of Books, 1990.

– *Speech Acts*. Cambridge: Cambridge University Press, 1962.

Shannon, Claude. "Programming a Computer for Playing Chess." *Philosophical Magazine* 41, no. 314 (March 1950). Archived from the original (PDF) on 23 May 2020.

Shannon, Murray, and Bernard Baars. "Applying Global Workspace Theory to the Frame Problem." *Cognition* 98 (2005): 157–76.

Sherman, Justin, "Dumbed Down AI Rhetoric Harms Everyone." *WIRED*, 26 May 2021.

Singer, Peter W. "Isaac Asimov's Laws of Robotics Are Wrong," *Brookings*, 18 May 2009.

– *Animal Liberation: A New Theory for Our Treatment of Animals*. New York: HarperCollins, 1975.

Smith, Barry. "AI and the Ontology of Complex Systems." Guest lecture, University of Toronto. 23 November 2021.

Smith, Brian Cantwell. *The Promise of Artificial Intelligence: Reckoning and Judgment*. Cambridge, MA: MIT Press, 2019. https://doi.org/10.7551/mitpress/12385.001.0001.

Smith, Maria. "The Use of Artificial Intelligence in a 'Woke' Society." *Berkeley D-Lab*, 27 September 2019.

Smith, Russell. "How Algorithms Are Changing What We Read Online." *Walrus*, 15 September 2020.

Snyder, Timothy. *On Tyranny: Twenty Lessons from the Twentieth Century*. New York: Crown, 2017.

Sollinger, Daniel, dir. *Immortality or Bust*. Documentary, 2019. https://www.immortalityorbust.com/.

Soper, Spencer. "Fired by Bot at Amazon: 'It's You Against the Machine.'" *Bloomberg News*, 28 June 2021.

Spelke, Elizabeth. "Core knowledge." *American Psychologist* 55, no. 11 (November 2000): 1233–43.

Spinoza, Baruch. *Theological-Political Treatise*. Edited by Jonathan Israel. Translated by Michael Silverthorne and Jonathan Israel. Cambridge: Cambridge University Press, 2007.

Stanley, Jason. *How Fascism Works: The Politics of Us and Them*. New York: Penguin Random House, 2018.

Suits, Bernard. *The Grasshopper: Games, Life, and Utopia*. 3rd ed. Peterborough, ON: Broadview Press, 2014.

Taylor, Charles. *Modern Social Imaginaries*. Durham, NC: Duke University Press, 2004.

Taylor, F.W. "The Principles of Scientific Management." in *The Early Sociology of Management and Organizations*, Volume 1. London: Routledge, 2005.

Tegmark, Max. *Life 3.0: Being Human in the Age of Artificial Intelligence*. New York: Knopf, 2017.

Todorov, Tzvetan. *The Fantastic: A Structural Approach to a Literary Genre*. Ithaca: Cornell University Press, 1975.

Tolentino, Jia. "The Gig Economy Celebrates Working Yourself to Death." *New Yorker*, 22 March 2017.

Trench, Marianne, dir. *Cyberpunk*. Documentary. Produced by Peter von Brandenburg, 1990.

Tribe, Lawrence H. *Abortion: The Clash of Absolutes*. 1990. Rev. ed. New York: Norton, 1992.

Turing, A.M. "Computing Machinery and Intelligence." *Mind* 59, no. 236 (October 1950): 433–60.

Tzu, Lao. *Tao Te Ching.* Translated by D.C. Lau. Hong Kong: Chinese University Press, 1989.

Uexküll, J. *Theoretical Biology*. New York: Harcourt, Brace & Co, 1926.

Uriagereka, Juan. "Multiple Spell-Out." *Current Studies in Linguistics* 32 (1999): 251–82.

Vallor, Shannon. *Technology and the Virtues: A Philosophical Guide to a Future Worth Wanting*. Oxford: Oxford University Press, 2016.

Valpy, Michael. "The Young Will Inherit a Future They See as a Sham." *Toronto Star*, 8 December 2013.

Veblen, Thorstein, and John Kenneth Galbraith. *The Theory of the Leisure Class*. Boston: Houghton Mifflin, 1973.

Vinge, Vernor. "The Coming Technological Singularity: How to Survive in the Post-Human Era." In *Vision-21: Interdisciplinary Science and Engineering in the Era of Cyberspace*, edited by G.A. Landis, 11–23. NASA Publication CP-10129, 1993.

Walzer, Michael. *Just and Unjust Wars: A Moral Argument with Historical Examples*. New York: Basic Books, 1977.

Warhaft, Marci. *The Good Stripper: A Soccer Mom's Memoir of Lies, Loss, and Lapdances.* Toronto: Sutherland House, 2020.

Wark, Wesley. *Gamer Theory.* Cambridge, MA: Harvard University Press, 2007.

Weber, Max. *The Protestant Ethic and the Spirit of Capitalism.* Translated by Talcott Parsons. New York: Scribner's, 1958.

Weiner, Norbert. *Cybernetics, Or Control and Communication in the Animal and the Machine.* 2nd ed. Cambridge, MA: MIT Press, 1961.

Weinrib, Lloyd L. *Natural Law and Justice.* Cambridge, MA: Harvard University Press, 1987.

Whitehead, Alfred North. *Process and Reality.* London: Free Press, 1979. First published 1929 as the Gifford Lectures (New York and Cambridge).

Whyte, Kenneth. "Bestsellers: What It Takes." *SHuSH*, 18 September 2020.

Wickes, Jade. "Two Thirds of UK Youth Miss Lockdown." *The Face*, 22 March 2022.

Winterston, Jeanette. *12 Bytes: How We Got Here, Where We Might Go Next.* New York: Grove Press, 2021.

Wittgenstein, Ludwig. *Philosophical Investigations.* Translated by G.E.M. Anscombe. Oxford: Basil Blackwell, 1953.

Wright, Crispin. "Rule-Following without Reasons." *Ratio* 20, no. 4 (2007): 481–502.

Wylie, Philip. *Generation of Vipers.* New York: Farrar & Rinehart, 1942.

Zalloua, Zahi. *Being Posthuman: Ontologies of the Future.* New York: Bloomsbury, 2021.

Zwicky, Jan, and Robert Bringhurst. *Learning to Die.* Regina, SK: University of Regina Press, 2018.

Index

Page numbers in italics refer to figures.